Intellectual Path Dependence in Economics

Is economics always self-corrective? Do erroneous theorems permanently disappear from the market of economic ideas? *Intellectual Path Dependence in Economics* argues that errors in economics are not always corrected. Although economists are often critical and open-minded, unfit explanations are nonetheless able to reproduce themselves. The problem is that theorems sometimes survive the intellectual challenges in the market of economic ideas even when they are falsified or invalidated by criticism and an abundance of counter-evidence.

A key question which often gets little or no attention is: why do economists not reject theories when they have been refuted by evidence and falsified by philosophical reasoning? This book explores the answer to this question by examining the phenomenon of intellectual path dependence in the history of economic thought. It argues that the key reason why economists do not reject refuted theories is the epistemic costs of starting to use new theories. Epistemic costs are primarily the costs of scarcity of the most valued element in academic production: time. Epistemic scarcity overwhelmingly dominates the evolution of scientific research in such a way that when researchers start off a new research project, they allocate time between replicable and unreplicable research.

This book is essential reading for anyone interested in the methodology, philosophy and history of economics.

Altug Yalcintas is an historian and philosopher of economics. He is an Associate Professor at the Economics Department of Ankara University, Turkey.

Intellectual Path Dependence in Economics

Why economists do not reject refuted theories

Altug Yalcintas

LONDON AND NEW YORK

First published 2016
by Routledge
2 Park Square, Milton Park, Abingdon, Oxon OX14 4RN

and by Routledge
711 Third Avenue, New York, NY 10017

First issued in paperback 2017

Routledge is an imprint of the Taylor & Francis Group, an informa business

© 2016 Altug Yalcintas

The right of Altug Yalcintas to be identified as author of this work has
been asserted in accordance with the Copyright, Designs and Patent Act
1988.

All rights reserved. No part of this book may be reprinted or reproduced
or utilised in any form or by any electronic, mechanical, or other means,
now known or hereafter invented, including photocopying and recording,
or in any information storage or retrieval system, without permission in
writing from the publishers.

Trademark notice: Product or corporate names may be trademarks or
registered trademarks, and are used only for identification and explanation
without intent to infringe.

British Library Cataloguing in Publication Data
A catalogue record for this book is available from the British Library

Library of Congress Cataloging in Publication Data
Names: Yalcintas, Altug.
Title: Intellectual path dependence in economics : why economists do not
reject refuted theories / Altug Yalcintas.
Description: Abingdon, Oxon; New York, NY : Routledge, 2016.
Identifiers: LCCN 2015040322
ISBN 9781138016170 (hardback)
Subjects: LCSH: Economics–Philosophy.
Classification: LCC HB72 .Y35 2016
DDC 330.1–dc23
LC record available at http://lccn.loc.gov/2015040322

ISBN 13: 978-1-138-49555-5 (pbk)
ISBN 13: 978-1-138-01617-0 (hbk)

Typeset in Times New Roman
by Cenveo Publisher Services

This volume is dedicated to Dr Ali Fikirkoca (1975–2014) who was a close friend, a hardworking colleague and a bright scholar of innovation and evolution at Ankara University.

'[T]he moment a new theory has invalidated older views in any region of science, a thorough revision of that region should be carried out with the minimum of delay.'

John Desmond Bernal (1939, 329)

'Scientific honesty then consists of specifying, in advance, an experiment such that if the result contradicts the theory, the theory has to be given up.'

Imre Lakatos (1970, 96)

'If I am right in the criticisms of Quine I have been making (and in general line I am taking in this book [*Philosophy and the Mirror of Nature*]) the only way in which I can do *ontological* damage is to block the road of inquiry by insisting on a bad old theory at the expense of a good new theory.'

Richard Rorty (1979, 209, italics in original)

Contents

List of figures and tables		viii
Preface		ix

PART I
Epistemic responsibility of economists | | 1

1   Matters of opinion or questionable research practices? | | 3

PART II
The economic construction of sciences | | 43

2   Explaining epistemic hystereses | | 45

3   Sciences between Scylla and Charybdis | | 89

4   Error: a common tragedy in sciences | | 125

PART III
Concluding remarks | | 151

5   Economics as part of a system of research ethics | | 153

Index | | 168

Figures and Tables

Figures

1.1	The intellectual formation of the 'Coase Theorem'	10
1.2	Evolution of ideas in the absence of continual progression	12
3.1	Evolution of ideas when knowledge continuously progresses	116
3.2	A tree of intellectual life	117

Tables

1.1	Tabulation of cases	16
2.1	Costs in the economy and scholarly life	73
4.1	Events and their sizes	135

Preface

In *The Economics of Science: Methodology and Epistemology as if Economics Really Mattered* (1998), one of the finest works in the field of economics of scientific knowledge, James R. Wible argues that science can be explained in economic terms. Progress in science, Wible (ibid., 2) claims, 'is a consequence of focusing scarce scientific resources and the best scientific minds on the very best theories and their next best alternatives'. Wible's book is based on two assumptions: (1) scientists are economically rational actors and (2) sciences are self-corrective. These assumptions help Wible make the point that a systematic and empirical economics of scientific knowledge is possible.

In *Intellectual Path Dependence in Economics: Why Economists Do Not Refute Rejected Theories*, I also claim that science is an economic activity and agree with Wible that science can be explained in economic terms. However, although I think Wible's work has been intriguing for many authors in the literature on the economics of scientific knowledge (see Sent 2006), including myself, Wible's assumptions are unrealistic in the sense that his argument is not supported by strong cases in the history of economics where economists are *not* rational and sciences are *not* self-corrective. In the opening chapter of the present book, I outline what I mean by 'not rational' and 'not self-corrective': economists who are shown (and even convinced) that the 'Coase Theorem' is not the true message of Ronald H. Coase still use the 'Coase Theorem' in their models as though Coase implied an economy of zero transactions. The market of economic ideas has failed to correct an error that many economists, including Coase himself, have documented and invalidated. Softening the assumptions about rationality and self-correctiveness, we would have a more realistic economics of scientific knowledge which, borrowing the metaphor from Coase, not only works on the blackboard, but also in the scholarly world in which we live. A more realistic model would, then, be one in which scholars are not always rational and errors often remain uncorrected. In other words, scholars live in a world of positive *epistemic* costs (PEC).

In this book, I argue that scientists have over-produced the scientific knowledge in which various forms of questionable research practices (QRPs) are involved. QRPs are difficult to define with rigour. I regard QRPs as academic activities in which researchers impose social costs on the shoulders of the community of researchers and the general public. Examples of QRPs are various:

x *Preface*

publishing an article in two journals without telling this to the editors and readers, using inappropriate statistical techniques, not giving the reviewers access to the research materials that support the findings in an article, failing to disclose the financial sources used to write an article or a book, offering promotion to somebody in a research team or institution for sexual favours, as well as plagiarism, fabrication of data and manufacturing of data. QRPs undermine confidence in scientific research; they weaken or destruct intellectual morals, such as critical thinking, honesty and integrity. I argue that scholars who are involved in QRPs at universities, research institutes, museums and think-tanks lead to harmful consequences for the social and epistemic communities in which they live. Avoiding QRPs is an issue for maintaining a sustainable scholarly environment because the social and epistemic costs that come out of QRPs are not easily regulated, and their consequences remain often uncorrected. As a result, QRPs restrict the efficacy of the creative efforts of the community of scholars as a whole.

Wible's research programme does not conflict with my above claim about epistemic costs. However, a distinctive feature of his argument is that science is self-corrective. That is, an implication of Wible's research programme is that sciences eventually unlock divergent pathways and better theories are, sooner or later, selected. I disagree with Wible here. Although economists are often critical and open-minded, unfit explanations are nonetheless able to reproduce themselves. The problem is that theorems sometimes survive the intellectual challenges in the market of economic ideas even when they are falsified or invalidated by criticisms and an abundance of counter-evidence.

Why is that? The survival of theorems is an economic issue. Giving up a theorem is always intellectually costly. Scholars resist criticisms and counter-evidence by refusing to reject the theorems that are criticized and falsified. The theorems that dominate the market of economic ideas are so powerful that the efforts of critical and open-minded economists do not lead their opponents to change their minds and replace erroneous theorems with corrected ones. When the number of cases in which flawed theorems keep surviving increases, despite the efforts of economic critics, malpractices of scientists shift epistemic costs onto the shoulders of the members of scholarly community.

I call this emergence *intellectual path dependence*. Intellectual path dependence is a process where decentralized mechanisms of self-correction, such as G. W. Friedrich Hegel's negation (or dialectics) and Karl R. Popper's falsification (or critical rationalism), no longer produce the greatest academic value for the community of economists. The processes of intellectual path dependence are those in which 'invisible hand explanations' in sciences (Aydinonat 2008), which such philosophers of science as Michael Polanyi (1969), David Hull (1988) and Philip Kitcher (1993) presupposed in their analyses of the market of ideas, do not fully account for the enduring consequences of QRPs. In my view, invisible hand explanations in sciences produce the greatest scholarly value only when the mechanisms of self-correction fully work. The mechanisms of self-correction require economists, first and foremost, to reject refuted theories. When intellectual path dependence rules the processes of knowledge production, however,

Preface xi

economists are reluctant to adopt new theories. Then, processes of knowledge production are path dependent. The invisible hand in economics fails to work and the processes of self-correction cease to operate properly. The epistemic cost of filtering out the consequences of QRPs are high. QRPs thus stay in the game.

In this book, I propose that unorthodox branches of economics, especially the institutional and evolutionary political economy of Thorstein B. Veblen and his views on sabotage (1921 [2001], 1–26), K. William Kapp and his views on social costs (1950, 1–25), as well as Karl P. Polanyi and his views on self-regulating markets (1944 [2001], 71–80), can challenge conventional views not only in economics but also in science studies. Applying the analytical tools of evolutionary political economy in science studies, we would be able to demonstrate how manipulated and erroneous ideas are deliberately manufactured to be milestones of neoliberal theorizing in economics even when the originators of the theorems argue against such ideas. For instance, Ronald H. Coase has long been considered to be a prominent member of the Chicago School of Economics. However, absent Stigler's formulation of 'The Problem of Social Cost' in his *The Theory of Price* (1952 [1966]), would the influence of Coase on the Chicago School of Economics have been as significant as it is today? This is debatable. Had the 'Coase Theorem' Proper (that is, a theorem genuinely based on positive transaction costs) naturally been selected in the market of economic ideas, one may argue, such figures as John C. Commons and K. William Kapp would have been more influential figures in economics. 'Externalities' would have become internal in social and epistemic accounting. The issue of transaction costs would not only be a keyword to explain the *existence* of the business enterprises; transaction costs would account for the harmful consequences of the *functioning* of the business enterprises as well. Coase's critique of the orthodox economics, then, would not have been eclipsed and his significance for unorthodox economic theorizing (such as his views on the fallacies of the 'blackboard economics') would have been more visible. Most certainly, the theory of social costs would have been a popular research programme to which a greater number of economists would pay attention. Indeed, none of these has happened. The 'Coase Theorem' has blocked and weakened the criticism of the theory of social costs in economics and helped strengthen the Chicago School's theories of private property and freedom of contracts. The paradigmatic case of the 'Coase Theorem' suggests that George Stigler's view on Coase's view of transaction costs is the epistemic cost of the 'Coase Theorem'.

Further research on intellectual path dependence in economics can show that the ideologies of conservatism are not always formed merely of the right-wing political philosophies of scholars who wish to preserve the nature of social and political institutions as they are. Conservative ideologies are formed also of the consequences of errors, both in the right and in the left, remaining uncorrected in the scientific literature. Such errors do not disappear despite the efforts of critical scholars. The question then becomes: why can we not rid economics from conservatism? My answer to this question is *intellectual path dependence*: intellectual path dependence leads scholars to reproduce conservative ideologies in economics.

xii *Preface*

I contend that the 'Coase Theorem' has helped conservative ideologies in economics to reproduce. This 'theorem' has caused economists to lose contact with the actual markets. *After Coase*, or AC, the orthodox economists were able to justify why they should rather investigate the market on the blackboard (that is, the hypothetical model), instead of the actual market where the equilibrium is never easily reached and the ideals are never fully achieved. The 'Coase Theorem' was a tipping point that cut off the passage that connected the economists to the facts of the world; it separated the economists from the world in which they lived. The 'Coase Theorem' located the orthodoxy in economics into a fantasy world, a world that did not exist but was desired by orthodox economists. In this world, perfect markets replaced actual markets.

Perfect markets are extraordinary worlds in which economic agents, without senses of time, space and any social institution, easily achieve efficiency. Coase has, in fact, shown that a perfect market is not only empirically impossible to demonstrate, but also theoretically impossible to work on the blackboard. A positive transaction costs world is what we have got, Coase argues, and it is where we all live. Perfect markets do not exist; they are merely hypothetical.

Coase claims that the ideality of perfect markets lacks 'realisticness'. Unrealisticness, as the Coase Theorem Proper shows, is the prevalence of imperfections in the ways in which actual markets work. Since imperfect knowledge and imperfect competition prevail in the 'real' world, both in the economy and the academy, one cannot move from second 'best' solutions (e.g. reproduction of erroneous explanations) to first best solutions (e.g. truth seeking). Epistemic costs are hardly equal to private costs involved in the processes of knowledge production.

To sum up, it is unrealistic to assume that actual markets would function without cost. Epistemic costs, in this sense, are anything that separates the actual from the hypothetical, anything that keeps individuals away from institutions, conventions and ideologies. Ignoring the significance of institutions, conventions and ideologies, orthodox economists advocate an imaginary world in which every transaction can achieve efficiency and optimality. I thus agree with Jeanne L. Schroeder's definition of transaction costs here. She claims that 'transactions costs are ... Castration in the sense that they are the barrier that separates the Symbolic of actual markets from the Real of perfect markets' (Schroeder 1998–9).

A word of thanks

I thank the following colleagues and friends for reading the earlier versions of this book and providing me with helpful comments: Billur Aksoy, Bahar Araz, Ergün Ateş, Başak Bak, Utku Balaban, Nazan Bedirhanoğlu, Işıner Hamşioğlu, Corry Shores, Akın Usupbeyli and Zafer Yılmaz. I am also grateful to the Routledge editor, Laura Johnson, and the three anonymous referees for their criticisms and remarks. I was a visiting member of the Cambridge Social Ontology Group in the 2011–12 academic year. I thank Tony Lawson, Clive Lawson, Erkan Gürpınar and Sezgin Polat for insightful conversations in the coffee room of the Economics Department of the University of Cambridge.

During and after these conversations, I had the opportunity to rethink about the (artificial) tension between critical realism in economics and the rhetoric of economics (see 'Economic philosophy as economic criticism', Chapter 1). Erkan and I, at a later stage, co-authored a paper on social ontology and Thorstein B. Veblen (Gurpinar and Yalcintas 2015) in which we stressed the evolutionary ontological reasons why economists do not abandon theories when the dominant paradigm in economics is disputed. We argued that the 'drift' which Veblen thought would turn economics into an evolutionary science has now become an evolutionary process itself, in which economists are unable to displace non-evolutionary preconceptions in economics. I was the local organizer of an academic event on scientific misconduct in economics, entitled 'International Workshop on Scientific Misconduct and Research Ethics in Economics', which took place in Izmir, Turkey, August 2014. I thank James R. Wible, Steve T. Ziliak, Wilfred Dolfsma and Sarah Necker for their valuable contributions to the workshop. After the workshop, I had the chance to improve my views on the significance of QRPs in economics (see 'Replication failure as a questionable research practice', Chapter 2). I especially owe my gratitude to Steve Ziliak, my academic brother, who not only inspired but also encouraged me to write about the economics profession with more humour and irony. Since the workshop was over, James Wible and I have been co-editing a special issue of the *Review of Social Economy* on scientific misconduct in economics. The issue is to be published in March 2016.

Finally, I thank my wife, Funda Demir, and my father, Tayfun Yalçıntaş. My wife has convinced me that sometimes remaining locked into a pathway in life, knowingly and intentionally, is the best choice ever! (I would like to emphasize *sometimes* here.) 'Go with the flow,' she once said – and that's what I have done, so that this book came out. My father, tutor in mathematics, has helped me a lot in life. I cannot list everything here, but I wish to mention that the only formula in the present book (see Chapter 2), after his magic touch, looks much better than it once did. Thank you!

This book is based on the revisions of the articles I have published since my doctoral dissertation, 'Intellectual Paths and Pathologies: How Small Events in Scholarly Life Accidently Grow Big' (2009). I thank the editors and official representatives of the *American Journal of Economics and Sociology, Journal of the History of Economic Thought, Erasmus Journal for Philosophy and Economics, Journal of Philosophical Economics, Economics Bulletin, Culture Theory and Critique, Ankara University SBF Review* and *Journal of Economics and Political Economy* for allowing me to reuse the revised versions of the material that previously appeared in their outlets.

2015. 'Is Science Self-Corrective: A Book Review of James R. Wible's *The Economics of Science* (2014) [1998]'. *Journal of Economics and Political Economy* 2 (1): 223–8.

2013. 'The Problem of Epistemic Cost: Why Do Scholars Not Change Their Minds (about the "Coase Theorem")?'. *American Journal of Economics and Sociology* 72 (5): 1131–57.

2012. 'Between a Rock and a Hard Place: Second Thoughts on Laibman's *Deep History* and the Theory of Punctuated Equilibrium with Regard to Intellectual Evolution'. *Journal of Philosophical Economics* 6 (1): 1–22.

xiv *Preface*

2012. 'A Notion Evolving: From "Institutional Path Dependence" to "Intellectual Path Dependence"'. *Economics Bulletin* 32 (2): 1091–8.

2011. 'A Review Essay on David Laibman's *Deep History: A Study in Social Evolution and Human Agency*'. *Journal of Philosophical Economics* 5 (1): 168–82.

2011. 'On Error: Undisciplined Thoughts on One of the Causes of Path Dependence'. *Ankara University SBF Review* 66 (2): 215–33.

2010. 'Thesis Abstract: Intellectual Paths and Pathologies: How Small Events in Scholarly Life Accidentally Grow Big (2009)'. *Journal of the History of Economic Thought* 32 (4): 621–2.

2010. 'PhD Thesis Summary: Intellectual Paths and Pathologies: How Small Events in Scholarly Life Accidentally Grow Big (2009)'. *Erasmus Journal for Philosophy and Economics* 3 (1): 123–5.

2006. 'Historical Small Events and the Eclipse of *Utopia*: Perspectives on Path Dependence in Human Thought'. *Culture, Theory, and Critique* 47 (1): 53–70.

Altug Yalcintas, Ankara, September 2015.

References

Aydinonat, N. Emrah. 2008. *The Invisible Hand in Economics: How Economists Explain Unintended Social Consequences*. London and New York: Routledge.

Bernal, John Desmond. 1939. *The Social Function of Science*. London: George Routledge & Sons.

Gurpinar, Erkan, and Altug Yalcintas. 2015. 'One Long Argument in Economics: Explaining Intellectual Inertia in Terms of Social Ontology'. Paper presented at STOREP 2015 CONFERENCE, 'Shifting Boundries: Economics in the Crisis and the Challenge of Interdisciplinarity', Torino, 11–13 June.

Hull, David L. 1988. *Science as a Process: An Evolutionary Account of the Social and Conceptual Development of Science*. Chicago: University of Chicago Press.

Kapp, K. William. 1950. *The Social Costs of Private Enterprise*. Cambridge, MA: Harvard University Press.

Kitcher, Philip. 1993. *The Advancement of Science: Science without Legend, Objectivity without Illusions*. Oxford: Oxford University Press.

Lakatos, Imre. 1970. 'Falsification and the Methodology of Scientific Research Programmes'. In *Criticism and the Growth of Knowledge*, edited by Imre Lakatos and Alan Musgrave, 170–96. Cambridge: Cambridge University Press.

Polanyi, Karl. 1944 [2001]. *The Great Transformation*. Boston, MA: Beacon Press.

Polanyi, Michael. 1969. 'The Republic of Science: Its Political and Economic Theory'. In *Michael Polanyi: Knowing and Believing*, edited by M Grene, 49–72. Chicago: Chicago University Press.

Rorty, Richard. 1979. *Philosophy and the Mirror of Nature*. Princeton, NJ: Princeton University Press.

Schroeder, Jeanne L. 1998–9. 'The End of the Market: A Psychoanlaysis of Law and Economics'. *Harvard Law Review* 112 (2): 483–558.

Sent, Esther-Mirjam. 2006. 'Economics of Science: Survey and Suggestions'. *Journal of Economic Methodology* 6(1): 95–124.

Stigler, George Joseph. 1952 [1966]. *The Theory of Price*. 3rd edn. New York: Macmillan.

Veblen, Thorstein B. 1921 [2001]. *The Engineers and the Price System*: Batoche Books.

Wible, James R. 1998. *The Economics of Science: Methodology and Epistemology as if Economics Really Mattered*. New York: Routledge.

Part I
Epistemic responsibility of economists

1 Matters of opinion or questionable research practices?

George Stigler invited Ronald Coase to Chicago in 1959 to give a speech at a workshop that he organized. Coase accepted the invitation. After the workshop, Coase asked the learned audience of Chicago to hold a special meeting to discuss his approach to the 'rationale of property rights' which the Chicagoans thought was an error and Coase should delete from his 1959 article, 'The Federal Communications Commission'. The meeting was arranged. Eminent scholars of Chicago gathered at the residence of Aaron Director, the founder of the *Journal of Economics and Law*. Milton Friedman, Arnold Harberger and John McGee were at the meeting. 'How could such a fine economist like Coase think', his fellows at Chicago wondered, 'that there were costs involved in the operation of price mechanism in the market?' The discussion took about two hours. It was during this meeting that Coase convinced his Chicago colleagues of his argument. And so was it possible for the next generation of economists to know 'probably the most widely cited article in the whole of the modern economic literature'. 'I persuaded these economists that I was right,' reported Coase in his autobiographical 'Nobel Prize Speech' in 1991, 'and I was asked to write up my argument for publication in the *Journal of Law and Economics* … Had it not been for the fact that these economists at the University of Chicago thought that I had made an error in my article on "The Federal Communications Commission", it is probable that "The Problem of Social Cost [1960]" would never have been written' (Coase 1997, 10, see also Stigler 1988, 75–80).

Coase's classic 1960 article, 'The Problem of Social Cost', deserves special attention in the history of economic analysis. The main point of the article was to provide a criticism of the established theory of negative 'externalities'. According to Coase, accounts of negative 'externalities' were inadequate. The price mechanism was not easily able to solve the problems that arose out of the harmful effects of individual actions on others. Economists, since Arthur Cecil Pigou (1920 [1962]), have believed that taxes and other kinds of governmental regulations were the best ways of diminishing the negative effects of individual behaviour. In view of that, governments should restrain those responsible for the harmful effects of individual action in the market. Although this was not unwise, Coase argued, such a solution would depend on whether the 'gain from preventing the harm is greater than the loss which would be suffered elsewhere as a result

4 *Epistemic responsibility of economists*

of stopping the action which produces the harm' (Coase 1960). There is no single solution to every problem in the market. Economists should be more concerned with the consequences that happen in actual cases – not merely with the consequences that happen on the blackboard only.

For Coase, the problem was to understand the causation between the parties in which one party is supposed to inflict harm upon the other. The problem was of a reciprocal nature: 'To avoid the harm to B would inflict harm on A,' wrote Coase. 'The real question that has to be decided is: should A be allowed to harm B or should B be allowed to harm A? The problem is to avoid the more serious harm.' Carrying out market transactions (such as conducting negotiations with parties, drawing up a contract, reaching an agreement about the terms of the contract and so on) were costly – 'sufficiently costly at any rate,' wrote Coase, 'to prevent many transactions that would be carried out in a world in which the pricing system worked without cost' (Coase 1960, 15). In other words, the positive transactions cost world in which we live does not always allow parties to conduct negotiations that end up with an efficient (re-)allocation of resources and rights. Under positive transaction costs, 'the initial delimitation of rights does have an effect on the efficiency with which the economic system operates' (Coase 1960, 16). Then, assigning private property rights (no matter to whom) might be a solution to the problem of social cost as negative 'externalities' are not self-corrective. That is, in the world we live we need a legal system that prevents one party from inflicting harm on another, instead of a ruling state that punishes, by way of introducing taxes, the party responsible for the harm. The problem is, therefore, to decide on the appropriate social arrangement for possible harmful effects. This requires a case-by-case investigation of different ways of handling the problem.

Coase introduced his view in 1960. But the 'Coase Theorem' became established in economic theory only after Stigler's third edition of his *The Theory of Price* (1966). (The first edition of the book appeared in 1952. It did not mention any of Coase's works.) According to Stigler, Coase's 1960 article raised important issues about the efficiency of markets, government intervention and property rights. In a famous passage, Stigler said:

> [t]he Coase theorem thus asserts that under perfect competition private and social costs will be equal. It is a more remarkable proposition to us older economists who have believed the opposite for a generation, than it will appear to the young reader who was never wrong, here.

> (Stigler 1966, 113)

The 'theorem', as economists know it, has since become an important topic of investigation.

A common misrepresentation regarding Coase's contribution is that the 'Coase Theorem' is elaborated as if Coase himself argued there were no transaction costs in the market. Many of the most cited articles on the 'Coase Theorem' (such as Kahneman *et al.* 1990, Jolls *et al.* 1998, Hoffman *et al.* 1994, Elhauge 1991), as well as many dictionaries and textbooks of economics published in the USA and

Europe (such as Rutherford 1995, 75; Varian 2003, 542–3; Harrison 1995, 56–60; Cooter and Ulen 1997, 79–84) still describe the 'Coasian world' as a world of zero transaction costs. This rich literature focuses a lot of attention on the 'Coase Theorem' rather than what Coase really said in 1960. In fact, 'The Problem of Social Cost' had received the attention of economic scholarship before Stigler. Articles published between 1960 and 1966 helped 'The Problem of Social Cost' to become known among economists. R. Turvey (1963), S. Wellisz (1964), G. Calabresi (1965) and E. J. Mishan (1965) are among the authors who considered and reviewed Coase's article in their contributions to economic theory in the early 1960s. (ISI Web of Science reports that 'The Problem of Social Cost' was cited 12 times between 1960 and 1966, whereas it was cited 72 times from 1966 to 1972, and 734 times until Coase was awarded the Swedish Bank Prize in 1991.) Most of these articles were interested in the debates regarding the divergence between private and social costs and none of them strayed away from the assumption of positive transaction costs.

A great score of institutionalists, including Veblen (1904) and Kapp (1950), stressed the fact that social costs as well as spill-overs were intentional and systematic. Books published before the 1960s pointed out that harmful effects of individual production were, in fact, internal to the capitalist system. However, insofar as the problems with social costs in market economies are concerned, none of these scholars were as influential as Stigler in getting a 'theorem' established in the literatures of economics and law. Today, publications citing 'The Problem of Social Cost' and applying positive transaction costs in their economic analysis, such as Nicita and Pagano (2008), Robson and Skaperdas (2008) and Medema (2011a, b), are still a minority. This controversy has evolved into such a state that, in a number of publications, including Williamson (1985) and many others (such as Kelman 1979, Hojman and Hiscock 2010), authors clearly express the controversy on the meaning and implications of the 'Coase Theorem'; nevertheless, most of these authors keep applying the assumption of zero transaction costs in their analysis.

An example of this is the following:

> It is noteworthy that this important and influential paper ['The Problem of Social Cost'] is in two parts. The first part features frictionlessness; the second qualifies the earlier discussion to make allowance for frictions. Much of the follow-on literature, including franchise bidding, is largely or wholly preoccupied with frictionlessness or deals with frictions in a limited or sanguine way.
>
> (Williamson 1985, 348, 22nd footnote)

Williamson might be right. But this is not an excuse to analyze 'franchise bidding' as if there were no friction in the market. Williamson's perspective does not help the literature to move away from the sin of Stigler's ideologization.

An interesting case to investigate closely is raised by Gary North, a Christian Reconstructivism activist and founder of the Institute for Christian Economics. North argues that the 'Coase Theorem' raises a number of moral issues: the 'Coase Theorem', North argues,

6   *Epistemic responsibility of economists*

assigns zero economic value – and therefore zero relevance – to the sense of moral and legal right associated with a wilful violation of private ownership. The theorem ignores the economic relevance of the public's sense of moral outrage when there is no enforcement by the civil government of owners' legal immunities from invasion, even if this invasion is done in the name of some 'more efficient' social good or social goal.

(North 1992, 27)

In other words, the victims of, say, pollution, claims North, would not sue the polluter in civil courts. Or, restrictions on kidnappers would be impossible. North thus considers the 'Coase Theorem' 'one of the most morally insidious pieces of academic nonsense ever to hit the economics profession' (ibid.). According to North, the epistemological problem of social costs becomes an ethical one and economics happen to be 'wicked'. He poses an important question:

Who should make the initial distribution of an ownership right to whomever 'values it the most'? How does this sovereign agent know scientifically which potential owners 'are likely to value them [ownership rights] the most'? In short: By what standard of value does he make the initial distribution?

(Ibid., 30)

North falls into the same trap as Stigler: Coase did not say this. He did not assume individuals would have no commitment to any sense of justice. He pointed out the impossibility of a world without transaction costs. If Coase were asked the questions in the above quote, he would argue that judges should certainly intervene in the types of disputes mentioned above to find fair solutions. He would argue that there are reasons for governments to enter markets to protect the rights of different parties. Some economists – certainly, the followers of Stigler – might be considered 'wicked', if one subscribes to North's vocabulary. Economics, however, cannot be considered wicked. Coase does not suggest economists should be value-free and morally neutral. Many economists, like Coase himself, and unlike Stigler and his followers, care about justice, equity, etc. The problem of social cost means also the problem of ethics and justice. It is the problem of caring about the social consequences of individual doings. 'Externalities' can be morally significant, too, especially when one's action harms the utility of another and violates the others' rights. North, likewise, states that 'the issue of economic efficiency therefore cannot be separated from the issue of judicial equity' (North 1992, 45). But he, just like the followers of Stigler, fails to see that Coase never intended the 'Coase Theorem'.

The controversy over the 'Coase Theorem' is that, in a number of important articles and books, that of Stigler (1952 [1966]) being the first, it has been analyzed as if Coase argued that the world in which we live is a world of zero transaction costs. This 'theorem', however, was not a proper formulation of Coase's message. Coase did not argue that the pricing system worked without costs. The reason why he used the example of zero transaction costs was (1) heuristic (Zerbe 1980) and (2) he showed that even under the assumption of zero transaction costs, the Pigouvian system was 'inadequate' and 'incorrect' (Medema 1995). The misunderstanding about the original message of Coase came out in Coase's 'Nobel Prize Lecture' in 1991. Almost 50 years after Coase first published his 'The Problem of Social Cost', the consequence of the initial condition under which Coase's contribution was first formulated (Stigler 1952 [1966]) is not eliminated. *The market of ideas*, in Coase's own terms (Coase 1974, 1977), has failed to correct the error fully even today. 'The Problem of Social Cost' has been, ironically, an occasion for economists to discuss one of the most obvious facts in a market economy that has been well known since Adam Smith: the consequences of *zero* transaction costs (see McCloskey 1998a, 239–40; Medema 2009, 11).

In effect, Stigler's interpretation of Coase (1960) has made Coase's contribution disappear. The 'Coase Theorem', in actuality, had been stated long before Coase, and therefore does not belong to the works of Coase, but of Adam Smith (McCloskey 1998a). In other words, the 'Coase Theorem' existed even before Coase. One would never need the theorem, as Coase himself reports also, to say that 'people will use resources in the way that produces the most value' (Hazlett 1997). This amounts to saying that we are living in a world without transaction costs. However, Coase believed to the contrary: we live in a world of positive transaction costs. The naming of the 'Coase Theorem' is, therefore, erroneous because the theorem meant the opposite of what Coase wrote in his works. There may be a few exceptional occasions outside the blackboard world in which transaction costs are so low (still positive though) as to be taken into consideration. Coase did not exclude this possibility. Nevertheless, the origin of the theorem is controversial since the message of the 'Coase Theorem' is not what Coase meant in 1960. Implications of the theorem are not always useful because the assumption of a zero transaction costs world is too restrictive and presupposes a world that does not comply with the facts of the world.

Coase raised the issue himself in (Coase 1988, 15). He said:

> What my argument does suggest is the need to introduce positive transaction costs explicitly into economic analysis so that we can study the world that exists. This has not been the effect of my article. The extensive discussion in the journals has concentrated almost entirely on the 'Coase Theorem,' a proposition about the world of zero transaction costs. This response, although disappointing, is undesirable.

Deirdre McCloskey pointed out the issue as well. McCloskey considers Stigler to be one of the worst historians of economic thought. Stigler 'used the history as an ideological tool', she says, 'and was ruthless in doing so. He read a lot but was defective in paying attention. Thus the Coase Theorem' (McCloskey 1998b).

The 'Coase' theorem as understood by George Stigler or Paul Samuelson is actually Adam Smith's theorem (Smith 1776 [1966]). It is wholly explicit in F. Y. Edgeworth (1881, 30ff, 114); and with all the bells and whistles in

8 Epistemic responsibility of economists

> Arrow and Debreu (1954). Smith, Edgeworth, Arrow, Debreu, with many others, noted that an item gravitates by exchange into the hands of the person who values it the most, if transactions costs (such as the cost of transportation) are not too high. Why a student of economic thought like Stigler would call this old idea in economics 'remarkable' I do not know, though it is not the only strange reading that Stigler gave. Applying it to pollution rights is unremarkable. As Paul Samuelson said sneeringly about the 'Coase' theorem: Where's the theorem?
>
> (McCloskey 1998a, 240)

This shows that the error has been detected and reported a number of times for decades. Then, quite naturally, one would expect the error to be corrected. The findings show, however, that this has not happened. Mechanisms of the scientific invisible hand, so to speak, one of which is the mechanism of *replication*, has not operated desirably in the market of ideas and the error been left uncorrected.

The specificity of the 'Coase Theorem' is the following: although Coase had the concept of transaction costs already in mind in the 1930s, the theorem is known to originate from 'The Problem of Social Cost'. However, revisiting the original works of Ronald Coase, who stated that market mechanisms always worked at a cost, one concludes that academic economics has failed to apply, spread and be proud of one of the most innovative and powerful ideas in the history of economic analyses in its very original and authentic form. Why was the 'Coase Theorem' coined after 'The Problem of Social Cost', not after one of his earlier works, and why was it established differently from how Coase proposed? Can the evolutionary history of the 'Coase Theorem' be an example of *intellectual path dependence* in which positive epistemic costs (PEC) cause the market of economic ideas to fail? Is Stigler's view on the contribution of Coase a matter of opinion or a questionable research practice (QRP)?

In his *Memoirs* (Stigler 1988, 75) Stigler says that 'in 1960, Ronald Coase criticized Pigou's theory *rather casually*' (italics added). What Stigler means by 'rather casually' is not clear. Does Stigler intend to say that welfare economics and the economics of law are two different fields of research and Coase's critique of the Pigouvian welfare system has become a significant contribution to the economic analysis of law? Or does he mean that Coase's critique lacks the ideological element that would state that markets could actually work and the condition for markets to work is to assume that there are no transaction costs? It is more likely that Stigler had the intention of using Coase to show that competitive markets could work. Stigler did, in fact, not have much to do with the truism that the market operated under positive transactions. Stigler never claimed that markets with positive transaction costs never existed. But neither did he abstain from asking for financial support from corporations and conservative foundations (Nik-Khah 2010). All in all, Stigler achieved an ideological twist that helped orthodox economics ignore markets where transaction costs were high by assuming perfect competition in which private costs were equal to social costs. Coase's critique of the Pigouvian system was thus transformed into a theoretical tool promoting the ideology of orthodox economics. Had Stigler not manipulated

Coase's idea of positive transaction costs, Coase would not have been known as one of the most influential economists of the twentieth century, making a chief 'contribution' to the intellectual history of the neoliberal thought collectives at the London School of Economics (Tribe 2009) and the Chicago School of Economics (Horn and Mirowski 2009) from the 1960s onwards. Chicago economics was (and still is) the dominant paradigm that challenges critical streams of thought in economics. It may not come as a surprise that Coase owes much of his success to the Chicagoans, a group to which he later belonged.

How has this process of ideologization run? Figure 1.1 shows the intellectual formation of the 'Coase Theorem' in graphical terms. (For a detailed description of this model, see Sydow *et al*. 2005, Sydow and Schreyögg 2010.) In this scenario, first-generation models include influential articles whose findings, by virtue of innovative research programmes, are (re-)formulated in original ways. Second-generation models often take the form of textbooks and secondary or follow-up research, the findings of which are primarily borrowed from first-generation models and strengthen the ideological power of the 'contribution'. *Replication failure* works as the engine of this process of positive feedback which causes the significance of the first-generation model to increase and transform a 'contribution' into a constitutive part of the orthodox ideology in economics.

The main reason that such contradictions in the history of ideas do not disappear easily (or at all) is that this history does not always function to fix errors fully. In other words, the market of ideas does not operate like a perfect market, and the effects of several small events, such as errors and misrepresentations in analyses, often remain uncorrected for long periods due to high *epistemic costs* of replicating old findings.

Every time a second-generation model cites Stigler on the 'Coase Theorem' the (mis-)interpretation is reinforced and smoothing out the irregularity in the pathway on which 'The Problem of Social Cost' is locked becomes more costly. Economists use Stigler's results, build upon his work and seek out recognition and prestige among their peers. In this way, the economic literature over-invests in Stigler's *The Theory of Price* (1952 [1966]). The growing popularity of the 'Coase Theorem' and second-generation models increasingly reinforce each other. The scholarly life of economists is a PEC world in which negative 'externalities' (e.g. misrepresentations of ideas) are not always and perfectly self-corrective. Positive feedback loops in the world in which intellectuals live and operate (such as journals, conferences and other informal meetings), which does not allow perfecting solutions to come about so easily. Errors frequently remain uncorrected.

Epistemic costs involved in the formation of the 'theorem' decrease the chances of replicating the findings of the original article. Scarcity of resources, such as time constraints due to pressures to publish and write grant proposals (Frey 2003, Klamer and van Dalen 2002), plays the most important role here: researchers' limited time does not allow them to re-examine the results of the models in previous generations. Likewise, had economists replicated Stigler's 1966 interpretation by way of simply revisiting 'The Problem of Social Cost' for

10 *Epistemic responsibility of economists*

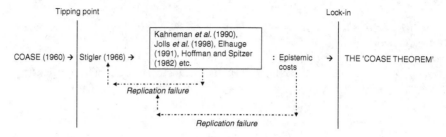

Figure 1.1 The intellectual formation of the 'Coase Theorem'

Note: The diagram, by way of using symbols representing sequential stages and mechanisms between stages in the most simplistic form, depicts the transmission mechanism in the market of economic ideas in which scholarly processes of decision-giving authors after Stigler's 1966 book transform into the 'Coase Theorem'. Arrows with dots (---▸) correspond to replication failure in which second-generation models (Kahneman *et al.*1990, Jolls *et al.* 1998, etc.) do not test the findings of the first-generation model (Stigler 1966) and principally rely on (i.e. reproduce) available results in the market. Colon (:) signifies the costs generated during the transaction between second generation models and Stigler (1966). In the case of the 'Coase Theorem', epistemic costs are the opportunity costs of allowing time to replicate the results of Coase (1960). Such costs disallow intellectuals to retest the result of Stigler (1966) and lock them into a particular research programme – the 'Coase Theorem'. Bold arrows between stages (➔) show the direction of the working mechanism. Tipping point is where the erroneous interpretation of Stigler was published in 1966. Lock-in is the stage in which the 'Coase Theorem' is accepted as the established message of Coase (1960). The diagram indicates that inputs in the market of economic ideas such as errors in interpretation, via the mechanism of replication failure, lead to a particular result – such as the 'Coase Theorem'.

themselves, the assumption of zero transaction costs would perhaps not have had such an impact on the way economists understood Coase's original contribution. Economists who believed that Coase's contribution was important could and should have rechecked the 'theorem' in 'The Problem of Social Cost' instead of simply reproducing the conclusions in Stigler's 1966 book. Yet economists did not do so until recently. Empirical findings (Butler and Garnett 2003, Medema 2010) show that whereas almost all the articles on or about the 'Coase Theorem' cite Stigler 1966, some of the most cited articles most heavily focused on it do not even cite Coase's 1960 article, such as Kahneman *et al.* 1990. For instance, in my doctoral thesis, entitled 'Intellectual Paths and Pathologies' (2009), I closely examined the most cited and the latest articles mentioning the 'The Problem of Social Cost' in order to see whether (and in what ways) economists have used the 'Coase Theorem' in their works. I found that three-quarters of the articles that I examined still misrepresented 'The Problem of Social Cost' (Yalcintas 2009, 3–23). Such empirical studies suggest that the 'Coase Theorem' has a long past but a short history: the 'theorem' has been around for 50 years (perhaps more) but Coase's actual contribution is not as old. Today, the 'Coase Theorem' has turned into a case of intellectual path dependency in which a small event (a (mis-)interpretation of an original contribution) grew so large (the 'Coase Theorem') that it has dominated all discussion of Coase's contribution and caused his original contribution to be entirely lost until recently. If the

Matters of opinion or questionable research practices? 11

researchers had (economic) incentives to replicate Coase (1960), the 'Coase Theorem' could have been 'corrected' long ago. Coase reported:

> I would not wish to conclude that, while consideration of what would happen in a world of zero transaction costs can give us valuable insights, these insights are, in my view, without value except as steps on the way to the analysis of the real world of positive transaction costs. We do not do well to devote ourselves to a detailed study of the world of zero transaction costs, like augurs divining the future by the minute inspection of the entrails of a goose.
>
> (Coase 1981, 187)

Coase is right: it is questionable how well economists would do, devoting themselves to the 'Coase Theorem'. But, still, economists 'stick to their guns' (Jolink and Vromen 2001), especially when they are charged about issues on which they already have strong opinions. Perhaps it is the nature of economic scholarship that scholars refuse to change their minds about the ideological consequences of their models. More sophisticated accounts of the evolutionary social ontology of academic workmanship, such as the one tried in this book, might be needed to resolve the complications in the life story of ideas. In fact, ideas do not come out of nothing. Scholarship has a life. It evolves, it transforms, and sometimes it gets stuck. Scholarship cannot overcome every difficulty. Such difficulties are easily visible to an eye that has not been blinded by the once-powerful idea of continuous progression and growth of knowledge in academic scholarship. A PEC worldview may help us understand why some views have survived in academic scholarship yet are inefficient and have not yielded desirable outcomes as expected. The question now is the following: is it possible to avoid misreadings, over-emphases and errors? According to the PEC worldview of science, it is not. However, what is more important than preventing such failures from happening is discovering institutional remedies that uncover and correct errors as soon as possible. In order to be able to do this, one should be knowledgeable about the epistemic costs of academic scholarship and the consequences that such costs give rise to.

What if Stigler had never formulated the 'Coase Theorem' in 1966? It is not a matter of minor theoretical detail in economics, in which the error could simply be corrected by doing a little historical and philosophical research on Coase's 1960 article. The significance of the problem in the case of the 'Coase Theorem' is that the error has metastasized into a number of fields of social research and it is not entirely possible to undo the consequences of the applications of the 'theorem' in economic and juridical matters. The 'Coase Theorem' has been one of the most popular and cited theorems in economics, law and political science. As of January 2015, Coase's 'The Problem of Social Cost' was cited 4,544 times, according to Thomson Reuters' Web of Knowledge, whereas George Akerlof's 'The Market for Lemons: Quality, Uncertainty, and Market Mechanism' was cited 4,035 times, Armen A. Alchian and Harold Demsetz's 'Production, Information Costs, and Economic Organization' 2,911 times and Kenneth J. Arrow's 'The Implications of Learning by Doing' 2,051 times.

12   *Epistemic responsibility of economists*

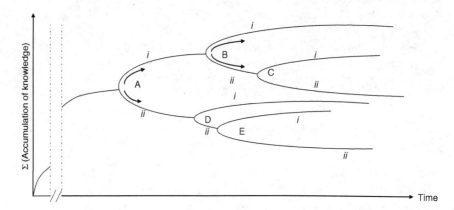

Figure 1.2 Evolution of ideas in the absence of continual progression

I propose to respond to the above question of 'what if' in terms of the theory of intellectual path dependence, in the hope that we are able to move beyond the life story of the 'Coase Theorem' *per se* and arrive at a sophisticated methodological tool that might provide valuable insight into similar cases in the history of economic ideas and, additionally, of all ideas where economists do not reject refuted theories and errors remain uncorrected for long periods of time. I claim that, under conditions of intellectual path dependence, it is impossible to achieve continual progression in the evolutionary history of (economic) ideas. Path dependence in intellectual history, or intellectual path dependence, means that the initial conditions of certain ways of thinking sometimes lock us in to particular pathways. Such pathways occur when consequences of small events irreversibly catch intellectuals in their complex web and are amplified over time. The distinctive property of such conditions is that the evolution of ideas does not necessarily lead to any predefined end point. Historical small events trigger shifts in the course of events and this leads to positive or negative consequences that move the system away from its systematic course. After small events take place, complex webs of academic scholarship function in one of the following ways (see Figure 1.2): (i) as a short-cut that moves the system to a better state and elevates it to higher levels of order which could only be reached within longer time spans if there had been no interruptions or (ii) as a hindrance that breaks the system down and disallows intellectuals to proceed further and achieve scientific progress. When historical small events become a hindrance (ii), a small uncorrected error sometimes feeds back a negative cumulative effect on the progress of scientific knowledge. When they operate as a short-cut (i), however, the conditions that turn an event into a starting point of a new pathway can be the breaking point of an old one such that they unlock the old course of events bearing path dependent properties and perhaps lead to more complex evolutionary pathways. This would mean an upward movement of the

Matters of opinion or questionable research practices? 13

system to more coherent and sophisticated levels. Within intellectual paths, setting a new start in motion is not easy (and sometimes impossible) for a number of reasons. Such impossibility could be a chance for improvement (that is, further sophistication) of the evolution of ideas; however, the direction of the evolution of events after such bifurcation points depends completely on the conditions that take place afterwards.

What is wrong with economists?

For about a decade or so, economists, both orthodox and unorthodox, have thought about the question of 'What is wrong with economics?' (Reiss 2011). Historians and philosophers of economics looked for plausible answers to the following questions. Why has economics failed to introduce realistic assumptions? Why have economists kept teaching and researching monolithic methodologies? Why have econometric models become less able to make plausible predictions? (For a collection of essays on these questions, see Fullbrook 2004, 2003, Cohen 2007, Krugman 2009, Coy 2009, Elliot 2010, Rothman 2011, Colander 1991, Kirman 2010, Woo 1986.) Public figures discussed the questions in the popular media, especially after the 2008 Financial Crisis (Chakrabortty 2012, Harvey 2012, Davidson 2012, Greeley 2012, Milne 2013, *The Economist* 2011, Johnson 2012). Challenges to orthodox economical thinking are not new (Marx 1859, Veblen 1909, Hoover 1926, Ward 1972, Bell and Kristol 1981) and, as the list of references in this page suggests, they are just too many and varied. (See also Colander *et al.* 2009, Lawson 2009, Mirowski 2010, Worrell 2010, Fox 1997.) As recent works on the same questions show, the scale and scope of concern among economists are growing. I argue that intellectual path dependence offers an original answer to these questions. Let me elaborate.

There is a myth among researchers, as well as the general public, that science is capable of correcting errors that might have happened in its past due to questionable practices of scientists. There has been a common thought that refuted, erroneous and invalidated theories are eventually eliminated or revised in social and natural sciences. It is assumed that, as time goes by, truer theories would replace nullified hypotheses by standard means of sciences such as negation and falsification. An unending process of trial and error would gradually help scientific knowledge to 'grow'. In this way, sciences would 'progress' into 'higher' stages of understanding.

Arguing that the world is governed by reason, Friedrich Hegel wrote the following:

> At issue there are shapes of consciousness, each of which dissolves itself in being realized, has its own negation for result – and thereby has gone over to a higher shape. The one thing needed to *achieve scientific progress* … is the recognition of the logical principle that negation is equally positive.
>
> (Hegel 1812 [2010], 33, italics in original)

14   *Epistemic responsibility of economists*

In *The Social Function of Science* (1939, 329), John Desmond Bernal claimed that 'the moment a new theory has invalidated older views in any region of science, a thorough revision of that region should be carried out with the minimum of delay'. In his *Conjectures and Refutations: The Growth of Scientific Knowledge* (1963, 216), Karl Popper argued that:

> [T]he history of science, like the history of all human ideas, is a history of irresponsible dreams, of obstinacy, and of error. But science is one of the very few human activities – perhaps the only one – in which errors are systematically criticized and fairly often, in time, corrected. This is why we can say that, in science, we often learn from our mistakes, and why we can speak clearly and sensibly about making progress there.

Last, but not least, John Kenneth Galbraith claimed '[e]conomics is not durable truth; it requires continuous revision and accommodation. Nearly all its error is from those who cannot change' (Galbraith 1981, 125).

Self-correction in science means that errors, mistakes and misinterpretations are automatically cleared off if and when scientists have the opportunity to exchange ideas freely. As Wible remarks, too,

> [f]rom an economic point of view, science seems to move forward most rapidly when structured as small-numbers pluralism. Progress in science, to the extent that it occurs, is a consequence of focusing scarce scientific resources and the best scientific minds on the very best theories and their next best alternatives.
>
> (Wible 1998, 2)

Although I think that scientists vigorously debate viewpoints of other scientists, I argue that sciences and humanities are *not* always self-corrective, neither in the short nor the long run. Under conditions of intellectual path dependence, where the standard procedures of scientific reasoning such as dialectics and critical rationalism do not clear the market of ideas from the consequences of enduring errors and mistakes, errors remain uncorrected. The invisible hand in science does not properly work.

How can this happen? As Figure 1.1 also demonstrates, first-generation models include influential articles whose findings, by virtue of innovative research programmes, are (re-)formulated in original ways. After the first-generation models, findings are popularized and spread in the market. Second-generation models often take the form of textbooks and secondary or follow-up research, the findings of which are primarily borrowed from first-generation models. Second-generation models are so influential that they frequently cite first-generation models as well as each other and, as a result, their citation figures increase logarithmically. *Their* results are thus established in the market. The findings of the first-generation models are not often replicated because of high opportunity costs of allowing time for retesting the findings of others. Reputation and power also affect the selection process of researchers where scholars utilize the works of reputable authors to legitimize their own findings (Sterman and Wittenberg 1999). For instance, research conducted by Nobel laureates and powerful institutions with which Nobel laureates are affiliated (such as RAND Corporation, see Mirowski 2002, 153–231) are highly credited and further research is often directed by the outcomes of such authors' work. During all of this, access to financial resources and possibilities of finding research partners play prominent roles. This intermediary phase is thus (1) economically constructed so that the growing popularity of the first- and second-generation models operates under increasing returns, (2) the search for research funds is highly influential on the way further research (and its methodology) is conducted and (3) epistemic costs determine whether to replicate the findings of the original research programme.

Now, my point is that during the process of path formation, there is no guarantee that errors, no matter how small or how big, are corrected. Who can ever know that findings and methodology of a particular piece of scholarly publication, if and when the findings and methodologies are not tested for validity, do not contain any mistakes? And who can ever assure that mistakes in the finding and methodologies, if and when they are not tested for validity, will eventually be corrected?

Errors in the history of economics

Steven Pinker argues that 'the defining practices of science, including open debate, peer review, and double-blind methods, are explicitly designed to circumvent the errors and sins to which scientists, being human, are vulnerable. Scientism does not mean that all current scientific hypotheses are true; most new ones are not, since the cycle of conjecture and refutation is the lifeblood of science' (Pinker 2013, n.p.). I agree with Pinker that scientists are vulnerable to errors. But, is refutation really the lifeblood of sciences? I doubt it. As the case of the 'Coase Theorem' suggests, among others in the history of economic thought, controversies in the history of economics do not resolve easily (if at all). Theories, ideas and viewpoints are not always cleansed of controversial content.

In the history of economic ideas, we detect numerous instances of error in the ways economists analyse the phenomena they live by. Errors often cause the evolution of the economic literature to 'change tracks'. Stanley Jevons once argued that 'that able but wrong-headed man, David Ricardo, shunted the car of Economic science on to a wrong line, a line, however, on which it was further urged towards confusion by his equally able and wrong-headed admirer, John Stuart Mill' (Jevons 1871, 45). Jevons thought that Malthus and Senior had a better understanding of 'true doctrines'. But the influence of Ricardo and Mill was powerful. 'It will be a work of labour', Jevons claimed, 'to pick up the fragments of a shattered science and to start anew' (ibid., li–lii). It is a hard task, he argued, though a must for those who would like to see the advance of economic science.

Table 1.1 Tabulation of cases

The model or the case	What is wrong with the model or the case?	The original model(s) replicated or the original case(s) reconsidered	The source(s) replicating the model or reconsidering the case	Comment
Several passages from *The Wealth of Nations* (1776)	Adam Smith is claimed to have plagiarised from the works of physiocrats.	Smith (1776).	Rothbard 1995 [2006].	No serious research has been conducted about this issue.
The 'Coase Theorem'	Ronald Coase claims that the world in which we live is a world of positive transaction costs. The 'Coase Theorem' implies zero transaction costs.	Stigler 1952 [1966].	McCloskey (1998a), Medema (2009).	The error has not been fully corrected.
Statistical significance tests	Economists have misused the statistical significance tests.	Several articles published in the *American Economic Review* in the 1980s and the 1990s.	Ziliak and McCloskey (1996, 2004a, b, 2008).	Misused statistical significance tests are not corrected. Articles are not retracted.
The case of QWERTY	The original case of path dependence in economics, QWERTY, is misleading: QWERTY, contrary to what has been claimed, is an efficient keyboard system.	David (1985).	Liebowitz and Margolis (1990), Kay (2013), Vergne (2013).	Errors in the original case study are well documented. But QWERTY is still widely used as an example of path dependence in economics.
Stereotyping and confirmation bias in econometrics	The claim that 'women are more risk averse than men' is not supported empirically.	Several articles on risk aversion published in top journals of economics, finance and psychology.	Nelson (2014, 2015a, 2015b).	No measures to prevent stereotyping and confirmation bias are taken.

Software packages	Solutions are often inaccurate. Many software packages have bugs.	Several software packages, including EViews, LIMDEP, SHAZAM, TSP and spreadsheets such as MS Excel, Open Office Calc and Gnumeric	McClullough (1998, 1999a, 1999b, 1999c)	The software packages that contain well-known statistical flaws are still in the market; discrepancies in the algorithms and codes remain uncorrected.
'Debt intolerance ceiling'	The model contains coding errors. It also excludes data that would have changed the results of the model.	Reinhart and Rogoff (2010a, b).	Herndon *et al.* (2013b).	Austerity plans relied heavily on the original article by Reinhart and Rogoff. No economist has ever been accused of fraud or manipulation of data.
The Chicago Boys	Several Chicago-trained economists played roles in the neoliberal transformation of the Chilean economy in the 1970s.	Policies made by several economists and bureaucrats.	Valdés (1995).	No economist has officially been accused of conflict of interest or ideological manipulation.
The role of military funds in the USA after the WWII	Research units at several corporations and institutions sponsored the development of game theory and operations research.	Harmful consequences of the ties of universities to corporations and institutions in the USA.	Mirowski (2002).	No economist or institution has officially been accused of mismanaging research monies.
The 2008 financial crisis	Economists in reputable economics departments in the USA are claimed to have contributed to the materialization of the 2008 Financial Crisis.	Several cases documented in *Capitalism: A Love Story* (2009), *Inside Job* (2010), *Margin Call* (2011), *Too Big to Fail* (2011).	Harvey (2012), Colander *et al.* (2009), Chakrabortty (2012), Milne (2013).	No economist has ever been accused of fraud or fabrication and manipulation of data.

18 *Epistemic responsibility of economists*

William Coleman points at the consequences of the issue as well. He argues:

> [I]nstead of moving further away ('ahead') from the past, economic thought has sometimes moved 'forward into the past' as old problems recur, and older theories live again. Thus in the 1970s slow growth of the UK economy promoted Roger Bacon and Walter Eltis to advance classical growth like diagnoses of this sluggishness: too few producers. Similarly, the war between post-Keynesians and Monetarists in the same period was reminiscent of the 1840s controversy between the Banking School and the Currency School.
>
> (Coleman 2005, 111)

Likewise, the South Sea Bubble was repeated when Wall Street crashed in 1929. Families were torn apart at the time; people turned into beggars (see Mackay 1841 [1995], 46–88; Colbert 2001, 13–14).

Mark Blaug (1962 [2003], ix) states that 'great chunks of the history of economic thought are about mistakes in logic and gaps in analysis ... [mistakes which were] propelled forward by the desire to refine, to improve, to perfect'. What if the intellectual history of economics has been full of errors? For many historians of economics, this is quite 'normal' because error in the making of civilizations is merely a result of the imperfect nature of human understanding. For them, errors are sooner or later corrected; more important than errors are corrections. However, the intellectually path dependent evolution of economics suggests that self-correction processes are often complex and that there is no guarantee that corrections would waive all of the irreversible effects of the past with a finger snap. In other words, every error amounts to a compromise (small or big) in the continuity of history where the success of social and intellectual projects relies on uninterrupted maintenance of ongoing scholarly conversation and empirical back-ups in old theories. When errors do not disappear easily and without causing further trouble, they make a long-lasting idea in history impossible – the idea that perfection in the world of scholars is achievable.

An example of long-lasting errors in the history of ideas is statistical significance tests in economics. Statistical significance tests are tools that tell the testers whether a relationship between two variables exists in statistical terms. However, statistical significance tests do not reveal how powerful the relationships between the variables are. Steve T. Ziliak and Deirdre N. McCloskey (Ziliak and McCloskey 1996, 2008, 2004b) argue that sciences are about magnitudes of relationships and scientists should ask the question 'How much?' rather than ask 'whether'. In *The Cult of Statistical Significance: How the Standard Error Costs Us Jobs, Justice, and Lives* (2008), Ziliak and McCloskey claim that medical scientists, psychologists and economists have failed to do that. Examining 182 papers published in the *American Economic Review* during the 1980s, the authors report that 70 per cent of the articles did not distinguish statistical significance from economic significance and 96 per cent of the articles misused statistical significance tests. Ziliak and McCloskey conducted the same survey for the empirical papers of the next decade and concluded that the case had not improved.

Matters of opinion or questionable research practices? 19

Economists have, since the 1980s, not ceased to make the same error. Ziliak and McCloskey (2008, 80) write,

> Of the 187 relevant articles published in the 1990s, 79 percent mistook statistically significant coefficients for economically significant coefficients (as compared to 70 percent in the earlier decade). In the 1980s a disturbing 53 percent had relied exclusively on statistical significance as a criterion of importance at its first use; in the 1990s, an even more disturbing 60 percent did.

The substitution of existence for size is an error that has lasted in economics for decades. The statistical significance tests are one of the examples of important intellectual paths in the scholarly life of economics for which setting a new path in motion has long been impossible (Altman 2004). Ziliak and McCloskey (2004b, 250–1) conclude:

> The textbooks are wrong. The teaching is wrong. The seminar you just attended is wrong. The most prestigious journal in your scientific field is wrong ... Perhaps you feel frazzled by what Morris Altman (2004) called the 'social psychological rhetoric of fear', the deeply embedded path dependency, that keeps the abuse of significance in circulation. You want to come out of it. But perhaps you are cowed by the prestige of Fisherian dogma. Or, worse thought, perhaps you are cynically willing to be corrupted if it will keep a nice job.

One of the consequences of intellectual path dependence in economics is that the efforts of critics who claim that mathematical and econometric techniques in economics are often inaccurate are partially or totally ignored. B. D. McCullough, professor of decision sciences at Drexel University, has published many articles on errors in computation and the reliability of mathematical techniques in economics (see, for instance, McCullough 1998, 1999a, 2000). He has argued that computer solutions are often inaccurate and many software packages have bugs. His works provide evidence that some of the software packages yield a specific solution which another package fails to produce. Econometric textbooks rarely mention which software packages in the market produce more accurate results. McCullough (1999c) claims that:

> the market provides us with what we want; and we want speed, user-friendliness, and the latest econometric features ... Frequently there is a trade-off between speed and accuracy, and often the fastest way to compute is not the most accurate way to compute.

In a number of case studies (McCullough 1999b, McCullough and Heiser 2008, McCullough and Yalta 2013), he has shown that different packages produce different solutions to the same problem. He thus concludes that many software packages produce untrustworthy outcomes.

20 *Epistemic responsibility of economists*

> Researchers conducting nonlinear estimation typically make no effort to guard against such inaccurate answers ... We surveyed ten econometrics texts; while each advocated the use of computer software to produce a solution to nonlinear estimation problems, none suggested verifying the solution produced by a software package. The general position of econometrics texts and researchers is that the 'solution' produced by a nonlinear solver may be accepted uncritically.
>
> (McCullough and Vinod, 2003, 873–4)

The software packages that contain well-known statistical flaws are still on the market; discrepancies in the algorithms and codes remain uncorrected.

Debates on the significance of the enduring consequences of errors which econometric techniques cause is a debate on which many economists, orthodox and unorthodox, would like to express an opinion. The increasing number of economists who claim that there is a multitude of errors in the history of economics caused by econometric research suggests that the theory of intellectual path dependence has applications in many sub-fields of economics. Some economists are asking for 'greater transparency' in econometrics (see, for instance, Levy and Peart 2008, 2013). Some others claim that the mathematical language that is used in econometric textbooks fails to express the causal concepts. Bryant Chen and Judea Pearl (2013, 4) argue that 'not only have [econometric models] failed to penetrate the field, but even basic causal concepts lack precise definitions and, as a result, continue to be confused with their statistical counterparts'. Julie Nelson has published articles on the persistent consequences of stereotyping and confirmation bias in econometrics (see Nelson 2014, 2015a, b). Nelson argues that the claim that 'women are more risk averse than men' is not supported empirically. Nelson (2014, 1) defines stereotyping as 'the tendency to draw on overly simple beliefs about groups to make judgments about individuals'; and confirmation bias is 'the tendency to perceive and seek out information that confirms one's pre-existing beliefs, and avoid information that conflicts'. Economists often start to research a particular topic with beliefs in 'sex differences'. As the data is collected and models are constructed, it seems obvious that such differences reflect an underlying reality. The beliefs of economists feed the consequences of data and models, and vice versa. It is assumed that members within a group are identical; the degree of overlap of male and female distributions are not debated. Differences of scores on risk-related variables are overlooked. Nelson reports that articles with the following titles thus appear very often: 'Will Women be Women?' (Beckmann and Menkhoff 2008), 'Girls will be Girls' (Lindquist and Säve-Söderbergh 2011). As a consequence, '[a] whole literature can, apparently, drift in a particular direction', Nelson (2014, 14) argues, 'due to widespread (though possibly erroneous) cultural beliefs combined with generally accepted (but in actuality, non-rigorous) methodological practices'.

Economists have also questioned the usefulness of the notions and analytic tools used in economics. It is ironic that these considerations are almost totally absent from many of the economics textbooks these days. For instance, in *The*

Aggregate Production Function and the Measurement of Technological Change (2013), Jesus Felipe and John J. S. L. McCombie argue that the aggregate production functions, such as Cobb–Douglas and constant elasticity of substitution (CES) production functions, which are commonly used in real business-cycle (RBC) theory and short-run models of unemployment, are 'not even wrong' because, to say the least, the structures of many production industries, within an economy and across economies, are not even similar, but such functions assume that they are identical. Felipe and McCombie (2013, 4) ask: 'Does it make any sense to combine the values of each of the outputs and the inputs of the two industries and estimate a production function that purportedly represents the underlying combined technology of these two industries?' In *GDP: A Brief but Affectionate History* (2014), Diane Coyle questions the usefulness of gross domestic product (GDP), a keystone notion broadly used in national income accounting, as a measurement of a country's economic wellbeing. She argues that the economic policy-makers have long seen GDP as an important indicator to gauge the success of an economy. But it is an 'artificial, complicated, and abstract' conception, Coyle (ibid., 5) claims, which has undesirably affected the livelihood of several peoples in history. GDP has been defined differently and it has served different purposes in the hands of economic and social policy-makers since it was first formulated in the 1930s. After all, GDP is not a one-size-fits-all methodology to measure the welfare of an economy. '[GDP] is a measure designed for the twentieth-century economy of rapid innovation and intangible, increasingly digital, services', Coyle argues. 'How well the economy is doing is always going to be an important part of everyday politics, and we're going to need a better measure of "the economy" than today's GDP' (ibid., 6). Likewise, Julian Reiss, in his *Error in Economics: Towards a More Evidence-based Economics* (2008), claims that such economical concepts and measurements as Consumer Price Index, ratio spectrum auctions and natural experiments on minimum wages, are based on poor evidence. They wrap up theory, value judgements and evidence in single indices. Specificities of particular cases and heterogeneities of context are ignored. Many concepts and measurements in 'theory-based economics', Reiss concludes, are erroneous.

William A. Barnett does not challenge the notions and conceptual tools in economics. However, in *Getting It Wrong* (2012), Barnett claims that, especially prior to the 2008 Financial Crisis, the formulas used by economic policy-makers had become obsolete because the data were inaccurate. If business firms and governments had acquired best-practice data, Barnett argues, they could have better assessed systemic risks and decreased their leverages.

Individual and collective actions of economists who are involved in political and criminal activities have been examined as well. Economists who are involved in QRPs have caused the scientific credibility of economics to diminish in the public eye. For instance, in his *Pinochet's Economists: The Chicago School of Economics in Chile* (1995), Juan Gabriel Valdés outlines the role that the 'Chicago Boys' played in the radical transformation of Chilean society where a

22 *Epistemic responsibility of economists*

military coup abolished the democratic government in 1973. Valdés remarks that the policies of the Chicago-trained economists in Chile:

> anticipated a fashion – financial abundance, assaults on the state, the denigration of government intervention, the celebration of rapid enrichment, the 'yuppie' boom, and complete disregard for social policies – a fad that some neo-liberal intellectuals and especially economists felt would distinguish western 'modernity' in the closing years of the century.
>
> (Ibid., 3)

Philip Mirowski provides a detailed account of the intellectual reorganization of economics by military funds in the USA after the World War II when 'research units organized for military purposes', such as RAND Corporation and Rad Lab, sponsored the applications of game theory, operations research and experimental economics to military tactics. '[I]t was the military', Mirowski claims, 'that acted as the executive science manager in charge of economics in the postwar period' (Mirowski 2002, 562–3).

For further cases, readers may be interested in reading an online discussion that took place on Eh.net, a website owned and operated by the Economic History Association, between May and July 2005. The discussion was initiated by John Womack's question: 'Why teach the history of error?' It later evolved into a discussion on several cases and aspects of errors in the history of economics. The discussion has been outlined in (Fiorito and Samuels 2006).

Economic philosophy as economic criticism

So what? What if errors and QRPs are common in economics? Many cases in the history of economics suggest that patterns of failure, in which economic scholarship adheres to erroneous explanations, do not fit in many accounts of the philosophers and historians of economic science who explain how economists choose theories with conventional explanations. Coexistence of refutations and erroneous explanations requires further reflection on the conditions under which economists choose not to modify their explanations. I argue that an economic critique of academic scholarship, based on the theory of intellectual path dependence, should, in the first place, be able to account for the simple question: *why do economists refuse to change their minds when their theories are refuted by evidence and falsified by philosophical reasoning?*

Academic scholarship is an economical process in which scholars do not always react to changes in forces rapidly. Often, there are lags of response, causing epistemic hystereses that hold paradigms or research programmes dependent not only on the current state but also on the history of the past states. A way for economists to fight epistemic hystereses is to listen to their critics. In literature, cinema, theatre and many other branches of humanities, criticism is an essential part of the profession. However, unlike humanities and arts, criticism is not a part of the economic discipline at any rate. Art critics and literature critics are highly credited for their criticism and remarks on works by painters and novelists, whereas there are not many scholars in the economics profession doing the work of somebody whom we might call an economic critic. In fact, Philip R. P. Coelho *et al.* (2005) report that, from the period of 1963 to 2004, the percentage of articles and pages devoted to critical commentary in *American Economic Review*, *Economic Journal, Journal of Political Economy, Quarterly Journal of Economics* and *Review of Economics and Statistics* have declined sharply. In the second half of the 1960s, more than 30 per cent of the articles published in the *Quarterly Journal of Economics* were devoted to critical commentary. In the 2000s, it declined to less than 10 per cent. In the same period, nearly 15 per cent of the articles published in the *Economic Journal* were devoted to critical commentary. In the 2000s this figure decreased to nil. A major reason for the insufficient number of economic critics in economics is that the publication of critical commentary is costly to economics journals. 'The opportunity cost of publishing a comment (and the almost inevitable reply)', Robert Whaples (2006) claims, 'is that the journal cannot publish as many standard articles. Standard articles are cited more frequently, and hence probably are more effective in building and maintaining the prestige of the journal.' Another reason for the diminishing number of economic critics is that economists, who are very good at colonizing such disciplines as philosophy, sociology, history and psychology, are not tolerant of philosophers, sociologists, historians and psychologists who offer critical comments on the state of economics. Economists are not keen to be accountable for their own ways of thinking and writing.

An economic critic is a scholar whose primary research interest is the methodological and rhetorical assessment of the works of economists. Economic critics provide epistemological criticisms and remarks on the works by 'practising economists'. The significance of economic criticism does not necessarily originate from a particular ideology and political view, but lays in scholars' critical intention to evaluate the works of economists. Evaluations of economic critics can avoid the unmerited strengthening of particular schools in economics; their evaluations may challenge the established views.

Can economic philosophers fill in this gap? In my view, many economic philosophers have expressed their disillusionment with orthodox economic theories. The works of economic philosophers are a source of inspiration in terms of seeing inadequacies in economic theorizing. Concerned by the unresponsiveness of the community of economists about the significance of the problem, economic philosophers have long been critical of the economical methodology and rhetoric of the orthodoxy in economics. Economic philosophy today is a branch of the philosophy of social science where its practitioners study the epistemological, ontological and rhetorical issues in economic argumentation such as rationality, positivism, ethics and causation.

Economic philosophy 'is to be understood simply as philosophy of science applied to economics' (Blaug 1980 [1987], xi). The number of publications and average number of citations that each publication gets within economic philosophy have increased over the past few decades. There are now a considerable number of independent journals for economic philosophy (*Economics and*

24 *Epistemic responsibility of economists*

Philosophy, Journal of Economic Methodology, Journal of Philosophical Economics, Erasmus Journal of Philosophy and Economics, Revue de philosophie économique, Oeconomia – History/Methodology/Philosophy and *Economic Thought: History, Philosophy, and Methodology*), as well as a number of history of economic thought and unorthodox economics journals (such as *History of Political Economy, Journal of Economic Issues, Cambridge Journal of Economics, Kyklos* etc.). Additionally, printing houses (such as Routledge) are increasingly publishing peer-reviewed articles and books on philosophical topics within economics. A number of graduate programmes, mainly in Europe, such as those at Erasmus University, the London School Economics, the University of Bayreuth, the University of Helsinki and Kingston University, have been launched, granting graduate degrees in Economics and Philosophy. Scholars in economic philosophy are prominent figures not only in philosophy, but also in economic history and the history of economic thought. From a scholarly point of view, economic philosophy has become an established field of research in social sciences.

Today, economic philosophy is intellectually diverged, if not totally separated, from the scholarly agenda in the applied fields of economics. Economic philosophy as economic criticism, or *economic philosophizing*, is transforming economics into a science of asking questions about the findings, methodologies and models of economics, instead of only finding out answers to the problems of the economy such as inflation, rates of unemployment, growth and so forth. Economic philosophy as economics criticism would allow economists to reflect on the ways in which they understand and explain the world around them; it would make them conscious about the validity and the applicability of the knowledge economists produce. Economic criticism would certainly improve the quality of economic scholarship.

One of the debates in economic philosophy since the 1980s has mainly been concerned with the possibility of whether it is possible to frame a meta-theory that would help economists produce better economics. The emergence of many traditions in economic philosophy was the result of the debates that took place in the intellectual pathways that postmodernism and social constructivism have generated against the positivist philosophy of science since the 1960s (Hands 2001, 1–12; Boylan and O'Gorman 1995, 8–35). Since then, debates over topics like the growth of knowledge, prediction, explanation and other issues introduced by philosophers of science, such as Thomas Kuhn, Imre Lakatos and Paul Feyerabend, have taken place with specific interest to economics. For instance, eminent philosophers of science in the traditions of neo-pragmatism, such as Stanley Fish, George Lakoff and Richard Rorty, greatly influenced Deirdre N. McCloskey (McCloskey 1994b, 1990b, 1985), one of the most influential figures in economic philosophy since the 1980s. McCloskey's 'The Rhetoric of Economics' (1983) and *The Rhetoric of Economics* (1985) proved a catalyst, prompting an intense debate between the rhetoric of economics and realism in economics, lasting until the end of the 1990s. McCloskey has long been the proponent of the argument that methodological inscriptions in economics in the

Matters of opinion or questionable research practices? 25

form of '3 x 5 cards' were not useful. McCloskey (1990a, 1994a) makes a distinction between 'philosophical analysis' and 'rhetorical analysis', claiming that philosophical analysis is a compilation of techniques to break concepts into smaller pieces so as to eliminate inconsistencies around the issue and produce true (or truer) claims on or about the facts of the world. By contrast, rhetorical analysis 'does not deal with Truth directly; it deals with conversation' (McCloskey 1985, 28).

According to McCloskey, a conversation is the performance of intellectual actors in scholarly circles so as to convince their peers about new ideas. McCloskey claims that economic conversations feature a 'meta-economical hierarchy': at the bottom is methodology (with a small 'm') – that is, the toolbox of a practising economist. In the middle is Methodology (with a capital 'M') – that is, the rules that demarcate 'science' from 'non-science' such as the Popperian programme of falsifiability. And at the top of the hierarchy lay 'conversational norms' that 'we implicitly adopt by the mere act of joining what our culture thinks of as conversation' (McCloskey 1984, 580): 'Don't lie; pay attention; don't sneer; co-operate; don't shout; let other people talk; be open-minded; explain yourself when asked; don't resort to violence or conspiracy in aid of your ideas' (McCloskey 1994b, 99).

McCloskey's critique of economics has been supported and embraced, partially or wholly, by such economic philosophers as Arjo Klamer, Philip Mirowski, Jack L. Amarglio, David F. Ruccio, Julie Nelson, Steve Ziliak and Irene van Staveren. Nevertheless, she has been criticized by philosophical realists. Proponents of realism in economics, including Tony Lawson and Uskali Mäki, among others, have claimed that it is both possible and useful to underlabour for economics and that it helps '[clarify] the cognitive schemes, conceptual tools, etc., at work behind scientific practices' (Lawson *et al.* 1996). Realism, a philosophical movement that aims at accounting for the internal social mechanisms giving rise to particular social outcomes, argues that social reality is structured. Deeper structures of society are not always observable and can be different from the empirical surface phenomena. Underlying structures of social phenomena, as well as its powers and mechanisms, determine the world as we experience it. Lawson argues that economies and societies are open systems in which components of systems interact with other components in their environment in various ways. Open systems are compilations of dynamic processes where events are over-determined by multiple causes. Orthodox economics, however, is dominated by methodologies that presuppose closed systems in which causation runs in isolated environments. In closed systems, relations between events are constant. Countervailing forces have no effect on the system. Orthodox economics, relying upon analyses of closed systems, requires event regularities that hold that when event x occurs, then event y occurs. According to Lawson, event regularities can operate only under certain conditions. Such conditions are not generalizable. In other words, open systems lack regularities and constants. In order for economics to provide valid explanations of the world in which we live, economists should aim to uncover

26   *Epistemic responsibility of economists*

hidden structures and underlying mechanisms that account for the causal relationships between events. What is wrong with economics, according to Lawson, is not only that economists fail to account for the structures and mechanisms operating on ontological levels, but also that economics departments are unwilling to employ scholars who propagate methodologies alternative to mathematical models and econometrics which rely on deductivist explanations.

It has long been considered that rhetoric of economics and realism in economics are two opposed traditions in economic philosophy. Although proponents of the rhetoric of economics and realism in economics deeply disagree on a number of issues, such as whether economic reality exists independently from each of us or whether better economic methodology is a condition for better economics, I suggest we appraise the significance of the debate between rhetoric of economics and realism in economics on the basis that both have been significant criticisms of orthodox economics. Indeed, one observes more corresponding concerns between rhetoric of economics and realism in economics over the current state of economics than inconsistent views on longstanding philosophical issues. For instance, the debate between rhetoric of economics and realism in economics, especially during the 1990s, has been shaped more by disagreements about their different worldviews than on their criticism of orthodox economics. However, as Lawson has argued (Lawson 2006, 502), critical views in economics could be considered as a division of labour, 'as approaching the same totality but with a distinguishing set of concerns, emphases, motivating interests and (so) questions'. In *Economics and Reality* (1997), Lawson mentions McCloskey thrice (five times including footnotes) and in *Reorienting Economics* (2003) only once (thrice including footnotes). (Lawson does not cite Klamer at all.) In none of his works is Lawson as critical of McCloskey as he is critical of the deductivist methodology in economics. Moreover, Lawson makes several claims parallel to McCloskey's, such as that:

> the essential mode of inference sponsored by transcendental realism is neither induction nor deduction but one that can be styled *retroduction* or *abduction* or 'as if' reasoning. It consists in the movement, on the basis of analogy and metaphor among other things, from a conception of some phenomenon of interest to a conception of some totally different type of thing, mechanism, structure or condition that, at least in part, is responsible for the given phenomenon.
>
> (Lawson 1997, 24)

Lawson also acknowledges the divergence between 'official' methodologies and 'unofficial' methodologies (or, in McCloskey's terms, big M and small m methodologies) when he says that there is an 'incongruity between official and actual stances on methodology' (ibid., 39). Disagreements between Lawson and McCloskey came later, as Lawson's critical ontology evolved into an anti-postmodernist social theory while McCloskey's criticism has been explicitly a part of postmodernist critical theory.

Matters of opinion or questionable research practices? 27

Disagreements between the two of the most prominent economic critics notwithstanding, let us assess the consequences of their critical efforts with regard to the present state of 'practising economics'. How effective have rhetoric of economics and realism in economics been so far? How reactive have 'practising economists' been to the philosophical challenges since the 1980s? In my view, hostility in economics towards economic criticism leads to the issue of 'legitimation' in the sense in which Jean-François Lyotard uses the term. How is it that the scientific community of scholars does not consider statements of conditions regarding internal consistency and experimental verification to be included in the economic rhetoric (Lyotard 1979 [1999], 8)?

For various reasons, scholars regard new theorems invalidating established ones as illegitimate. Historians and philosophers of science have offered plenty of sophisticated explanations for scientists' resistance to scientific discoveries (for instance, Kuhn 1957, McCalman 2009, Hellman 1998). I find most of these explanations convincing. Such explanations are important for us to understand the reasons motivating scholars, preventing them from changing their opinions about the facts of the world. For instance, in numerous accounts, sources of resistance to epistemic novelty are said to be psychological and social. As Bernard Barber (1961, 597) argued:

> there has also been a tendency, where some explanation of the sources of resistance is offered, to express a psychologistic basis – that is, to attribute resistance exclusively to inherent and ineradicable traits or instincts of the human personality … But it must also include the cultural and social dimensions – those shared and patterned idea-systems and those patterns of social interaction that also contribute to resistance.

In the final chapter of the book, I also reassess this issue and argue that such factors as 'unwillingness' and 'docility', among others, retard scholarly processes in which competing theorems are disseminated and reproduced by diversification. Diversification is an intellectually healthy process in which opinions deviate from established explanations. Diversification is a mechanism that increases the wealth of scholarly communities in terms of growing number of theorems, ideas, viewpoints, methods and so forth. However, I claim that competition among scientific explanations time and again generates intellectual losers. An epistemic community may be hostile to divergent thinking and insistent on old methods when members of epistemic community are forced to choose between 'normal research' and 'revolutionary research' (Kuhn 1977). Scholars may combat epistemic innovations because the 'essential tension' between tradition and change amounts to abandoning intellectual commitments in favour of new ones. As Joel Mokyr (1992, 335) argues with regard to technological revolutions, 'the manipulation of nature for the material benefit of humanity has been accompanied by an odd mixture of pride, greed, guilt, and fear'. Intellectual evolution is no different. But could this be all there is? Why do scholars not change their minds despite powerful criticism from within (namely, proponents of rhetoric and realism) and outside of economics?

28 *Epistemic responsibility of economists*

I claim that we can develop an economic account of the epistemic hysteresis in economics. My hypothesis is that economic conservatism is the *reason d'être* of the pervasiveness and prevalence of hostility against criticism in economics. Economic conservatism is the ideology that resists the remarks provided by economic critics, especially when economic criticism requires economists to lock out the established pathways of thought. When economic conservatism becomes the predominant ideology in scholarly processes, private costs of rejecting a theory are no longer equal to the social costs of doing so. As a consequence, scholars consider the option of refusing to reject falsified and invalidated theorems. It might be impossible for economists to detect whether a theorem is flawed and unsupported by evidence. For instance, it is often impossible to replicate economic models because original and new data might be copyrighted and its use (except by the original author) might be prohibited. Under such circumstances, members of the scholarly community cannot be excluded from the usage of models and theorems which might be flawed empirically. Although it is in the self-interest of the community of scholars that economics is reorganized in such a way that economists are able to prevent harmful consequences of QRPs from happening, ideologies of orthodox economics do not easily allow the reproduction of the criticisms by unorthodox economists by way of, say, not publishing unorthodox research in high-impact journals. Just as economists who argue that we all have moral duty towards the society in which we live in order to eliminate the free-rider 'problem', so should economic scholars have moral duty to do what it requires us to waive epistemic costs or perhaps 'moral costs' (Frey 2003). This is one of the ways to increase the intellectual welfare of the community of economic scholars. The alternative might be the 'tragedy of the commons' (Hardin 1968) where 'rational' scholars behaving according to their ideological self-interests, in effect, lead to consequences that contradict the scientific community's long-term interests. These ideologies and other non-scholarly beliefs and habits of thought (Gurpinar and Yalcintas 2015) eventually turn into processes of self-deregulation (or, better, self-*de*correction) where criticism is not intended to alter the behaviour of researchers when errors in lines of reasoning are pointed out and counter-evidence is provided. As a result, competition among rival theories does not always lead to the displacement of erroneous theories. Instead, 'fitter' theories are pulled out of the academic conversation.

Lack of cooperation between economic critics and those defending others who are criticized (i.e. economic conservatives) puts the issue of sustainability of economic scholarship in jeopardy, leading a group of scholars to over-exploit specific epistemic resources and pathways on which they eventually become dependent. Intellectual path dependence is a significant phenomenon, especially when seemingly small, unfavourable decisions in the past cause undesirable consequences in the future – 'tyranny of small decisions' (Kahn 1966). Under conditions of intellectual path dependence, we might have to cease talking about the possibility of the so-called growth of knowledge or so-called truths. The 'truths' do not reveal themselves if no one is held responsible for the social and epistemic costs of refusing to use falsified and invalidated theorems. Indeed,

Matters of opinion or questionable research practices? 29

economic conservatives may be unwilling to give up social and epistemic benefits of keeping using the theorems at the expense of other members of the scholarly community. In this way, erroneous theorems and models are over- and re-produced.

The question as to why economists do not change their minds is conditioned by another question: why should they? One is obliged to show that there is a condition in which economists should consider their critics. When scholars confront their critics, scholars have some rhetorical strategies to make deals with their critics. For instance, they hedge their claims, use polite or modest arguments, praise others, or appeal to authority in order to fortify their position (Myers 1989). Economists do the same. The response to Milton Friedman's article, 'The Quantity Theory of Money: A Restatement' (1956), in which he debated how monetary changes affected the economy, is a case in point. After publishing this article, Friedman was criticized by many scholars, including Karl Brunner, Allan Meltzer, James Tobin, Don Patinkin and Paul Davidson, on the basis that his article lacked a model and empirical results to support the claim he made. However, Friedman took all the challenges seriously, responded to them in a scholarly manner and, as a result, he modified what he initially claimed in the article, although he did not provide a model or further empirical findings to support his claim (Backhouse 1993). In a rhetorical examination of Friedman's responses, Tony Dudley-Evans (1993) found that 63 per cent of Friedman's replies were actually bald on-record, 23 per cent hedging and 10 per cent praise and acceptance. Although the debate over Friedman's theoretical framework went on for many years and Friedman modified his views in some respects (although without providing a model and empirical findings), the impact of the original article has lasted, regardless of what the critics said about the original claim (see also Bloor and Bloor 1993). How did this happen?

N. Gregory Mankiw (1990) provided a response to this question. Surveying the reasons why applied macroeconomists did not change the ways in which they analyzed the economy from the 1970s to the 1990s, despite the fact that academic macroeconomists offered better ways of understanding the economy, Mankiw argues that 'we should not expect these recent developments, no matter how promising, to be of great practical use in the near future. In the long run, however, many of these developments will profoundly change the way all economists think about the economy and economic policy' (ibid., 1647). Mankiw is optimistic about (applied) economists who eventually adapt new theories. He points out that changing one's mind is in fact a process, an ongoing interpretation, in which economists require time to adapt new theories that economists test and think about. If there are errors in economic theorizing, they survive only for a period of time, at the end of which economists change their minds and errors go extinct. Mankiw seems to agree with Daniel Kahneman's well-known argument in his *Thinking, Fast and Slow* (2011) that 'slow-thinking' individuals fix unconscious errors of reasoning as the individuals make considered decisions over time. Mankiw's (and Kahneman's) view may be true for individual economists who are analytical and vigilant in the long run. His views may apply to a number of

30 *Epistemic responsibility of economists*

individual economists who are able to think slowly. However, *economists as a community* seem to be content with 'fast thinking' only. As many of the above cases suggest, from 'Coase Theorem' to confirmation bias in econometric modelling, economists as a community are often gravely locked into conventional ways of thinking, or System 1, even in the long run. As time goes by, economists become less enthusiastic about experimenting novel ways of thinking. Adapting novel ideas is harder for groups of scholars than individuals.

Historians and philosophers of economics often argued that individual scholars repeatedly changed their minds throughout their careers. For instance, Joseph A. Schumpeter remarked that the views of Adam Smith in *The Theory of Moral Sentiments* (1759 [2002]) and *The Wealth of Nations* (1776 [1966]) were irreconcilably different. Schumpeter coined the term 'Das Adam Smith Problem', which today refers to the discussion on whether Adam Smith changed his views on sympathy, previously expressed in the earlier of the works cited above, when later writing *The Wealth of Nations* (1776 [1966]), in which self-interest played the key role (Montes 2003). In *For Marx* (1969), Louis Althusser argued that 'Young Karl Marx', the author of *The Manuscripts* in 1844, changed his views on the economy, society and philosophy as he grew older. Deirdre McCloskey is also a well-known example of a scholar who changed her mind several times in her career. 'I have been most things in my life,' says McCloskey (2000, 27),

> a positivist social engineer, a Joan Baez socialist, and a man. Now I'm a free market feminist, a quantitative postmodernist, and a woman. I'm not ashamed of these changes of mind. Keynes replied to the complaint that he changed his mind on free trade, 'When I get new information I change my mind. What do you do?'

John B. Davis (2013, 46) claims that Mark Blaug changed his position on the rational construction of ideas as well. Later in his career, Blaug 'expressed serious doubts about what rational reconstructions achieve, while also making an argument for historical reconstructions'. Blaug thought that, as Davis argues, there is always a risk of 'loss of content' in current ideas because current ideas are less original and well founded. Finally, in a recent study, investigating the 'ideological migration' of the winners of Swedish Bank Prize in Economic Sciences in Memory of Alfred Nobel between 1969 and 2012, Daniel Klein reports that '[a] person might believe the better idea of two ideas, but for bad reasons. Once his reasons are found bad, he migrates to a different idea, even though other good reasons justify the first. Such might not be the tendency, but certainly it can happen' (Klein 2013, 228). Klein supports his claim by 'meta-evidence' in his research, showing that 16 economics laureates have grown more classical liberal in their later careers whereas five have grown less so.

In recent years, economics journals have retracted a number of articles in which the editors think the conclusions are reached after QRPs. Solmaz Filiz Karabağ and Christian Berggren (2012) document some of the retracted articles published in management and economics journals. Searching the databases of Business Source Premier, Emerald, ScienceDirect and JSTOR, which include the most prestigious management and economics journals, the authors report that 31 articles in management journals and six articles in economics journals have been retracted. Some of the other retracted articles which are not covered in this paper include the following: 'An Agent-Based Decision Support Model for the Development of E-Services in the Tourist Sector' by Frank Bruinsma *et al.* (2010) was retracted in 2014; 'A Framework for Market Discipline in Bank Regulatory Design' by Paul Hamalainen *et al.* (2005) was retracted in 2009; 'Coordinating Ordering, Pricing and Advertising Policies for a Supply Chain with Random Demand and Two Production Modes' by Sheng-Dong Wang *et al.* (2010) was retracted in 2010; and 'The Role of Deliberate and Experiential Learning in Developing Capabilities: Insights from Technology Licensing' by Ulrich Lichtenthaler and Miriam Muethel (2012) was retracted in 2014. The growing number and rate of retractions in economics, albeit too low in relation to the number and rate of retraction in biomedical sciences, suggest that economics journals are willing to take the initiative in clearing the consequences of some of the QRPs printed in their outlets. Many academic journals, such as *American Economic Review*, now require authors to submit a Disclosure Statement about the sources of financial support that the authors used (Glandon 2010; see also the statement of the American Economic Association (AEA), 'The American Economic Review: Data Availability Policy', available on the AEA's website). Also, several other journals, such as *Journal of Money, Credit, and Banking*, *Econometrica*, *Journal of Political Economy* and *Review of Economic Studies*, require the authors to reveal their data and codes in order to make sure that the findings of the articles are replicable in future. *Econ Journal Watch*, inviting authors to submit articles on previously published works in economics, serves the function of debating already published papers. *Econ Journal Watch* invites the original authors to respond to their critics as well.

In a number of individual cases in arts and sciences, authors withdraw their literary and artistic works by their own consent, even though they are not involved in any form of QRPs. Some of these authors claim that the published material causes grave moral damage to themselves. Some others claim that they have changed their views on a research subject on which they published articles and books. In both cases, the artists and authors claim their *moral rights*, as opposed to the copyrights which the publishers possess, on their artworks and their articles (Hansmann and Santilli 1997, Rigamonti 2006, Fortunet 2011). For instance, Jean Paul Sartre, in 1969, claimed his right of withdrawal against his publisher for his *L'existentialisme est un humanisme* (1946). In another well-known case, Charlie Chaplin vs Leslie Frewin Publishers Ltd (1996), the son of Charlie Chaplin sued to block the publication of his father's life story in which Charlie Chaplin harshly criticized his parents. In both cases, the jurisdiction recognized the authors' right of withdrawal. However, the cases were rejected. The difficulty with claiming one's moral right in such cases is obvious: it is not fully possible to retain all the published

32   *Epistemic responsibility of economists*

material from the market. The consequences of an artwork and a book, once they reach the market, are irreversible. Nevertheless, the significance of the issue of moral rights for authors and artists is that those who claim their moral rights are concerned about the possible harmful consequences of their actions for the community of scholars and artists. Even though both cases were unsuccessful and the published material not withdrawn, it is an important signal to actual and potential readers that the authors changed their feelings and thoughts about the published material. In economics, to the best of my knowledge, there is not any case in which the author(s) wished to withdraw his or her own article or book.

In order to help researchers to overcome the difficulty of deciding which scholarly content to trust, CrossRef, 'an association of scholarly publishers that develops shared infrastructure to support more effective scholarly communications' (see their website at http://www.crossref.org/), introduced a new online service, called CrossMark, to verify that the researchers are reading the most recent reliable versions of the articles and books downloaded from the internet. CrossRef now adds a CrossMark logo to every scholarly item downloaded from the CrossRef member publisher. Researchers simply click on the logo. A status box on-screen checks if the document is current. If there have been any corrections, updates, or retractions or withdrawals about the downloaded item, updates are reported to the researchers.

Technological innovations, such as CrossRef, certainly have an improving impact on ensuring the integrity of the published items. However, in my view, QRPs are issues of morality that may not be resolved with technological innovations. The issue of morality in academic scholarship is significant because the individual and social actions of scholars practising research in questionable ways inflict harm upon others. This puts research integrity under serious risk. QRPs cause the erosion of academic trust among scholars. Personality, reputation and honour of the community of scholars are thereby damaged. QRPs downgrade the social value of academic scholarship. Most importantly, QRPs lead to intellectual path dependencies that make it impossible to achieve continuous growth of knowledge. The intellectual welfare of economics can be increased only if scholars care about the moral consequences of their decisions and actions.

Fortunately, a significant number of scholars, students and organizations have become intellectual activists in order to fix the damage caused by QRPs in economics and to safeguard their moral rights on economics knowledge. For instance, Daniel Kahneman, a 'Nobel Laureate' economist and psychologist, issued an open letter in September 2012, entitled 'A Proposal to Deal with Questions about Priming Effects'. In this letter, Kahneman argued the following:

> I see a train wreck looming. I expect the first victims to be young people on the job market. Being associated with a controversial and suspicious field will put them at a severe disadvantage in the competition for positions.

Matters of opinion or questionable research practices? 33

Because of the high visibility of the issue, you may already expect the coming crop of graduates to encounter problems.

(Ibid., 1)

Also, in a letter endorsed by many 'heterodox economists' and sent out to Robert E. Hall, then the President of the AEA, it was stated that '[e]conomics is unusual among the social science professions in that it lacks professional ethical codes or guidelines' (Epstein *et al.* 2011, 2). As a response to the concerns of critical economists as well as many other orthodox economists, the Executive Committee of the AEA 'adopted extensions to its principles for authors' disclosures of potential conflicts of interest in the AEA's publications' (AEA 2012, 1). In a recent paper, Wolfgang Stroebe *et al.* report that 'institutions can almost certainly encourage good practice more than they do at present. At the outset, clear norms and codes of conduct should exist and procedures for investigating fraud should be known, sound, and impartial' (Stroebe *et al.* 2012, 681).

Economics students, too, have been investing significant amounts of time for improvements. In 2001, French students of economics rose up against the monopoly of orthodox theory in undergraduate programmes and prepared a petition for a more realistic and pluralistic economics. Many students in the UK, USA and elsewhere joined the protests and signed the petition. Recently, students in the UK, mainly at the University of Manchester and University of Cambridge, have started new movements. Articles on the students' request to change the teaching syllabus in the UK were published in the popular media (Inman 2013a, Chakrabortty 2013, Ward-Perkins and Earle 2013, Inman 2013b). Many economists worldwide endorsed the claims by the students and expressed supportive views in public. In one of these statements, Marco Schneebalg, the Vice President of the Cambridge Society for Economic Pluralism, claimed that:

The shape of the world economy has changed dramatically over the last twenty years, but the economic curriculum has not. Curriculum reform is necessary and long overdue to overhaul some of the outdated concepts that are still being taught. A re-introduction of the intellectual dynamism of pluralism would reinvigorate the discipline. The last twenty years have seen the dotcom bubble burst and the worst financial crisis since the Great Depression. It's fair to say that economists failed to anticipate the coming of the crisis or its magnitude once it had arrived.

(Schneebalg 2014, n.p.)

The Institute for New Economics Thinking (INET), a non-profit organization that funds, as they put it (at http://ineteconomics.org/about/mission), 'the efforts of scholars all over the world as they change the way economics is studied, considered, and thought', also supports efforts of reform in economics, including restructuring undergraduate syllabi in economics. INET's project, entitled 'Curriculum Open Access Resources in Economics', or 'Core Econ', offers new content and methods of teaching economics curriculum at undergraduate economics departments. It is stated that:

34 *Epistemic responsibility of economists*

The CORE curriculum will equip students to understand how the economy has evolved and how it works by bringing advances in economics research over the past three decades, lessons from economic history, and the comparative experience of different countries into the curriculum.

(http://core-econ.org/)

Academic decency and dignity – that is, a rhetoric that accepts the standards of morality and respectability on scholarly issues – matter more than marshalling the analytic tools of the ordinary rhetoric of economics. Academic decency and dignity will help reform the predicament in economics, which, in the next part of this book, I regard as a consequence of epistemic hystereses in economic scholarship.

References

AEA (American Economic Association). 2012. Press release. Available at: https://www.aeaweb.org/PDF_files/PR/AEA_Adopts_Extensions_to_Principles_for_Author_Disclosure_01-05-12.pdf

Althusser, Louis. 1969. *For Marx*. London: Allen Lane.

Altman, Morris. 2004. 'Statistical Significance, Path Dependency, and the Culture of Journal Publication'. *Journal of Socio-Economics* 33 (5): 651–63.

Arrow, Kenneth J., and Gerard Debreu. 1954. 'Existence of an Equilibrium for a Competitive Economy'. *Econometrica* 22 (3): 265–90.

Backhouse, Roger E. 1993. 'The Debate over Milton Friedman's Theoretical Framework: An Economist's View'. In *Economics and Language*, edited by Willie Henderson, Tony Dudley-Evans and Roger Backhouse, 103–31. London and New York: Routledge.

Barber, Bernard. 1961. 'Resistance by Scientists to Scientific Discovery'. *Science* 134 (3479): 596–602.

Barnett, William A. 2012. *Getting It Wrong: How Faulty Monetary Statistics Undermine the Fed, the Financial System, and the Economy*. Cambridge, MA: MIT Press.

Beckmann, Daniela, and Lukas Menkhoff. 2008. 'Will Women Be Women? Analyzing the Gender Difference among Financial Experts'. *Kyklos* 61 (3): 364–84.

Bell, Daniel, and Irving Kristol (eds). 1981. *The Crisis in Economic Theory*. New York: Basic Books.

Bernal, John Desmond. 1939. *The Social Function of Science*. London: George Routledge & Sons.

Blaug, Mark. 1962 [2003]. *Economic Theory in Retrospect*. 5th edn. Cambridge: Cambridge University Press.

Blaug, Mark. 1980 [1987]. *The Methodology of Economics: How Economists Explain*. Cambridge: Cambridge University Press.

Bloor, Meriel, and Thomas Bloor. 1993. 'How Economists Modify Propositions'. In *Economics and Language*, edited by Willie Henderson, Tony Dudley-Evans and Roger E. Backhouse, 153–68. London and New York: Routledge.

Boylan, Thomas A., and Paschal F. O'Gorman. 1995. *Beyond Rhetoric and Realism in Economics: Towards a Reformulation of Economic Methodology*. London and New York: Routledge.

Bruinsma, Frank, Karima Kourtit, and Peter Nijkamp. 2010. 'An Agent-Based Decision Support Model for the Development of E-Services in the Tourist Sector'. *Review of Economic Analysis* 2: 232–55.

Matters of opinion or questionable research practices? 35

Butler, Michael R., and Robert F. Garnett. 2003. 'Teaching the Coase Theorem: Are We Getting It Right?'. *Atlantic Economic Journal* 31 (2): 133–45.

Calabresi, Guido. 1965. 'The Decision for Accidents: An Approach to Non-fault Allocation of Costs'. *Harvard Law Review* 78 (4): 713–45.

Chakrabortty, Aditaya. 2012. 'Economics has Failed Us: But Where are the Fresh Voices'. *Guardian*, 16 April.

Chakrabortty, Aditaya. 2013. 'Mainstream Economics in Denail: The World has Changed'. *Guardian*, 28 October.

Chen, Bryant, and Judea Pearl. 2013. 'Regression and Causation: A Critical Examination of Six Econometrics Textbooks'. *Real-World Economics Review* 65: 1–20.

Coase, Ronald H. 1959. 'The Federal Communications Commission'. *Journal of Law and Economics* 3 (1): 1–44.

Coase, Ronald H. 1960. 'The Problem of Social Cost'. *Journal of Law and Economics* 3 (October): 1–44.

Coase, Ronald H. 1974. 'The Market for Goods and the Market for Ideas'. *American Economic Review* 64 (2): 384–91.

Coase, Ronald H. 1977. 'Advertising and Free Speech'. *Journal of Legal Studies* 6 (1): 1–34.

Coase, Ronald H. 1981. 'The Coase Theorem and the Empty Core: A Comment'. *Journal of Law and Economics* 24 (1): 183–7.

Coase, Ronald H. 1988. *The Firm, the Market, and the Law*. Chicago: University of Chicago Press.

Coase, Ronald H. 1997. 'Biography of Ronald H. Coase'. In *Nobel Lectures in Economic Sciences (1991–1995)*, edited by Torsten Persson, 3–20. Singapore: World Scientific Publishing Co.

Coelho, Philip R. P., Frederick De Worken-Eley III and James E. McClure. 2005. 'Decline in Critical Commentary, 1963–2004'. *Econ Journal Watch* 2 (2): 355–61.

Cohen, Patricia. 2007. 'In Economic Departments, a Growing Will to Debate Fundamental Assumptions'. *The New York Times*, 11 July.

Colander, David. 1991. *Why Aren't Economists as Important as Garbagemen? Essays on the State of Economics*. New York and London: M. E. Sharp, Inc.

Colander, David, Michael Goldberg, Armin Haas, Katarian Juselius, Alan Kirman, Thomas Lux and Birgitte Sloth. 2009. 'The Financial Crisis and the Systematic Failure of Academic Economics'. *Critical Review: A Journal of Politics and Society* 21 (2–3): 249–67.

Colbert, David. 2001. *Eyewitnesses to Wall Street: 400 Years of Dreamers, Schemers, Busts and Booms*. New York: Broadway Books.

Coleman, William Oliver. 2005. 'Taking Out the Pins: Economics as Alive and Living in the History of Economic Thought'. *Economics Papers: A Journal of Applied Economics and Policy* 24 (2): 107–15.

Cooter, Robert, and Thomas Ulen. 1997. *Law and Economics*. 2nd edn. Reading, MA: Addison-Wesley.

Coy, Peter. 2009. 'What Good are Economists Anyway?'. *Bloomberg Businessweek*, 16 April.

Coyle, Diane. 2014. *GDP: A Brief but Affectionate History*. Princeton, NJ: Princeton University Press.

David, Paul A. 1985. 'Clio and the Economics of QWERTY'. *American Economic Review* 75 (2): 332–7.

36 *Epistemic responsibility of economists*

Davidson, Paul. 2012. 'What Makes Economists So Sure of Themselves, Anyway?'. *Naked Capitalism*. Available at: http://www.nakedcapitalism.com/2012/01/paul-davidson-what-makes-economists-so-sure-of-themselves-anyway.html. Accessed June 2014.

Davis, John B. 2013. 'Mark Blaug on the Historiography of Economics'. *Erasmus Journal for Philosophy and Economics* 6 (3): 44–63.

Dudley-Evans, Tony. 1993. 'The Debate over Milton Friedman's Theoretical Framework: An Applied Linguist's View'. In *Economics and Language*, edited by Willie Henderson, Tony Dudley-Evans and Roger Backhouse, 132–52. London and New York: Routledge.

The Economist. 2011. 'Marginal Revolutionaries'. 31 December.

Edgeworth, Francis Ysidro. 1881. *Mathematical Physics*. London.

Elhauge, Einer R. 1991. 'Does Interest Group Theory Justify More Intrusive Judicial Review?'. *The Yale Law Journal* 101 (1): 31–110.

Elliot, Larry. 2010. 'Rescuing Economics from Its Own Crisis'. *Guardian*, 8 November.

Epstein, Gerald *et al.* 2011. Letter. Available at: link.reuters.com/mak54r. Accessed December 2015.

Felipe, Jesus, and J. S. L. McCombie. 2013. *The Aggregate Production Function and the Measurement of Technical Change: 'Not Even Wrong'*. Cheltenham: Edward Elgar.

Fiorito, Luca, and Warren J. Samuels. 2006. 'Robert Hoxie's Introductory Lecture on the Nature of the History of Political Economy [1916]: The History of Economic Thought as the History of Error'. *Research in the History of Economic Thought and Methodology* 24-C: 49–97.

Fortunet, Edouard. 2011. 'The Author's Moral Right to Withdraw a Work (droit de repentir): A French Perspective'. *Journal of Intellectual Property Law and Practice* 6 (8): 535–41.

Fox, Glenn. 1997. *Reason and Reality in the Methodologies of Economics: An Introduction*. Cheltenham: Edward Elgar.

Frey, Bruno S. 2003. 'Publishing as Prostitution? – Choosing Between One's Own Ideas and Academic Success'. *Public Choice* 116 (1–2): 205–23.

Friedman, Milton. 1956. 'The Quantity of Money: A Restatement'. In *Studies in the Quantity Theory of Money*, edited by Milton Friedman, 3–21. Chicago: University of Chicago Press.

Fullbrook, Edward (ed.). 2003. *The Crisis in Economics: The Post-Autistic Movement – The First 600 Days*. London: Routledge.

Fullbrook, Edward (ed.). 2004. *A Guide to What is Wrong with Economics*. London: Anthem Press.

Galbraith, John Kenneth. 1981. *A Life in Our Times: Memoirs*. Boston: Houghton Mifflin.

Glandon, Philip. 2010. Report on the American Economics Review Data Availability Compliance Project. Available at: https://www.aeaweb.org/aer/2011_Data_Compliance_Report.pdf. Accessed February 2015.

Greeley, Brendan. 2012. 'Are Economics PhDs Learning the Wrong Thing?'. *Bloomberg Businessweek*, 1 June.

Gurpinar, Erkan, and Altug Yalcintas. 2015. 'One Long Argument in Economics: Explaining Intellectual Inertia in Terms of Social Ontology'. Paper presented at STOREP 2015 CONFERENCE, 'Shifting Boundries: Economics in the Crisis and the Challenge of Interdisciplinarity', Torino, 11–13 June.

Hamalainen, Paul, Maximilian Hall and Barry Howcroft. 2005. 'A Framework for Market Discipline in Bank Regulatory Design'. *Journal of Business Finance and Accounting* 32 (1–2): 183–209.

Hands, D. Wade. 2001. *Reflection without Rules: Economic Methodology and Contemporary Science Theory*. Cambridge: Cambridge University Press.

Matters of opinion or questionable research practices? 37

Hansmann, Henry, and Marina Santilli. 1997. 'Authors' and Artists' Moral Rights: A Comparative Legal and Economic Analysis'. *Journal of Legal Studies* 26 (1): 95–143.

Hardin, Garrett. 1968. 'The Tragedy of the Commons'. *Science* 162 (3859): 1243–8.

Harrison, Jeffrey L. 1995. *Law and Economics in a Nutshell.* St Paul, MN: West.

Harvey, J. Terry. 2012. 'How Economists Contributed to the Financial Crisis'. *Forbes*, 2 June.

Hazlett, Thomas W. 1997. 'Looking for Results: Nobel Laurate Ronald Coase on Rights, Resources, and Regulation'. *Reason.* Available at: http://reason.com/archives/1997/01/01/looking-for-results. Accessed June 2014.

Hegel, Georg Wilhelm Friedrich. 1812 [2010]. *The Science of Logic.* Cambridge: Cambridge University Press.

Hellman, Hal. 1998. *Great Feuds in Science: Ten of the Liveliest Disputes Ever.* New York: Wiley.

Herndon, Thomas, Michael Ash and Robert Pollin. 2013. 'Does High Public Debt Consistently Stifle Economic Growth? A Critique of Reinhart and Rogoff'. *PERI Working Paper Series 322.*

Hoffman, Elizabeth, and M. L. Spitzer. 1982. 'The Coase Theorem: Some Experimental Tests'. *Journal of Law and Economics* 25 (1): 73–98.

Hoffman, Elizabeth, Kevin McCabe, Keith Shachat and Vernon Smith. 1994. 'Preferences, Property Rights, and Anonymity in Bargaining Games'. *Games and Economic Behavior* 7 (3): 356–80.

Hojman, David, and Julia Hiscock. 2010. 'Interpreting Suboptimal Business Outcomes in Light of the Coase Theorem'. *Tourism Management* 31 (2): 240–9.

Hoover, Glenn E. 1926. 'The Present State of Economic Science'. *Social Forces* 5 (1): 57–60.

Horn, Rob van, and Philip Mirowski. 2009. 'The Rise of the Chicago School of Economics and the Birth of Neoliberalism'. In *The Road from Mont Pélerin: The Making of the Neoliberal Thought Collective*, edited by Philip Mirowski and Dieter Plehwe, 139–78. Cambridge, MA: Harvard University Press.

Inman, Phillip. 2013a. 'Academics Back Students in Protests against Economics Teaching'. *Guardian*, 18 November.

Inman, Phillip. 2013b. 'Economics Students Aim to Tear up Freemarket Syllabus'. *Guardian*, 24 October.

Jevons, William Stanley. 1871. *The Theory of Political Economy.* New York: Macmillan.

Johnson, Robert. 2012. 'Economists: A Profession at Sea'. *Time*, 19 January.

Jolink, Albert, and Jack J. Vromen. 2001. 'Path Dependence in Scientific Evolution'. In *Evolution and Path Dependence in Economic Ideas*, edited by Pierre Garrouste and Stavros Ioannides, 205–24. Cheltenham: Edward Elgar.

Jolls, Christine, Cass R. Sunstein and Richard H. Thaler. 1998. 'A Behavioral Approach to Law and Economics'. *Stanford Law Review* 50 (5): 1471–550.

Kahn, Alfred E. 1966. 'The Tyranny of Small Decisions: Market Failures, Imperfections, and the Limits of Economics'. *Kyklos* 19 (1): 23–47.

Kahneman, Daniel. 2011. *Thinking, Fast and Slow.* New York: Farrar, Straus and Giroux.

Kahneman, Daniel. 2012. 'A Proposal to Deal with Questions about Priming Effects'. Available at: http://www.nature.com/polopoly_fs/7.6716.1349271308!/suppinfoFile/Kahneman%20Letter.pdf. Accessed December 2015.

Kahneman, Daniel, Jack L. Knetsch and Richard H. Thaler. 1990. 'Experimental Tests of the Endowment Effect and the Coase Theorem'. *Journal of Political Economy* 98 (6): 1325–48.

38 *Epistemic responsibility of economists*

Kapp, K. William. 1950. *The Social Costs of Private Enterprise*. Cambridge, MA: Harvard University Press.

Karabağ, Solmaz Filiz and Christian Berggren. 2012. 'Retraction, Dishonesty and Plagiarism: Analysis of a Crucial Issue for Academic Publishing, and the Inadequate Responses from Leading Journals in Economics and Management Disciplines'. *Journal of Applied Economics and Business Research* 2 (3): 172–83.

Kay, Neil M. 2013. 'Rerun the Tape of History and QWERTY Always Wins'. *Research Policy* 42: 1175–85.

Kelman, Mark. 1979. 'Consumption Theory, Production Theory, and the Ideology in the Coase Theorem'. *Southern California Law Review* 52 (3): 669–98.

Kirman, Alan. 2010. 'The Economic Crisis is a Crisis for Economic Theory'. *CESifo Economic Studies* 56 (4): 498–535.

Klamer, Arjo, and Hendrik P. van Dalen. 2002. 'Attention and the Art of Scientific Publishing'. *Journal of Economic Methodology* 9 (3): 289–315.

Klein, Daniel B. 2013. 'The Ideological Migration of the Economics Laureates: Introduction and Overview'. *Econ Journal Watch* 10 (3): 218–39.

Krugman, Paul. 2009. 'How did Economists Get It So Wrong?'. *The New York Times*, 6 September.

Kuhn, Thomas S. 1957. *The Copernican Revolution: Planetary Astronomy in the Development of Western Thought*. Cambridge, MA: Harvard University Press.

Kuhn, Thomas S. 1977. 'The Essential Tension: Tradition and Innovation in Scientific Research'. In *The Essential Tension: Selected Studies in Scientific Tradition and Change*, 225–39. Chicago: University of Chicago Press.

Lawson, Clive, Mark Peacock and Stephen Pratten. 1996. 'Realism, Underlabouring and Institutions'. *Cambridge Journal of Economics* 20 (1): 137–51.

Lawson, Tony. 1997. *Economics and Reality*. London: Routledge.

Lawson, Tony. 2003. *Reorienting Economics*. London: Routledge.

Lawson, Tony. 2006. 'The Nature of Heterodox Economics'. *Cambridge Journal of Economics* 30 (4): 483–505.

Lawson, Tony. 2009. 'The Current Economic Crisis: Its Nature and the Course of Academic Economics'. *Cambridge Journal of Economics* 33 (4): 759–77.

Levy, David M., and Sandra J. Peart. 2008. 'Inducing Greater Transparency: Towards the Establishment of Ethical Rules for Econometrics'. *Eastern Economic Journal* 34: 103–14.

Levy, David M., and Sandra J. Peart. 2013. 'The Ethics Problem: Towards a Second-Best Solution to the Problem of Economic Expertise'. Available at: http://s3.amazonaws.com/chssweb/documents/15754/original/Collective_Action_Problem_of_Economists.pdf?1400607026

Lichtenthaler, Ulrich, and Miriam Muethel. 2012. 'The Role of Deliberate and Experiential Learning in Developing Capabilities: Insights from Technology Licensing'. *Journal of Engineering and Technology Management* 29 (2): 187–209.

Liebowitz, Stan J., and Stephen E. Margolis. 1990. 'The Fable of the Keys'. *Journal of Law and Economics* 33 (1): 1–25.

Lindquist, Gabriella Sjögren, and Jenny Säve-Söderbergh. 2011. '"Girls will be Girls", especially among Boys: Risk-taking in the "Daily Double" on Jeopardy'. *Economics Letters* 112 (2): 158–60.

Lyotard, Jean-François. 1979 [1999]. *The Postmodern Condition: A Report on Knowledge*. Minneapolis: University of Minnesota Press.

Mackay, Charles. 1841 [1995]. *Popular Delusions and the Madness of Crowds*. London: Three Rivers Press.

Mankiw, N. Gregory. 1990. 'A Quick Refresher Course in Macroeconomics'. *Journal of Economic Literature* 28 (December): 1645–60.

Marx, Karl. 1859. *Zur Kritik der Politischen Ökonomie*. Berlin: F. Duncker.

McCalman, Iain. 2009. *Darwin's Armada: Four Voyages and the Battle for the Theory of Evolution*. New York: W. W. Norton Co.

McCloskey, Deirdre N. 1983. 'The Rhetoric of Economics'. *Journal of Economic Literature* 21 (2): 481–517.

McCloskey, Deirdre N. 1984. 'Communications: Reply to Caldwell and Coats'. *Journal of Economic Literature* 22 (2): 579–80.

McCloskey, Deirdre N. 1985. *The Rhetoric of Economics*. Madison: University of Wisconsin Press.

McCloskey, Deirdre N. 1990a. 'Formalism in the Social Sciences, Rhetorically Speaking'. *The American Sociologist* 21 (1): 3–19.

McCloskey, Deirdre N. 1990b. *If You're So Smart: The Narrative of Economic Expertise*. Chicago: University of Chicago Press.

McCloskey, Deirdre N. 1994a. 'How to Do a Rhetorical Analysis and Why'. In *New Directions in Economic Methodology*, edited by Roger Backhouse, 319–71. London and New York: Routledge.

McCloskey, Deirdre N. 1994b. *Knowledge and Persuasion in Economics*. Cambridge: Cambridge University Press.

McCloskey, Deirdre N. 1998a. 'Good Old Coase Theorem and the Good Old Chicago School: A Comment on Zerbe and Medema'. In *Coasean Economics: Law and Economics and the New Institutional Economics*, edited by Steven Medema, 239–48. Boston: Kluwer Academic.

McCloskey, Deirdre N. 1998b. 'Other Things Equal: The So-called Coase Theorem'. *Eastern Economic Journal* 24 (3).

McCloskey, Deirdre N. 2000. 'Postmodern Market Feminism: A Conversation with Gayatri Chakravorty Spivak'. *Rethinking Marxism* 12 (4): 27–37.

McCullough, B. D. 1998. 'Assessing the Reliability of Statistical Software: Part I'. *The American Statistician* 52 (4): 358–66.

McCullough, B. D. 1999a. 'Assessing the Reliability of Statistical Software: Part II'. *The American Statistician* 53 (2): 149–59.

McCullough, B. D. 1999b. 'Econometric Software Reliability: EViews, LIMDEP, SHAZAM and TSP'. *Journal of Applied Econometrics* 14 (2): 191–202.

McCullough, B. D. 1999c. 'The Numerical Reliability of Econometric Software'. *Journal of Economic Literature* 37 (2): 633–65.

McCullough, B. D. 2000. 'Is It Safe to Assume that Software is Accurate?'. *International Journal of Forecasting* 16 (3): 349–57.

McCullough, B. D., and David A. Heiser. 2008. 'On the Accuracy of Statistical Procedures in Microsoft Excel 2007'. *Computational Statistics and Data Analysis* 52 (10): 4570–8.

McCullough, B. D., and H. D. Vinod. 2003. 'Verifying the Solution from a Nonlinear Solver: A Case Study'. *American Economic Review* 93 (3): 873–92.

McCullough, B. D., and A. T. Yalta. 2013. 'Spreadsheets in the Cloud – Not Ready Yet'. *Journal of Statistical Software* 52 (7). Available at: www.jstatsoft.org/v52/i07/paper

Medema, Steven. 1995. 'Finding His Own Way: The Legacy of Ronald Coase in Economic Analysis'. In *The Legacy of Ronald Coase in Economic Analysis*, edited by Steven Medema, ix–lxix. Northampton, MA: Edward Elgar.

Medema, Steven. 2009. *The Hesitant Hand: Taming Self-Interest in the History of Economic Ideas*. Princeton, NJ: Princeton University Press.

40 *Epistemic responsibility of economists*

Medema, Steven. 2010. 'The Coase Theorem in the Textbooks, 1960–1979: The Case of Intermediate Microeconomics'. Working Paper, University of Colorado, Denver.

Medema, Steven. 2011a. 'A Case of Mistaken Identity: George Stigler, "The Problem of Social Cost", and the Coase Theorem'. *European Journal of Law and Economics* 31 (1): 11–38.

Medema, Steven. 2011b. 'The Coase Theorem: Lessons for the Study of the History of Economic Thought'. *Journal of the History of Economic Thought* 33 (1): 1–18.

Milne, Seumas. 2013. 'Orthodox Economists Have Failed Their Own Market Test'. *Guardian*, 20 November.

Mirowski, Philip. 2002. *Machine Dreams: Economics Becomes a Cyborg Science.* Cambridge: Cambridge University Press.

Mirowski, Philip. 2010. 'The Great Mortification: Economists' Responses to the Crisis of 2007–(and Counting)'. *The Hedgehog Review* 12 (2): 28–41.

Mishan, Ezra J. 1965. 'Reflections on Recent Developments in the Concept of External Effects'. *Canadian Journal of Economics and Political Science* 31 (1): 3–34.

Mokyr, Joel. 1992. 'Technological Inertia in Economic History'. *The Journal of Economic History* 52 (2): 325–38.

Montes, Leonidas. 2003. 'Das Adam Smith Problem: Its Origins, the Stages of the Current Debate, and One Implication for Our Understanding of Sympathy'. *Journal of the History of Economic Thought* 25 (1): 63–90.

Myers, Greg. 1989. 'The Pragmatics of Politeness in Scientific Articles'. *Applied Linguistics* 10 (1): 1–35.

Nelson, Julie A. 2014. 'The Power of Stereotyping and Confirmation Bias to Overwhelm Accurate Assessment: The Case of Economics, Gender, and Risk Aversion'. *Journal of Economic Methodology* 21 (3): 211–31.

Nelson, Julie A. 2015a. 'Are Women Really More Risk-averse than Men? A Re-analysis of the Literature Using Expanded Methods'. *Journal of Economic Surveys* 29 (3): 566–85.

Nelson, Julie A. 2015b. 'Not-So-Strong Evidence for Gender Differences in Risk Taking'. *Feminist Economics*: 1–29. doi: 10.1080/13545701.2015.1057609.

Nicita, Antonio, and Ugo Pagano. 2008. 'Law and Economics in Retrospect'. In *New Institutional Economics: A Guidebook*, edited by Eric Brousseau and Jean-Michel Glachant, 409–24. Cambridge: Cambridge University Press.

Nik-Khah, Edward. 2010. 'George Stigler'. In *The Elgar Companion to the Chicago School of Economics*, edited by Ross Emmett, 337–41. Cheltenham: Edward Elgar.

North, Gary. 1992. *The Coase Theorem: A Study in Economic Epistemology*. Tyler, TX: Institute for Christian Economics.

Pigou, Arthur Cecil. 1920 [1962]. *The Economics of Welfare*. London: Macmillan.

Pinker, Steven. 2013. 'Science is Not Your Enemy: An Impassioned Plea to Neglected Novelists, Embattled Professors, and Tenure-less Historians'. *New Republic*, 6 August.

Popper, Karl R. 1963. *Conjectures and Refutations: The Growth of Scientific Knowledge.* New York: Harper and Row.

Reinhart, Carmen M., and Kenneth Rogoff. 2010a. 'Growth in a Time of Debt'. *NBER Discussion Paper No. 15639.*

Reinhart, Carmen M., and Kenneth Rogoff. 2010b. 'Growth in a Time of Debt'. *American Economic Review: Papers and Proceedings* 100 (May): 573–8.

Reiss, Julian. 2008. *Error in Economics: Towards a More Evidence-Based Economics.* London: Routledge.

Matters of opinion or questionable research practices? 41

Reiss, Michael. 2011. *What Went Wrong with Economics: The Flawed Assumptions that Led Economists Astray*. London: Goldhurst Press.

Rigamonti, Cyrill P. 2006. 'Deconstructing Moral Rights'. *Harvard International Law Journal* 47 (2): 353–412.

Robson, Alex, and Stergios Skaperdas. 2008. 'Costly Enforcement of Property Rights and the Coase Theorem'. *Economic Theory* 36 (1): 109–28.

Rothbard, Murray N. 1995 [2006]. *Economic Thought Before Adam Smith: An Austrian Perspective on the History of Economic Thought, Vol I*. Auburn, AL: Ludwig von Mises Institute.

Rothman, Joshua. 2011. 'Why American Science isn't Working'. *The Boston Globe*, 24 September.

Rutherford, Donald. 1995. *Routledge Dictionary of Economics*. London: Routledge.

Schneebalg, Marco. 2014. 'The Need for a New Economics'. *Varsity - Independent Student Newspaper for the University of Cambridge*. Available at: http://www.varsity. co.uk/comment/6702. Accessed June 2014.

Smith, Adam. 1759 [2002]. *The Theory of Moral Sentiments*. Cambridge: Cambridge University Press.

Smith, Adam. 1776 [1966]. *An Inquiry into the Nature and Causes of the Wealth of Nations*. London and New York: W. Strahan and T. Cadell A. M. Kelley.

Sterman, John D., and Jason Wittenberg. 1999. 'Path Dependence, Competition, and Succession in the Dynamics of Scientific Revolutions'. *Organization Science* 10 (3): 322–41.

Stigler, George Joseph. 1952 [1966]. *The Theory of Price*. 3rd edn. New York: Macmillan.

Stigler, George Joseph. 1988. *Memoirs of an Unregulated Economist*. Chicago: University of Chicago Press.

Stroebe, Wolfgang, Tom Postmes and Russell Spears. 2012. 'Scientific Misconduct and the Myth of Self-Correction in Science'. *Perspectives on Psychological Science* 7 (6): 670–88.

Sydow, Jörg, and Georg Schreyögg (eds). 2010. *The Hidden Dynamics of Path Dependence: Institutions and Organizations*. New York: Palgrave Macmillan.

Sydow, Jörg, Georg Schreyögg and Jochen Koch. 2005. 'Organizational Paths: Path Dependency and Beyond'. Conference Paper Presented at the 21st EGOS Colloqium, Berlin.

Tribe, Keith. 2009. 'Liberalism and Neoliberalism in Britain, 1930–1980'. In *The Road from Mont Pélerin: The Making of the Neoliberal Thought Collective*, edited by Philip Mirowski and Dieter Plehwe, 93–138. Cambridge, MA: Harvard University Press.

Turvey, Ralph. 1963. 'On the Divergence between Social Cost and Private Cost'. *Economica* 30 (119): 309–13.

Valdés, Juan Gabriel. 1995. *Pinochet's Economists: The Chicago School of Economics in Chile*. Cambridge: Cambridge University Press.

Varian, Hal R. 2003. *Intermediate Microeconomics: A Modern Approach*. 6th edn. New York: Norton.

Veblen, Thorstein. 1904. *The Theory of Business Enterprise*. New York: C. Scribner's Sons.

Veblen, Thorstein. 1909. 'The Limitations of Marginal Utility'. *Journal of Political Economy* 17 (9): 620–36.

Vergne, Jean-Philippe. 2013. 'QWERTY is Dead; Long Live Path Dependence'. *Research Policy* 42: 1191–4.

42 Epistemic responsibility of economists

Wang, Sheng-Dong, Yong-Wu Zhou and Jun-Ping Wang. 2010. 'Coordinating Ordering, Pricing and Advertising Policies for a Supply Chain with Random Demand and Two Production Modes'. *International Journal of Production Economics* 126: 168–80.

Ward-Perkins, Zach, and Joe Earle. 2013. 'Economics Students Need to be Taught More than Neoclassical Theory'. *Guardian*, 28 October.

Ward, Benjamin. 1972. *What's Wrong with Economics*. New York: Basic Books.

Wellisz, Stanislaw. 1964. 'On External Diseconomies and the Government Assisted Invisible Hand'. *Economica* 31 (124): 345–62.

Whaples, Robert. 2006. 'The Costs of Critical Commentary in Economics Journals'. *Econ Journal Watch* 3 (2): 274–82.

Wible, James R. 1998. *The Economics of Science: Methodology and Epistemology as if Economics Really Mattered*. New York: Routledge.

Williamson, Oliver E. 1985. *The Economic Institutions of Capitalism: Firms, Markets, Relational Contracting*. New York: Free Press.

Woo, Henry K. H. 1986. *What's Wrong with Formalization in Economics?: An Epistemological Critique*. Newark, CA: Victoria Press.

Worrell, DeLisle. 2010. 'What's Wrong with Economics?'. Address by the Author, Governor of the Central Bank of Barbados, to the Barbados Economic Society (BES) AGM, Bridgetown.

Yalcintas, Altug. 2009. 'Intellectual Paths and Pathologies: How Small Events in Scholarly Life Accidentally Grow Big'. PhD Thesis, Erasmus Institute for Philosophy and Economics, Erasmus University, Rotterdam.

Zerbe, Richard O., Jr. 1980. 'The Problem of Social Cost in Retrospect'. *Research in Law and Economic* 83 (2): 83–102.

Ziliak, Stephen Thomas, and Deirdre N. McCloskey. 1996. 'Standard Error of Regression'. *Journal of Economic Literature* 34 (1): 97–114.

Ziliak, Stephen Thomas, and Deirdre N. McCloskey. 2004a. 'Significance Redux'. *Journal of Socio-Economics* 33 (5): 665–75.

Ziliak, Stephen Thomas, and Deirdre N. McCloskey. 2004b. 'Size Matters: The Standard Error of Regression in the American Economic Review'. *Journal of Socio-Economics* 33 (5): 527–46.

Ziliak, Stephen Thomas, and Deirdre N. McCloskey. 2008. *The Cult of Statistical Significance: How the Standard Error Costs Us Jobs, Justice, and Lives*. Ann Arbor: University of Michigan Press.

Part II
The economic construction of sciences

2 Explaining epistemic hystereses

Epistemic costs

The economic construction of sciences means that the production, exchange, and consumption of knowledge have intellectual consequences that we can explain in terms of epistemic costs involved in processes of scientific research. What are epistemic costs?

Epistemic costs are the social costs of knowledge production that are significantly higher than the private costs of doing research. Social costs involve, as William Kapp remarks, 'direct and indirect losses suffered by third persons or the general public' (Kapp 1950, 13). We can apply Kapp's views on the processes of scientific knowledge production. Direct and indirect losses suffered by third persons in the academy occur when intellectual vices and academic wrong doings such as plagiarism, fraud and the deterioration of data take place. Individual scholars are occasionally able to shift some of the harmful consequences of their behaviour onto the general scholarship. Such scholarly mechanisms as refereeing and reviewing, the ethics of scholarly behaviour and certain codes of action, all of which include the issue of liability and also help increase the productivity of scientific processes, cannot fully correct or cure the harmful consequences of individual scholarship.

Issues of social costs and (negative) 'externalities' have been widely debated in economics since Adam Smith's *The Wealth of Nations* (1776 [1966]). The works of Alfred Marshall, Paul Samuelson and Arthur Cecil Pigou have received particular attention from scholars who have been interested in such issues as pollution and global warming, government subsidies for education and health services, and property rights. Although economists have long been aware of the spill-over effects of economic activities, it is not only economic activities that lead to social costs. Spill-over effects and unintended consequences of academic scholarship cause (positive and negative) 'externalities' as well. Seen from the lenses of 'externalities' as a generalized conception for all types of human activity – economic, social and epistemological – epistemic costs should be comprehended as the intended and unintended consequences of the social and economic activities of scholars. 'Externalities' undermine the epistemic benefits of scholarly communities.

46 *The economic construction of sciences*

Before we move on further, let me briefly touch upon some of the types of private costs that matter for scholarly activities:

- Costs of writing grants, filling in forms, administrative tasks and attending meetings and conferences (Rockwell 2009, Kean 2006).
- Communication and collaboration costs (Agrawal and Goldfarb 2008, Bhattacharjee 2008, Bonilla 2014).
- Costs of R&D and expenses of electricity, equipment and infrastructure (Stephan 2012, 82–110).
- Salaries (Hamermesh *et al.* 1982, Ehrenberg *et al.* 2007).
- Costs of copyrights, licensing and patenting and costs of exclusion (Stephan 2012, 51–60; Stiglitz 1986 [2000], 135).
- Cost of access to knowledge (Mokyr 2002, 7–9).

Cost of access to knowledge is the cost that is paid by the individual who wishes to acquire knowledge. It involves the costs of searching for useful knowledge. 'If someone "needs" to know something', Joel Mokyr argues,

> he or she will go to an expert for whom this cost is as low as possible to find out. Much of the way knowledge has been used in recent times has relied on such experts. The cost of finding experts and retrieving knowledge thus determines marginal access costs.
>
> (Mokyr 2002, 7)

Symbols, diagrams, notations and codes serve the purpose of reducing the costs of access to knowledge. Access costs increase if knowledge provides prestige, wealth and power to those who possess the knowledge. Copyrights increase access costs as well. Costs of access to knowledge also include the costs of running academic journals and publishing houses. It is sometimes too costly to publish articles in academic journals. High cost of access to knowledge prevents new journals and publishers from entering the academic economy. It is a factor that creates a hierarchy among journals and publishers based on impact factors (see, for instance, the debate and petition on the 'Cost of Knowledge' at http://thecostofknowledge.com/ (accessed June 2014) and Flood 2012).

A positive epistemic costs (PEC) worldview embraces a cost–benefit approach in epistemology. As Mokyr also claims in his *The Gifts of Athena* (2002), there is no such thing as a free lunch in epistemology. However, despite the significance and variety of the types of private costs in processes of production (see also Alchian and Demsetz 1972, Becker and Murphy 1992), I am particularly interested in the costs that arise out of the social costs of knowledge production. Social costs of knowledge production are the costs that diminish the social benefits and intellectual welfare of the community of scholars when scholars are involved in QRPs. The significance of social costs of knowledge production is that they risk the productivity of scholars who are not directly involved in the process of knowledge production.

Negative 'externalities' of the processes of knowledge production are endogenous to academic scholarship primarily because productivity losses are often the

Explaining epistemic hystereses 47

consequence of the lack or impossibility of a common law or custom against irresponsible acts of individual scholars. Academic scholarship is a social as well as an economic activity that often requires interaction and cooperation of universities with 'pecuniary employments' (Veblen 1919, 279–323) and 'thought collectives' (Plehwe 2009, Mirowski 2009). Individual scholars and research institutions interact and cooperate with business enterprises in such ways that salaries, research monies and academic and social facilities are financed and maintained by these businesses. Scholars working in advisory companies and those with funding opportunities largely controlled by corporate enterprises have a significant influence on the scholarly community as to the direction in which new research is conducted.

Such interactions and cooperations have far-reaching consequences for scholarly production. At organizational levels, many universities are institutionalized and managed in similar ways to corporate businesses. 'Competitive (or business) calculus', which simply covers the cost–benefit analysis within a business enterprise, is not the best way to assess the worthiness of academic work and allocation of research monies in certain fields, the results of which are socially significant but not always applicable or able to contribute to the ways in which profit-making businesses operate. As Kapp argues, '[n]either social costs nor social returns enter into the cost–price calculations of the private firms unless special provisions to this effect are made by law and by the systematic application of the principles of social insurance' (Kapp 1950, 8–9). The risk here is that academic scholarship might fail in similar ways to business enterprises.

The conception of epistemic costs refers to harmful effects of knowledge production processes causing disruption in the intellectual environment. Disruption in the intellectual environment may emerge when scholars keep reproducing erroneous explanations, invalidated methodologies and falsified data, so that reliable knowledge production is no longer available. We may call this the problem of *intellectual minima* or the scholarly tolerable level of QRPs. In analyses of intellectual minima, 'externalities' of knowledge production should be taken into account seriously. An effective approach on intellectual disruption would be an *ex ante* assessment of the process of knowledge production so as to prevent epistemic costs from increasing and impairing the intellectual environment. Kapp's critique with regard to environmental disruption is that no such assessment is involved in orthodox economics, in that social accounting is understood as a self-contained system isolated from the environment 'of which the economic system is a part and from which it receives important inputs and with which it is related through manifold reciprocal interdependencies' (Kapp 1976, 212–13). However, Kapp remarks, social accounting is an open system which is 'in continuous dynamic interaction with a more comprehensive social and political as well as physical system from which economic processes receive important organizing (and disorganizing) impulses and upon which they exert their own negative and positive influences' (ibid., 213). In my view, Kapp's critique can be extended so as to embrace *intellectual accounting* in the following way. A scholar who takes part in the processes of knowledge production does not operate

48 *The economic construction of sciences*

in an artificially closed environment. A scholar is in continuous interaction with other scholars within numerous scholarly networks. In a reciprocal manner, scholars receive inspirational and intellectual impulses, and they exert their own positive and negative influences in return. In an intellectual environment where the tiniest influences get into a 'mutual interaction of a multiplicity of factors' (Kapp 2011, 15), processes of knowledge production cannot be truly analyzed and realistically represented as isolated self-sustaining systems. Under such circumstances, one cannot assume that the intellectual system as a whole moves towards any sort of balance brought about by the mechanisms of self-correction in scholarly conversations. On the contrary, intellectual systems often diverge from static conditions where errors are automatically and continuously corrected towards dynamic conditions of self-reinforcing conflicts of interest, tensions among scholars and contradictions between theories.

Epistemic costs, to use Kapp's terminology, are 'unpaid' costs which, in my view, come about as a consequence of QRPs. 'Unpaid costs' in academic scholarship are often ignored by practising scientists and intellectual historians interested in (re-)constructing intellectual history in rationalistic ways. Epistemic costs are among the factors causing serious intellectual disruption that makes rational constructions in intellectual history virtually impossible. The impossibility of rational constructions may diminish the intellectual welfare of research communities. Intellectual welfare is the individual and collective ability of scholars to produce a sustainable environment where error-free explanations about the facts of the world are publicly available to others. In the production of intellectual welfare, negative 'externalities' should be minimally involved or not involved at all. The economics of scientific knowledge, then, is the science of finding out ways to minimize the epistemic costs that emerge as a consequence of the processes of knowledge production. From an economic point of view, it is vital that scholars reach a significant level of epistemic efficiency, say, by abiding with copyright laws and other scholarly conventions and virtues. There is, of course, no strict pattern or form of behaviour that would automatically help scholars correct past errors and replace erroneous explanations with error-free ones. In other words, while copyrights and scholarly conventions and virtues are often technical and formal issues, self-correction is almost always case-specific and concrete where scholars may have to sort out original, untried methods of correction. When epistemic costs are high – that is to say, when scholars need more time to correct errors than the time they require to produce knowledge – the levels of intellectual welfare can be so low that the prestige of scholars and research communities can be ruined. Scholarly processes unable to correct or replace refuted theories can cause serious damage to the intellectual environment at local and global scales. Scholars, individually or collectively, may not be able to exclude themselves from the negative 'externalities' involved in knowledge production processes which simply reproduce errors and invalidate theorems. In other words, scholarship cannot externalize the consequences of rejecting the obligation to refute erroneous explanations; epistemic costs often remain internal to the processes of knowledge production at varying degrees of significance.

Explaining epistemic hystereses 49

To paraphrase Kapp in his (1977) article, scholarship has an institutionalized built-in tendency to reinforce epistemic costs; the intellectual environment can be disrupted in a cumulative fashion.

I use scholarship here in order to refer to the production and exchange of every type of intellectual product with an epistemic utility. My intention is to point out the significance of the economic aspects of academic scholarship. As Matthew Gentzkow and Emir Kamenica (2014) remark, persuasion is often costly. The work of Gentzkow and Kamenica suggests, with respect to the decisions made by scholars, that there is an opportunity cost to each and every decision that scholars make while picking a theorem and rejecting a refuted one. It is not realistic to believe in the autarchy of academic scholarship where it is assumed that scholars work in a cost-free environment, operating with intellectual concerns alone (Johnson 1972). Producing, exchanging and using theories, ideas and viewpoints with an epistemic utility, scholars are knowledgeable about the ways in which they have to tackle with the costs of transacting and interacting in the scholarly world.

Epistemic costs arise because scholarship is not always a practice that a single scholar can undertake. A scholar can write a philosophical monograph on his or her own but monographs should, nevertheless, be read by critics and appreciated by an audience. It is not possible to complete a paper or a monograph on one's own. Scholarly collaboration is often necessary. It is the nature of scholarship that a scholarly work is a collective activity in the sense that scholars are dependent not only on the institutions of scholarship, but also on each other (March 2007).

The problem of epistemic costs is not solvable via maximizing a utility function: high epistemic costs cannot be compensated for by higher epistemic utilities that scholars gain from using refuted theories. Scholars cannot benefit from using an erroneous theory because reproducing an erroneous theory does not yield any epistemic utility at all. When epistemic costs are positive, copyrights, patents and licensing have positive functions. Such institutional and legal regulations limit the dissemination of erroneous theories. It is also often easy to track down the sources of errors in the processes of knowledge production when the system of copyrights, patents and licensing work well. However, the limited non-rivalrous and non-excludable nature of knowledge diminishes the total epistemic utility of the community of scholars because collective usage of an erroneous theory does not increase individual scholars' total utility. Since anyone can use it, an error involved in the logical structure of theories can rapidly disseminate in scholarly communities. The problem of epistemic cost should be resolved via *minimizing a cost function*, independent from the utility that the scholarly community would have gained if the scholars had abandoned a refuted theory.

The orthodox logic of maximizing a utility function is based on zero transaction costs: since transaction costs are zero, the only objective function is Max U, where the individuals aim at achieving the highest level of utility from the application of a theory. In case of PEC, however, the logic is reversed: since the utility of an erroneous theory equals zero, the only objective function is minimum epistemic cost (EC). This does not mean that if scholars abandon a refuted theory,

50   *The economic construction of sciences*

they would yield no utility. They do. However, when scholars abandon a refuted theory, they have a different objective function because they replace the refuted theory with a new theory, principally an error-free theory, yielding epistemic utility to scholars who use the theory. Now, unlike regular commodities with positive 'externalities', negative 'externalities' of knowledge production should in the first place be waived so that the harmful effects of scientific misconduct are minimized. In other words, further usage of a refuted theory would not yield any utility at all. The objective function of a scholarly community under conditions of PEC should, therefore, be a function to be minimized.

The objective function of a scholarly community, EC, which individual scholars should aim to minimize under conditions of PEC, can formally represented in a number of ways. Consider the following:

$$EC = \sum_{t=1}^{p} \left[n_t \left(1-r\right) m_t + m_t \right]$$

where
n: number of times a theory is used, $n > 1$
r: replicability of a theory, $0 < r < 1$
m: social costs caused by negative 'externalities' of knowledge production, $m > 0$
t: continuous periods of time $(1, 2, 3, …, p)$

How should scholars minimize epistemic costs? This equation suggests that a number of ways can be used to minimize the magnitude of the consequences of epistemic costs. Here, I assume that, within the period between t and p, theories are used more than once and the impact of negative 'externalities' of knowledge production under conditions of PEC is always positive. Therefore, $n > 1$ and $m > 0$. Then, scholars, first and foremost, want to increase the replicability of a theory. Replicability of a theory, as I elaborate in the following section, depends on the availability of data for testing the theory and the number of times the theory is replicated. If the data is available and the theory can easily be replicated with the data, the replicability of the theory is proportionally higher. If the theory has already been replicated with the data and the results are verified, then r equals 1. Replicability is lower when a theory is simply reproduced without being tested. In other words, epistemic costs are higher if scholars fail to replicate theories. Then, r converges to 0 (zero).

In order for scholars to minimize the epistemic cost function, they have to increase the replicability of a theory within a period of time. However, even when the replicability of a theory converges to and equals 1, epistemic costs are still positive because there are factors, other than the replicability of a theory, which increase the epistemic costs of using a theory. For instance, marginal epistemic costs, i.e. the amount of epistemic cost caused by the usage of a theory once more, might be equal to zero because the theory is fully replicated and the results are confirmed. Even then, total epistemic costs might still be positive due to such factors as ideologization, non-pluralist research practices of scholars, lack of research ethics and 'moral costs' (see below). In the equation, these factors are represented by the stock variable m. In order to decrease m, scholars, in principle, should acquaint themselves with the specificities of each single case and look for ways to resolve the issues related to QRPs by studying each case step by step. Therefore, m is also a variable representing the time-specificity of each case.

Epistemic costs, which are caused by negative 'externalities' of knowledge production (m), arise as a consequence of a number of factors. One of these factors is *ideologization*. Ideologization is the absence of opportunities to argue against the established theories in science. Joshua S. Gans and George B. Shepherd report cases where the best-known and cited articles by leading economists were rejected by top journals in economics, sometimes more than once, without an offer to revise and resubmit (Gans and Shepherd 1994, Shepherd 1995). Quoting Gracelia Chichilnisky, Gans and Shephard argue that '[t]he more innovative and interesting the paper, the more likely it is to be rejected' (Gans and Shepherd 1994, 177). Likewise, surveying 1,008 manuscripts submitted to three elite medical journals, Kyle Siler *et al.* (2014) found that, of the 14 most popular articles, 12 were desk-rejected; that is, editors of the three focal journals in medical science rejected some of the most cited articles without sending them out for peer reviewing. Such cases suggest that epistemic costs can also take the form of 'moral costs', as remarked by Bruno Frey (2003), arguing that it would be naive to assume that editors and anonymous referees always behave to the benefit of the scholarly community. Often, anonymous referees are inclined to judge papers based on whether their own work is appreciated, quoted and cited. 'Moral costs' are positive when referees reject a manuscript that they 'dislike' even though the manuscript would be beneficial for the scholarly community if the manuscript was accepted for publication. In such cases, 'moral costs' are positive and epistemic opportunities are gone, leading to non-remediable consequences. Scholars then refuse to change their minds because some epistemic factors, such as personal interests, prevent them from moving to other pathways of thought. In such cases, m is always positive.

Epistemic costs, which are caused by negative 'externalities' of knowledge production are positive also because many economic theories, which are 'unfit for purpose' (Fine 2013), are *artificially* selected. In living nature, being unfit does not mean that species become extinct. Likewise, in intellectual nature, economic theories, many of which are unfit for purpose, might survive. How can we account for the processes in which, as a result of the evolutionary selection mechanisms, the 'most foolish of the fools' often survives (Khalil 2000)? Artificial selection in the history of ideas refers to the human factors that cause some ideas to survive artificially. Theories are artificially selected when theories in intellectual history are intentionally isolated from other ideas in the hands of intellectual networks, publishing houses and editors. For instance, theories are more often than not reproduced by virtue of being published and republished by unauthorized publishing companies. As a consequence, they evolve in such ways that 'un-powerful' (or 'unfit') ideas are artificially kept alive. Under conditions of artificial selection, ideas are modified (or 'developed'), not by their original

52 *The economic construction of sciences*

authors or creators but by the editors and publishing companies, without the approval of their original authors and creators. These publications survive the challenges of intellectual life 'unnaturally' in the sense that many intellectual challenges are domesticated and thus errors, misinterpretations and flaws are systematically reproduced. When books and articles are domesticated, ideas do not change the established literature; on the contrary, under conditions of domestication, ideas are adapted to the established literature.

Artificial selection in intellectual history amounts to picking up specific theories for their specific traits intentionally. This allows some theories to reproduce faster than other theories. In this process, human control is essential. That is to say, the process runs 'artificially', not 'naturally'. Isolating theories from their parental theories, editors and publication houses achieves a controlled environment where theories are able to reproduce even under unfavourable conditions. Hence, theoretical variations, which could have emerged only over long time spans, are materialized within very short time spans; survival of some theories is dependent on the human element in their evolutionary history. The human element prevents theories from competing with other theories and becoming extinct. In other words, the *raison d'être* for some theories in intellectual history is the intervention of scholars in the works of other scholars not only by ways of criticism and other legitimate means of scholarly contribution (such as falsification), but also by manipulation, revision and other illegitimate means of QRPs. While scholars intervene in the works of other scholars so that original articles and books are no longer accessible to readers in general, this process might be taking place in the absence of the approval (even appreciation) of the owner of scholarly works. It is not realistic to assume the presence of good intentions during such processes at all times. New theories are parts of intellectual history and, content-wise, they have the same level of significance as theories that have emerged without such intentions. In other words, theories that emerge 'artificially' have the same status as the theories that emerge 'naturally'.

Just because there is human intervention in the evolution of ideas does not mean that the consequences of human intervention are always intended. Histories of species are independent from the history of humans who have caused the selection of species. Likewise, the life history of humans and the life history of theories do not overlap at all times. Theories have their own lives. They are borne. They grow up and mature. Sometimes they become extinct. One thing is for sure: specificities in the life history of theories are irreversible. Once a theory emerges, its effects on intellectual history might linger on so long that the present state of 'sophistication' cannot be precisely restored to its initial state.

In order to test the plausibility of the claim that some ideas are artificially selected, I conducted a bibliographical survey elsewhere on the economic manuscripts of Karl Marx and Friedrich Engels that have been translated into Turkish from the 1930s to date (Yalcintas 2012). My findings suggested that the great majority of the economic manuscripts of Marx and Engels, not only in Turkish but also in German, Russian, English and French, have been artificially selected:

Explaining epistemic hystereses 53

their works have not only been 'translated', but also modified in various ways by editors and publication houses.

The publication of many of the original works of Marx was facilitated by and the intellectual responsibility of Friedrich Engels, Karl Kautsky, August Babel and Eduard Bernstein. Indeed, in the absence of the 'contribution' of these scholars who knew Marx and his works well, Marxism would have been in a much poorer state than it is today. This viewpoint has long been shared in Marxian scholarship. For instance, in the 'Preface' of *Theories of Surplus Value* (1862 [1998], *Marx Engels Collected Works*, Vol. 30, 16–17), prepared by the Institute of Marxism-Leninism, CC CPSU, it is stated that:

> From Engels's statements quoted above it is clear that he attributed great importance to the manuscript *Theories of Surplus-Value*, and regarded it as Volume IV of *Capital*. But it is also evident that in 1884–85 Engels intended to remove from the text of this manuscript 'numerous passages covered by Books II and III'.
>
> Here the question naturally comes up: what should be our attitude with regard to this proposal or intention of Engels?
>
> Only Engels, the great companion and comrade-in-arms of Marx, and in a certain sense the co-author of *Capital*, could have removed from the manuscript *Theories of Surplus-Value* a whole series of passages. In order that the parts of the manuscript that remained after the elimination of these passages should not appear as disconnected fragments, it would have been necessary to work them over to a considerable extent and to link them together with specially written interpolations. And only Engels had the right to work over Marx's text in such a way.

However, consequences of editing and 'translating' Marx's works into other languages have been more than intended. Today, it is difficult, if not impossible – not only in Turkey, but also in many other countries – to access to the original German edition of Marx's *Das Kapital*. *Das Kapital*, including its first volume which was published in Marx's lifetime, has been edited and modified many times since the death of its author. The English translation of *Das Kapital* is composed of three parts and eight chapters whereas *Das Kapital* was published in seven parts and 25 chapters in 1867. Many of the works of Marx and Engels, such as *Grundrisse*, have been published only in shortened forms, followed by prefaces or subtexts that often include irrelevant, arbitrary and erroneous information about the authors and their publications. One of the first Turkish translations of Marx's works was published in 1933. It was only 128 pages. The most commonly used Turkish translations of *Das Kapital* and *Kritik der Politischen Ökonomie*, among others, were translated from their English or French editions. In many book stores across the country, several books, the authors of which are claimed to be Marx and Engels, exist under the following titles: *Sociology and Philosophy* (1975), *Secret Diplomacy in the Eighteenth Century* (1992) and *Woman and Family* (1992). Neither Marx nor Engels wrote any of these books.

54   *The economic construction of sciences*

My conclusion is that the works of prominent authors such as Marx and Engels and many other contemporary authors such as Ronald Coase should be read with awareness of the problems that might have arisen due to the conditions in which they have survived. Indeed, how did the theories of prominent authors survive? Has it always been dialectics and rational criticism that lead to the sophistication of theories over decades? Or have other factors, such as artificial selection, played significant roles as well? We know that Joseph Alois Schumpeter's *History of Economic Analysis* was published four years after the death of its author. Until the book was published, the author's wife, Elizabeth Boody Schumpeter, edited the book a number of times, making corrections to the manuscript (Schumpeter 1952 [1954]). Many books of Friedrich Nietzsche were published after the author's sister, Elisabeth Nietzsche, modified the original manuscripts of the author. This is how 'she prepared the way for the belief that Nietzsche was a proto-Nazi' (Kaufmann 1968 [1974], 8). Likewise, some of the works by Edmund Husserl, Martin Heidegger and Ludwig Wittgenstein, a number of novels by Franz Kafka, Leo Tolstoy and Mark Twain, a few of poems by Edgar Allan Poe, diaries of Anne Frank and manuscripts of Virginia Woolf were published after the death of the authors following the revisions of editors and publication houses. The good side of the story is that if editors and publication houses had not revised these manuscripts, these manuscripts would have never been available for the global audience. The not-so-good side of the story, however, is that most of the originals of the works of these authors are not accessible to readers today.

Often, books and articles are revised, edited and republished by friends and family members of authors as well as by experts who specialize in the works of the authors. For many historians of thought, this is not a problem at all because the completion of an intellectual or artistic product might require more than the lifetime of an individual, such as (in architecture) Cologne Cathedral, King's College Chapel and Sagrada Familia, the construction of which lasted more than one generation of designers. Among other examples are *Karl Marx/Friedrich Engels Collected Works*, completed in 29 years, and *Marx–Engels Gesamtausgabe (MEGA)*, expected to be published in 2025. It is evident that the intellectual lives of the works of Marx and Engels on political economy are independent from the intellectual lives of Marx and Engels. For many historians of thought the problem is not new. Indeed, many authors take precautions while they are still alive to ensure that their followers do not publish unauthorized manuscripts after their death. For instance, Adam Smith had his unpublished manuscripts burnt outside his residence a week before he died (Bell 1960). However, it is not realistic to assume that authors are always as meticulous in protecting the prospects for their manuscript. This is how manuscripts, awaiting the light of day in the personal libraries or drawers of the desks of authors, are posthumously published.

In what other ways can we minimize epistemic costs in intellectual history? One way, beyond those mentioned above, is to apply pluralist methodologies in science. It was stated in 'A Plea for a Pluralistic and Rigorous Economics',

Explaining epistemic hystereses 55

published as an announcement in the *American Economic Review* in 1992 and signed by 47 eminent economists, including three Nobel Prize winners, that:

> We the undersigned are concerned with the threat to economic science posed by intellectual monopoly. Economists today enforce a monopoly of method or core assumptions, often defended on no better ground that it constitutes the 'mainstream'. Economists will advocate free competition, but will not practice it in the marketplace of ideas.

In fact, pluralism *per se* is not a solution to the question 'What is wrong with economists?' because, one may argue, economics has already been marked by pluralism, in the sense that there have always been erroneous viewpoints in the profession. As John Rawls (2011, 63) once claimed with regard to democracy and political liberalism, '[t]hat a democracy is marked by the fact of pluralism as such is not surprising, for there are always many unreasonable views'. I thus call this *unreasonable pluralism in economics*. Unreasonable pluralism in economics can cause economists to miss the actual target. The actual target (that is, monotheism) in economics on which economists, both orthodox and unorthodox, should focus their attention, is the absence of creative thinking. Absence of creativity is one of the significant causes of the disability of economists to correct erroneous viewpoints. Reasonable pluralism or multiplicity of discourses, in my view, amounts to being open minded about alternative theories while scholars account for the facts of the world.

Avoiding ideologization is a way to deal with the problems of epistemic costs as well. Ideologization is insisting on belief systems and habits of thought, some of which yield no epistemic utility to scholars, when scholars have to make decisions under conditions of uncertainty. Imposing rules and legal enforcement, such as introducing intellectual property rights into the processes of refereeing in the form of 'moral costs' or requiring authors to take oaths, are among the ways to fight the consequences of scientific misconduct. Despite the fact that there are myriad methods of legal enforcement, none can cure the harmful effects of scientific misconduct and achieve integrity all together. Research ethics is always a better way to deal with the consequence of breaching scholarly integrity.

Conceptualizing knowledge as a public commodity (or, as it has been known, public 'good') is also useful on a number of accounts (David 2000, 2001). However, most of the original debates on science as public commodity have merely been on cases where science fails to contribute to industrial growth or where science fails to achieve optimality in resource allocation (Arrow 1962, Boulding 1966). The problem is not that the argument of knowledge as public commodity leads to knowledge being under-produced if it is left to the market alone (Stephan 1996). First of all, it is not always easy to make a flawless distinction between 'public' and 'private' (Kaul and Mendoza 2003). Various software programs that one can download on the internet are an example. In such programs, knowledge can be used in such ways that they can be divided into various components, then modified and re-edited, as long as contributors can claim

56 *The economic construction of sciences*

their *moral* rights on the final product. Indeed, the real issue is not whether the knowledge produced is 'public' or 'private'; it is whether morality is involved in the processes of knowledge production.

Moral rights, explicitly recognized in many countries after the Berne Convention for the Protection of Literary and Artistic Works (adopted in 1886, revised and amended in 1979), represent the non-monetary rights of the authors of articles, books and computer programs, such as the rights of prestige and attribution, which producers can claim when commodities are exchanged and consumed in the market. An example of moral rights is open-source software production in which software developers can modify and re-edit codes of software, principally on the condition that names of contributors are explicitly acknowledged. Second, knowledge is sometimes so restricted by intellectual property laws that even referees who review manuscripts for peer review journals do not have access to the data and algorithms that authors use in the manuscripts submitted to journals. A more significant problem that becomes observable when knowledge is conceptualized as public commodity is, therefore, that the private cost of knowledge production is not always equal to the epistemic cost of knowledge production. For instance, scientists often involve in QRPs where negative 'externalities' of research practices threaten scholarly integrity and independent referees are not able to monitor this even if they are required to do so. As Wible (1998, 2) argues, the *science of science* in general and the economics of scientific knowledge in particular have begun with the general problem of misconduct in science, which Wible considers as the main source for market failure in academic economics. In economics, market failure is characterized by a tendency towards moving away from or an inability to reach a Pareto optimum state of equilibrium. Failure in the market of ideas primarily involves genetic errors (as in automata theory) generated through and transmitted by generations of scholars: self-regulation of individual factors in interaction with the environment by way of reconstructing copies of themselves (Mirowski and Somefun 1998).

Types of QRPs include many forms of inappropriate or improper behaviour, such as plagiarism, fabrication and falsification of data. QRPs take different shapes in various disciplines. For instance, in medical sciences, one of the leading fields of research where scholars seriously investigate the causes and consequences of QRPs, there are strict regulations against using biohazardous materials and human and animal subjects in research. Although there has been important literature on the economics of scientific misconduct (Lacetera and Zirulia 2011, Enders and Hoover 2004), QRPs in economics have only recently received global attention as a distinct field of research. (See the special issues of the *Review of Social Economy* on 'Oaths and Codes in Economics and Business' (2013) and 'Scientific Misconduct and Research Ethics in Economics' (2016, in preparation).)

The literature on QRPs in various fields of research reveals important facts about the ways in which scientists conduct research in a given area. Most importantly, when researchers are involved in QRPs, consequences of the actions of scholars deviate from the 'normal' courses of scientific conduct. What is also striking, one might argue, is that being a scholar is not necessarily the equivalent of being a gentleman. John D. Bernal made this point in 1939 (xiii), writing that '[s]cience has ceased to be the occupation of curious gentleman or of ingenious minds supported by wealthy patrons, and has become an industry supported by large industrial monopolies and by the State'. Morton A. Meyers claims that '[s]cientists are subject to pride, greed, jealousy, and ambition, just like the rest of us' (Meyers 2012, 5). According to Murray N. Rothbard, Adam Smith was a 'shameless plagiarist'. Murray claims that:

> [Smith] acknowledge[ed] little or nothing and [stole] large chunks, for example, from Cantillon. Far worse was Smith's complete failure to cite or acknowledge his beloved mentor Francis Hutcheson, from whom he derived most of his ideas as well as the organization of his economic and moral philosophy lectures.
>
> (Rothbard 1995 [2006], 435)

Insofar as scientific misconduct is concerned, the well-known argument 'science is for society' has won the debate against the argument that 'science is for science' for the simple reason that scientific misconduct has started to generate undesirable consequences for society, and scholars ought to do something about it. Since misconduct in science became more common, science has been much further away from the service of scholars and the general public.

Replication failure as a questionable research practice

> Replication is the cornerstone of science. Research that cannot be replicated is not science, cannot be trusted either as part of the profession's accumulated body of knowledge or as a basis for policy ... [R]esearch that cannot be replicated lacks credibility.
>
> (McCullough and Vinod 2003, 888)

As the preceding argumentation suggests, epistemic costs are the costs of scarcity of the most valued element in academic production: time. When the element of time is considered, epistemic costs refer to the costs of contemplating what older generations wrote. A PEC view of decision-making processes in an open and homogeneous society holds that adoption of a new model of behaviour such as selecting a novel theory or abandonment of an old one depends on whether the benefits of a new behaviour exceed the associated epistemic costs. If the new model is attractive to the majority of the scholarly population and it does not significantly differ from the old patterns, the new behavioural innovation spreads among the population gradually. Individuals would reject behavioural innovations that are (re-)presented by a minority only and not reinforced by such factors as the reputation of a research project or research group, the harmony of interest that the scholars claim and the scholarly processes in which intellectuals set ideals for themselves as they achieve progress in their research. Sometimes individuals are constrained by one or all of these factors and such constraints narrow their choice set. Whether individuals will benefit from the constraints and

58　*The economic construction of sciences*

whether constraints will yield profitable results depend on the factor that is reinforced. The result will principally be determined on the basis of,

> subjective perception of the costs and benefits of an institutional alternative which might have its cause in changes in the related cost structures or social learning accompanied by changing mental models that lead to a new evaluation of the behavioural alternatives.
>
> (Stahl 2000, 281)

Epistemic scarcity overwhelmingly dominates the evolution of scientific research. When researchers start off a new research project, they allocate time between replicable and unreplicable research. It is through replication that theories and research programmes are checked in terms of their defensibility, consistency and coherency. Although replication should be an essential component of scholarly work, such an endeavour is not frequently handled by researchers because 'an economist might allocate a larger proportion of time to producing new publishable results devoting relatively less time and effort to the tasks required for replication' (Wible 1998, 25). Instead, authors, referees and editors of journals often assume that earlier findings are valid without retesting them in significant ways because replication takes time, and there is no reward for scholars in repeating others' work. Pressure to publish more articles is another factor that does not allow scientists to double-check their results. As a consequence, no significant research devotes time and effort to replicating the findings of earlier theories and research programmes without compensating their economic loss. Researchers, relying on the results of papers published in academic journals, simply reproduce their findings without examining their significance and validity (Mirowski and Sklivas 1991). Bypassing replication increases the probability of generic (i.e. reproductive) errors that had occurred in earlier studies but are not noticed in time. In academic scholarship, it is expected that such errors will be corrected as scientists do further research on the subject matter. But because of the costs of running such tests, some errors may pass unnoticed and be left uncorrected.

In daily language, replication and reproduction are used interchangeably. However, there are differences between the two. I use replication, in line with most authors in science literature, in the sense of testing the data and codes of a model or explanation for empirical validity and logical consistency. Reproduction, again according to many researchers in science literature, means that models or explanations are duplicated or applied to various cases without being tested. When replication does not take place, arguments, data and articles and books are simply reproduced without being questioned. Replication failure therefore means that authors reproduce the methodology, data and conclusions of the works of previous generations without checking the validity and veracity of these elements of the works. When authors do not replicate preceding papers and books, they simply copy and paste old methodologies, data and conclusions for the present research.

Replication failure amounts to the reproduction of old results – in that it reproduces the same intellectual value without producing any surplus meaning

(Feigenbaum and Levy 1996). Nevertheless, there are certain differences between replication failure and reproduction as well. Most of all, replication failure as a process implies perfect copies (of ideas) whereas reproduction implies imperfect copies (of ideas). It is by the reproduction of ideas, which is a very common mechanism of the selection of ideas, that we have a large population of explanations about unemployment, inflation, international trade, wages and so forth. It is due to the imperfect nature of the reproduction process that we have numerous explanations of the same phenomena. Economists, indeed, distort the meaning of variables and coefficients as well as the meaning of arguments that their colleagues put forth over generations. Reproductions of models made from earlier reproductions of models which contain miniscule errors can allow us to talk about a common ancestor of all economic models. But they no longer allow us to talk about continuous progression in economics. It is through this process of reproduction that game theory and operations research have emerged from the Cold War politics of the post-war era (Mirowski 2002). In more abstract terms, this process of reproduction causes so-called public benefits to emerge from private vices (Mandeville 1714 [1962]).

The residual of the difference between perfect copies of ideas and imperfect copies of ideas is errors. Errors are often immortal; as Kenneth E. Boulding (1966) once remarked, errors should perhaps be called 'bits' or 'memes' in the sense of 'capital stock of information' or the 'form of stock' as the measure of knowledge. This is how Richard Dawkins puts it in *The Selfish Gene* (1976 [2006], 16):

> We tend to regard erratic copying as a bad thing, and in the case of human documents it is hard to think of examples where errors can be described as improvements. I suppose the scholars of the Septuagint could at least be said to have started something big when they mistranslated the Hebrew word for 'young woman' into the Greek word for 'virgin,' coming up with the prophecy: 'Behold a virgin shall conceive and bear a son ...'.

Reproduction (i.e. imperfect copies) has been so prevalent in pop culture that a new form of art since the 1970s, namely hyper-realism, has created 'illusionary facts' of the world by reproducing features and details of objects unseen by the human eye. In my view, hyper-realism is an artistic genre that reproduces an image or a sculpture, as a whole or in part, simulating them in environments or contexts in which the image or the sculpture loses its connection to reality. In doing so, the photographer and sculptor are able to omit the 'narrative elements' of objects, by abstracting social, political and intellectual components from the context of which objects are a part. The product is a *false* reality, of course, although the intention of the artists is not to deceive the viewer; the intention is often to focus the viewer's attention on the corrupted condition in which the real object is located. Hyper-realist art is indeed a form of intellectual activism. (For the term 'intellectual activism,' see Yalcintas 2015.)

Magnifying details or features of objects, hyper-realists stress the fact that the world around us, imaginary and physical, might be deceiving our eyes, warning

60   *The economic construction of sciences*

us about the manipulated content of realistic objects. Hyper-realist products look like the original, but they are 'in fact' not; they are reproduced. Reproductions of hyper-realist artists are flat interfaces, usually without meaningful depth, standing between the person who observes and the object that is observed.

Hyper-realism in art, as I see it, is relevant for the philosophy of science because I think the reproduction of the models and theories about the facts of the world, in a similar fashion, gradually produces a false reality. In doing so, the theorists simplify the components of the facts of the world and abstract the components from the context of which the facts are a part. The intention of theorists, of course, is not to deceive the reader; their intention is to focus the reader's attention on the causation in which the facts take place. When the reality of theories is not questioned, theories eventually lose their meaning. In the absence of such questioning, the issues of realisticness (Mäki 1989, 1994) and verisimilitude (Popper 1963, 1972 [1979]), even when they are achieved, are not sufficient for readers to be convinced that theories tell them about the 'objective truth'. What we need is instead criticism of the 'given truths'. In other words, we need replications (not reproductions) of old findings in order to lock out the given intellectual pathways of thought.

Replication is often comprehended as a process where the validity of numerical data and results are tests by means of quantitative tools. This view is too limiting. Replication is not only an issue of concern for empirical sciences; replication is also a process in which the validity of non-quantitative hypotheses is checked to see whether the results follow the premises in a consistent manner. John Locke's conception of under-labouring can be considered as one of the oldest forms of replication in philosophy. Locke remarks in his *An Essay Concerning Human Understanding* (1869 [1836], ix) that under-labouring is the activity of 'clearing the ground a little, and removing some of the rubbish that lies in the way to knowledge'. To put it differently, under-labouring serves the purpose of assessing the ontological base on whether the conclusions are consistent with the premises. If they are not, the philosophers' task is to fix what potentially causes the problem. The philosophy of counterfactuals can also be seen as a form of replication in humanities because counterfactual reasoning is a way to test whether an event A is a conditional for the emergence of an event B. Indeed, this is how David Hume defines a 'cause': 'We may define a cause,' Hume writes in his *An Enquiry Concerning Human Understanding* (1748 [1999], 37),

> to be an object followed by another, and where all the objects, similar to the first, are followed by objects similar to the second. Or, in other words where, if the first object had not been, the second never had existed.

With counterfactuals, philosophers can replicate the emergence of a particular conclusion, and they can confirm or invalidate the significance of conditions in a course of events. Finally, we can interpret Stephan J. Gould's 'experiment of replaying life's tape' as a call for replication in order to check the significance of contingencies in a course of events. 'You press the rewind button,' Gould claims

Explaining epistemic hystereses   61

in his *Wonderful Life: The Burgess Shale and The Nature of History* (1989, 48), 'and, making sure you thoroughly erase everything that actually happened, go back to any time and place in the past ... Then let the tape run again and see if the repetition looks at all like the original.' Replicating the course of events by 'replaying life's tape', philosophers can tell whether an event is the consequence of contingencies or a part of a process in which there is no room for historical small events.

Replication is an analytical tool to detect errors that might have been involved in numerous stages of research practices. This tool not only functions to test whether raw data produce the proposed results, it also reveals the evolutionary pathways which scholars, intentionally or unintentionally, have taken in order to reach their goals. Replicated conclusions help reveal the causation in models in which particular results emerge out of particular hypotheses. Needless to say, breakdowns in causal relations do not produce proposed conclusions. Reproducing models and stories involving such breakdowns merely increases the intellectual significance of the harmful consequences of errors. Problems arise when errors lead to illogical anomalies. Some of these problems might be unfixable if they are not replicated in a timely fashion and if breakdowns are not fixed appropriately. Science is often not a self-correcting enterprise because replication has not been a common practice.

So far, I have written about replication in contrast to reproduction in the sciences and humanities. Replication failure, however, is a distinct entity and it possesses unique properties. Most of all, replication failure, as we know it, is a dynamic process in science in which the intentions of individuals are not necessarily a constituent of the working of the process. A dynamic process in science means that small errors that researchers make may become a part of the daily routine of scholarly life, mostly automatically, without the researcher intending to deceive the audience regarding his or her work. If the intention of the author was to deceive, legal action against the author could be required or implemented. However, replication failure, again, as we know it, is an 'innocent' form of behaviour where the consequences of a researcher's decision to allocate his or her time to working on the newest research, rather than replicating older models and findings, come about unintentionally.

I claim that this view of replication is limiting, too. Replication failure as a form of QRP amounts to becoming unable or unwilling to check and correct data which may *intentionally* be fabricated, falsified, or misrepresented. This issue is important because replication failure as a form of QRP might give rise to unethical consequences. Replication failure generates *vicious* cycles, as opposed to *virtuous* cycles, catching intellectuals into fashionable modes of thought through a positive feedback loop, enhancing the intellectual significance of seemingly negligible unethical behaviour of scholars. Vicious cycles are self-perpetuating processes creating temporary no-exit sequences of events with long-term effects on intellectual history. In contrast, virtuous cycles, as I see them, are self-perpetuating processes reinforcing the impact of desirable outcomes. When vicious cycles take

62 *The economic construction of sciences*

the form of 'Mr X depends on Mrs Y for the reliability of his results', 'Mrs Y depends on Mr Z for the reliability of her results' and 'Mr Z depends on Mr X for the reliability of his results', intellectuals' absence of interest in replication as a scientific virtue might grow in such a way that the unethical consequences of individual action may rapidly spread among the members of the community of scholars. Replication failure contributes to this process by discouraging intellectuals from using unconventional (i.e. virtuous) methods in their work. Vicious cycles are not necessarily unethical, but, in the absence of replication, reproducing identical types of behaviour might increase the pervasiveness of unethical behaviour. In cases of virtuous cycles, mechanisms of lock-in might still be in operation; however, consequences are often favourable. In other words, when vicious cycles emerge, positive feedback loops might cease to generate positive consequences for intellectuals.

Vicious cycles might turn into virtuous cycles when an unconventional behaviour is supported by other members of the scientific community, generating another cycle in the opposite direction. The 'Nobel Prize' Lecture of Ronald Coase is an exemplar of the type of unconventional behaviour calling the members of the scientific community to move in another direction. (See the previous chapter for details.) However, as I say, even after such interventions take place, consequences of vicious cycles might endure. As a matter of fact, the 'Coase Theorem' did not disappear from economics textbooks following Coase's several warnings. It is an example of a vicious circle in economics.

Researchers in humanities work under conditions similar to the conditions under which scientists work: in a nutshell, they all must have an idea, seek funds, develop the idea into a paper, present the paper at conferences and publish the paper. Time is not free for researchers in humanities and sciences. Researchers in sciences and humanities simply tend to reproduce interpretations, ideas and viewpoints published in journal articles and books by quoting and citing the authors. However, the nature of replication in the sciences and in the humanities are not identical. Replication for scientists is mostly checking the acceptability of data for current research whereas replication for researchers in the humanities might have nothing to do with data at all. For instance, philosophers, poets and novelists often only read and interpret books and journal articles written by others from a rhetorical and logical perspective; they are not always have concerned with checking the representations and re-descriptions as to whether they correspond to the 'truth'. In other words, philosophers and literary critics do not need, as Richard Rorty remarks, 'to think of knowledge as an assemblage of accurate representations' (Rorty 1979, 163); they are, rather, interested in whether the arguments work in a logical way. Arguments and metaphors that represent a specific phenomenon in creative fashions, without regard to the most recent works, are acceptable for philosophers, poets and novelists. This does not mean that they are not interested in the facts of the world; this only means their works are less prone to replication failure than the works of scientists who have to cite others' works frequently.

Nevertheless, researchers in humanities get themselves involved in incidents of QRPs as well. Philosophers, historians and other researchers in humanities can and do behave unethically not only when they publish copyrighted material without proper permission, but also when they rely on the interpretations of a reputable author without working on the original source that is interpreted. It is a common practice in humanities that researchers, without reading Aristotle, quote Richard Rorty interpreting John Dewey interpreting Friedrich Hegel interpreting Aristotle. Although no researcher is required to know everything about Aristotle in order to quote a passage from Rorty, replication failure in humanities might occur in the form of failing to check to see if an idea or a theorem belongs to a specific author or authors. As a matter of fact, there are plenty of influential articles that mention the 'Coase Theorem' without citing Ronald Coase's original 1960 article. Moreover, some of these articles cite George Stigler without also citing any of the works of Ronald Coase (see, for instance, Kahneman *et al.* 1990).

Replication failure is a process in which the community of scholars is not able to eliminate the breaches of responsible research practices. Also, since replication failure amounts to the reproduction of research results without them being checked, this type of failure is a dynamic mechanism that turns seemingly small errors into big ones. The end result of replication failure is, then, the enhancement of the intellectual significance of small errors, the consequences of which could have been prevented if the members of the community of scholars, such as referees, editors and potential readers had taken timely measures to verify the research. In other words, whereas replication is a procedure that can invalidate data and computer codes that researchers use, replication failure is a proactive mechanism averting the processes of eliminating invalid data, codes and conclusions. Replication failure operates like an automaton programmed to enhance the intellectual significance of small errors spreading on logarithmic speeds and scales. Once errors pass the eyes of the gatekeepers of academic scholarship, such as the reviewers and journal editors, without being replicated, it is not unlikely that tiny errors are reproduced by ways of citations in the works by members of the scholarly community. Errors are thus disseminated through networks with degenerating consequences for research integrity.

Replication failure operates in the following way: while a theory or research programme spreads among scholars due to its intellectual merit, there is also an economic side to the progress of every such programme. This economic side has to do with the costs arising out of the time necessary to replicate the results in the scope of other scholarly works. The economic development of a theory examines the dynamic relations among scholars as well as their products (such as publications and conference meetings) that positively feed back to each other in mutual support with further evidence and further argumentation. The qualitative resonance among scholars is unique: a small achievement or a small error in scholarly theorizing may spread quickly and broadly. Replication failure is one of these mechanisms in which either a harmful norm spreads widely and quickly in an academic community or a selected small change in the behavioural system of the community escalates further change and drives the system away from equilibrium. Replication failure is the inability or the unwillingness of scholars to

64   *The economic construction of sciences*

replicate the reasoning and check the validity of the methods and data used in past models and explanations.

Replication rarely takes place in academic scholarship. Many factors play important roles here. For instance, processes of inference and judgement are not individual but rather social phenomena. It is difficult to replicate certain experiments without the specialized knowledge of earlier researchers. Sometimes derived results of earlier works can be unreplicable: data may be lost, technical possibilities may not allow researchers to set up identical experimental environments, and there may be informational asymmetries. Moreover, attempts by rival scientists and graduate students to criticize and publish new findings on older data as part of their routine scientific work are construed as hostile acts (Wible 1998, 30). Scholars also argue that incentives inherent in empirical sciences, such as economics, discourage voluntary data-sharing and replicable research articles (Feigenbaum and Levy 1993).

The issue is not that all research fails to replicate earlier findings. A considerable amount of time is, in fact, devoted to the replication of results. And yet a certain proportion of findings are used without being tested by a significant method. Raymond de Vries *et al.*, conducting a survey among 51 scientists on 'perceptions of the behaviors that pose problems for the enterprise of science', quote one of their respondents who said the following. For this particular respondent, replication is not what (s)he is worried about because the quality of their data is not as high as it should be to allow him or her to replicate the results. The primary issue here is to 'cook' data or 'clean' data so that (s)he could get rid of unanticipated findings.

> Okay, you got the expected results three times on week one on the same preparation, and then you say, oh, great. And you go to publish it and the reviewer comes back and says, 'I want a clearer picture,' and you go and you redo it – guess what, you can't replicate your own results … Do you go ahead and try to take that to a different journal … or do you stop the publication altogether because you can't duplicate your own results? … Was it false? Well, no, it wasn't false one week, but maybe I can't replicate it myself … there are a lot of choices that are grey choices … They're not really falsification.
>
> (De Vries et al. 2006, 45)

The significance of replication failure is greater when the number of experiments conducted in a specific field is too small. Zacharias Maniadis *et al.* (2013, 20) argue that experimental economics 'can advance considerably if scholars begin to adopt concrete requirements to enhance the replicability of results, as for instance starting to actively encourage replications within a given study'. Their findings confirm others, including Ioannidis (2008, 2005), that argue that newly discovered associations are often untrue; when further experiments and several replications are conducted, it frequently becomes clear that many of the novel findings are inflated or false. As the authors argue, one swallow does not make a summer.

Explaining epistemic hystereses 65

Less visible forms of QRPs range from 'changing the design, methodology or results of a study in response to pressure from a funding source', to 'overlooking others' use of flawed data or questionable interpretation of data', to 'unauthorized use of confidential information in connection with one's own research' and to 'dropping observations or data points from analyses based on a gut feeling that they were inaccurate' (Martinson *et al.* 2005, 737). Researchers engaging in various forms of harmful behaviour pose challenges to the integrity of science. Conflict of interest, lack of accountability and fabrication of data decrease the frequency of success in the market of ideas, causing deviations from ethical norms in scientific research. Empirical studies on the pervasiveness of QRPs in science (Wadman 2005, Swazey *et al.* 1993, Geggie 2001, Martinson *et al.* 2006, Anderson *et al.* 1994, Al-Marzouki *et al.* 2005, McCabe *et al.* 2006, 2001, Stroebe *et al.* 2012, Fanelli 2009) provide evidence suggesting that the frequency of replication failure in the natural sciences, especially biosciences, is high. As the findings of a survey conducted by Martinson *et al.* (2005), who asked 6,965 researchers whether they had engaged in QRPs between 1999 and 2002, suggest, 'US scientists engage in a range of behaviours extending far beyond [falsification, fabrication, and plagiarism]. Attempts to foster integrity that focus only on FFP therefore miss a great deal' (ibid., 737).

One cannot overemphasize the fact that consequences of replication failure are often broad. Such consequences are sometimes irreversible. For instance, in a couple of frequently cited papers published after the 2008 Financial Crisis, Carmen M. Reinhart and Kenneth Rogoff argue that when a country's public debt is over 90 per cent of its GDP (so-called 'debt intolerance ceiling'), growth rates are several per cent lower (Reinhart and Rogoff 2010b, a). There is no difference between industrial economies and emerging economies. In emerging markets, however, higher public debt means higher inflation.

The methodology of their papers was empirical, based on a broad historical data (200 years) on the public spending of 44 countries. It is 'normally' expected that editors and referees make their data and model available to the community of readers and referees for such empirical papers. However, the papers were published in the prestigious yet un-refereed *NBER* and *American Economics Review: Papers and Proceedings*. The authors did not make their data available until recently.

In 2013, Thomas Herndon, Michael Ash, and Robert Pollin, researchers from the University of Massachusetts Amherst, took the case more seriously than the authors, editors and referees; they asked Reinhart and Rogoff, authors of the original article, for the Excel spreadsheets that contained the data used in their models. Three researchers replicated the data, as well as the model, and they found out that works of Reinhart and Rogoff featured coding errors (especially where no data were available for some of the European countries), exclusion of data (of Australia, Austria, Belgium, Canada and Denmark) and unconventional summary statistics. The finding of Herndon *et al.* is that:

> when properly calculated, the average real GDP growth rate for countries carrying a public-debt-to-GDP ratio of over 90 percent is actually 2.2 percent,

66   *The economic construction of sciences*

> not –0.1 percent as published in Reinhart and Rogoff. That is, contrary to [Reinhart and Rogoff], average GDP growth at public debt/GDP ratios over 90 percent is not dramatically different than when debt/GDP ratios are lower.
>
> (Herndon *et al.* 2013b, 3)

Austerity policies, they concluded, were unnecessary.

Reinhart and Rogoff responded to their critics in a newspaper article (Reinhart and Rogoff 2013). Herndon *et al.* complained about 'hate-filled, even threatening, e-mail messages, some of them blaming us for layoffs of public employees, cutbacks in government services and tax increases'. Nevertheless, they accepted that their papers involved errors. However, the papers were not retracted from *American Economic Review* (*AER*) and *NBER*. When Herndon *et al.* made their work publicly available as a working paper in 2013, austerity plans had already been implemented in the USA and Europe. It is not an exaggeration to argue that the US and European economies are now suffering from the consequences of an erroneous model that could have been corrected if the data and model were replicated (and refereed) prior to its publication.

The work by Herndon *et al.* was initially distributed as a PERI Working Paper Series of the University of Massachusetts Amherst. In December 2013, it was published in the *Cambridge Journal of Economics* (Herndon *et al.* 2013a). Commenting on the article's publication in the *Cambridge Journal of Economics*, Jakob Kapeller, editor of *Heterodox Economics Newsletter*, asked an important question that I think is of great importance with regard to the significance of the problem of replication failure in economics: why was this article not published in the *AER* but in the *Cambridge Journal of Economics* instead? Kapeller reports:

> Driven by intense curiosity I confronted Robert Pollin, the paper's corresponding author, with the question whether the paper has not been submitted to the AER, where the original article of Reinhart and Rogoff has appeared. He told me that 'The AER turned down our paper. Their reason was that the original Reinhart/Rogoff paper was published in their *Papers and Proceedings* issue of the AER, not in their issues in which papers are refereed. They said they have a strict policy of not publishing responses to the papers from their papers and proceedings issue.
>
> (*Heterodox Economics Newsletter*, 3 March 2014)

Can the policy of the *AER* be a result of the absence of criticism between authors and readers, signalling to us the coming of a serious problem in economics? Indeed, replication failure might generate a positive feedback loop between the reputation of authors and the citation of articles (or the reproduction of articles' impact) that are not even refereed in top economics journals and working paper series. If this is the case, then articles with unchecked findings could become increasingly cited, primarily because they were written by reputable authors and appear in the most prestigious outlets. Although many economics journals publish correspondence between authors and readers regarding the empirical and logical validity of previously published articles, only a small fraction of them encourage readers to replicate the results of previously published articles.

For most of the economics journals, publishing the replication results of refereed articles is not standard procedure. Reading *Secrets of Economics Editors* (Szenberg and Ramrattan 2014), an edited volume on the experiences of the editors of leading economics journals, ranging from *Journal of Economic Literature* to *Journal of Institutional Economics*, where editors openly discuss the difficulties resulting from referees' late submissions, plagiarism, conflict of interest and research ethics, one gets the impression that issues related to the replication of results do not rate among the most serious concerns of economics editors, although numerous editors, if not all, are aware of the problem that could come about in the absence of a replication policy. For instance, Campbell R. Harvey, editor of the *Journal of Finance* between 2006 and 2012, reports that the detailed replication policy that he drafted for the journal was rejected by more than half of the associate editors and advisers of the journal. 'Following a lively online debate about the policy', Harvey writes, 'in the end, it was shelved' (Harvey 2014, 79). The *Journal of Money, Credit, and Banking Project* (*JMCB Project*), which requires authors to make the software and data used in their articles available to readers, has been the first case in replication studies in economics. Findings of the *JMCB Project*, which run between 1982 and 1984, suggest that 'inadvertent errors in published empirical articles are a commonplace rather than a rare occurrence' (Dewald *et al.* 1986, 587). Besides, the *JMCB Project* also reveals that some of the results that published articles reach are not replicable because software and data are confidential, licensed, lost, or destroyed. Some of the programs that authors use in their research operate only with specific hardware that is no longer available in the market. In some cases, the authors claim, the results of replication are not publishable because there is not always a high degree of originality – for instance, in verifying the findings of past research; as a consequence, there are no rewards for potential researchers to replicate old findings. And, finally, authors sometimes prefer not to submit their data to the journal at all as they might see the process of replication as 'bullying' (Bohannon 2014).

The *JMCB Project* is not the first attempt to replicate software and data in published articles in economics. Dewald and Anderson (2014, 205) report that Ragnar Frisch wrote about the significance of replication studies in economics in the first issue of *Econometrica* in 1933. In 1975, the *Journal of Political Economy* implemented an editorial policy, too, that called for authors to provide underlying data to the readers of the journal; however, it did not get much attention from researchers. Later on, the section where the *Journal of Political Economy* published results of replications was removed (Dewald *et al.* 1986). The *JMCB Project* did not continue either; files and data that were produced after the *JMCB Project* were destroyed (Dewald and Anderson 2014, 208). Today, many economics journals have editorial policies requiring authors to make their software and data available to the public. Some of these journals, such as *Public Finance Review, Empirical Economics Journal of Human Resources, Labour*

68   *The economic construction of sciences*

Economics, American Journal of Business, Econometrica, Economic Journal, American Economic Review, Journal of Political Economy and *Review of Economics and Statistics*, now encourage potential readers to replicate the findings of published articles. These journals also archive data and programs used in the articles published (see also Kane 1994, Burman *et al.* 2010). A number of websites, such as replicationnetwork.com (run by Maren Duvendack) and replication.uni-goettingen.de (run by Jan Höffler), provide information and data on replication studies in economics. On the website of the American Economic Association (AEA), it is stated that:

> It is the policy of the *American Economic Review* to publish papers only if the data used in the analysis are clearly and precisely documented and are readily available to any researcher for purposes of replication. Authors of accepted papers that contain empirical work, simulations, or experimental work must provide to the *Review*, prior to publication, the data, programs, and other details of the computations sufficient to permit replication. These will be posted on the *AER* Web site. The Editor should be notified at the time of submission if the data used in a paper are proprietary or if, for some other reason, the requirements above cannot be met. (For more information on the AER's 'Data Availability Project', see also Glandon 2010.)

There is clearly a growing interest in replication studies in economics. Is this interest sufficient? I think it is practically impossible to know whether this interest would yield fruitful results in economics in the future because we do not know fully (1) how frequent the errors in empirical research have been and (2) how widespread and significant the consequences of undiscovered errors are. In a recent research by Maren Duvendack *et al.* (2015, 181–2), the authors claim that:

> conditional on the replication having been published, there is a high rate of disconfirmation. Over the full set of replication studies, approximately two out of every three studies were unable to confirm the original findings … nearly 80 percent of replication studies have found major flaws in the original research.

It is not realistic to assume that errors are isolated and their effects are local. Replication studies in economics would certainly help reduce the amount of errors in future research on the condition that economics journals discover new ways to diminish the epistemic costs of replication. But since most of the consequences of errors are irrevocable, it is likely that much of the past research in economics will remain unreplicated, even after this precious opportunity.

What if a theory or model is unreplicable? Karl Popper once argued that, in order for an argument to be scientific, the argument should be falsifiable. Scientists should try to disprove arguments, and only then science could progress. When Popper put this forth in the 1930s, he was claimed to be one of the most influential philosophers of science, who ended *philosophical positivism*, whose proponents claimed that for an argument to be scientific, the argument should be verified by empirical evidence. Since Popper, the debates in the philosophy of science have, of course, been varied and have become sophisticated. In the post-Popperian period, the philosophers of science are not only interested in falsification, verisimilitude and the like; they are also interested in the rhetoric of science, causation, evolutionary epistemology and so forth. However, since replication became an issue for the sciences, the philosophers of science seem to recede to the pre-Popperian era. Unreplicated findings do not comply even with the positivist view of science – that findings of science should be tested several times and the same findings should be produced in every test. The unreplicability of results suggests also the limits of the applicability of a Popperian view of critical rationalism, at least in empirical sciences such as economics, because replication failure is an obstacle limiting the power of criticism in empirical research. Therefore, one of the biggest issues these days is, again, verification, *not falsification* – in that, in multiple cases, scientists are not able to replicate the data and codes used in models. In other words, findings are not always fully verified. Then, it is not unlikely that forthcoming problems in the philosophy of science in the twenty-first century will very much resemble to the problems of the positivist era.

What if a model is replicated, and the results of replication do not match the results of the original model? First and foremost, it means that there is an inconsistency in the logics of the original model and the replication. After all, after replication, the results obtained do not always match the results made available by the original model. However, new results do not always refute the model that is replicated. As Michael A. Clemens (2015, 12) remarks,

> readers could confuse replication tests (signifying mistakes or worse) with robustness tests (signifying legitimately arguable choices). This may be part of why the responding authors clearly feel targeted for attack rather more than they feel engaged in collaboration to advance science.

Indeed, new results from replications can lead to new explanations that do not invalidate the original research; they can expand the scope of the original model. This is how academic conversations often proceed. Replicated results can be innovative. Or, replication can prove that the original results are plausible only under certain conditions. Also, failing to obtain identical results after replications does not mean that there is an ethical issue that scholars should have more seriously considered. For an ethical issue to be significant, researchers must have the intention to behave badly. And even when the researchers intend to behave badly, several scholarly mechanisms can still prevent harmful consequences.

Nevertheless, if it is proven after replicating the original model that there is definitely an error in the data, code and logic of the model, the erroneous model should either be abandoned or updated in the light of evidence and argument. If scholars refuse to do so, then there is an issue of research misconduct which can lead to intellectual path dependence. In order to prevent the literature from locking itself into undesirable pathways of thought, researchers should behave in such

70 *The economic construction of sciences*

a way that they minimize the harmful effects of using erroneous models. By so doing, researchers behave ethically.

Richard G. Anderson *et al.* (2005, 2) make a list of some of the elementary questions that come about when the market of economic ideas fail to replicate the results of an original article. 'How confident would you be of the published results in an empirical economics article', they ask, 'if:

- No one had ever attempted to replicate the results?
- Replication had been attempted – and failed?
- The original authors could not reproduce their own results?

One might think that the solution to the problem is simply to require that all empirical research be reproducible – but it is not quite so simple. Consider some more answers to the above question:

- If the results had been replicated using the original software package?
- If the results had been replicated using the original software package, but a newer version of the same package produced different results?
- If the results had been replicated using the original software package, but a different software package produced different results?
- If two would-be replicators, both using the original software package, found that one could replicate and the other could not?

None of the above questions look like the sophisticated questions that contemporary economic philosophers ask today. I thus contend that, no matter how profoundly economic philosophers criticize the research practices in economics, under conditions of replication failure, the results of economic models are unreliable. From a pre-Popperian positivist standpoint, economics is, to a considerable extent, unscientific. Economics cannot meet even the requirements of scholarship of the nineteenth century. From an evolutionary standpoint, economics is, to a considerable extent, intellectually path dependent.

I conclude that, although academic scholarship is often based on sophisticated reasoning, errors are sometimes part of established research programmes. In such cases, harmful consequences of scholarly behaviour are not 'external' to conducting research. When negative 'externalities' are systematic and intentional, one of the tasks of intellectual history should be tracing and accounting for the ways in which scholarly mechanisms operate so as to sustain harmful effects. The intellectual causation between the individual and scholarly production of errors, misinterpretations and distortions would then explain the ways in which individual costs are shifted to third parties. Harmful effects of individual scholarship are intrinsic and institutionalized in the structure of today's academic scholarship even though some of these harmful effects come about as chance events or on contingent bases, but processes that start off with small events eventually turn into processes that keep producing larger significant consequences as the processes become more and more complex.

Failure of the markets of ideas

> Scientific research is a market process, differing vastly in form but little in substance, from the comparable activities of grocers or manufacturers of computers. Individual scholars distribute themselves by the action of self-interest.
>
> (Stigler 1988, 84)

The metaphor of the market of ideas (and its failure) is certainly a helpful one. But it is also not a 'nothing but' argument and not without possible disadvantages (Dyer 1986, Mirowski 1987, Mirowski and Sent 2002). Most of all, it is distasteful for the social and political opponents of the current capitalist market system on the grounds, at least, that knowledge should not be commercialized in the hands of a group of captains of industry. Demands of the private sector to build up partnerships with research universities are not the only, and certainly the not best, ways of financing and organizing scientific research. Also, sceptics of the metaphor of the market of ideas are concerned, rightly, with the fact that most (if not all) of the market analysts have orthodox (or 'neoclassical') inclinations. However:

(1) *There is no compelling reason to comprehend the history of economic thought in terms of 'neoclassical markets' in which agents with perfect information are able to make optimal decisions in their own interests.* Just as the analyses of the market of goods and services do not require the assumption of perfect markets, so do the market of ideas not require, implicitly or automatically, an understanding of the neoliberal conceptualization of the processes in which scientific knowledge is produced. Markets of goods and services fail; and markets of ideas fail, too. When markets of ideas fail, errors are not corrected in the short and long runs.

(2) *The metaphor of a market of ideas is not necessarily a claim that ideas could and should be bought and sold in the same way as goods and services.* That is to say, there are no demand and supply curves in intellectual history – at least, in the sense that buyers and sellers of ideas do not come together to determine the 'price of an idea'. Instead, they come together in the public sphere (for example, at conferences, research labs, universities and think-tanks) to take part in the academic survival game.

(3) *The reasons for the failure of the market of ideas are internal to academic processes.* Academic scholarship fails due to the realization of risks involved in conducting research. Most of all, knowledge production suffers highly from power relations and surplus appropriation at various levels in research institutes and elsewhere. Besides, markets of ideas are institutionalized processes in which contingencies cause theorems to lock in to certain pathways. Moreover, certain pathways that come about as an outcome of ideologies and belief systems can collide with other pathways generating even bigger consequences for science in general. The metaphor of the market of ideas is an opportunity to account for the harmful consequences of the power of research funds in scholarly activities. This is very important because, today, academic scholarship has become such a system that the private vices of

72   *The economic construction of sciences*

intellectuals never turn into the public virtues of scholarship. In other words, markets of ideas are not able to self-regulate themselves so as to clear off or 'endogenise' negative externalities.

(4) *The fear of capitalism does not always amount to the fear of markets.* (For further argumentation on the fear of markets or 'emporiophobia' and 'agoraphobia', see Hodgson 1998, Rubin 2014, Ingber 1984.) Markets are not part of the economic sphere alone. Markets exist in economic as well as social and intellectual spheres. They are public spaces where people come together to interact, exchange ideas and accompany each other towards a common goal. Likewise, markets of ideas are public spaces with a number of academic institutions and intellectual conventions according to which individual scholars behave. On the one hand, the fear of markets amounts to the fear of communicating with people, of confronting the ideas that challenge one's own and of daring to live together and prosper. On the other hand, capitalism is a time- and place-specific form of markets, and the fear of capitalism is the result of political sentiments against predatory tendencies in global economies that cause poverty, inequality and injustice. It is true, capitalism hurts. But the metaphor of a market of ideas is not an argument for 'academic capitalism'. It is neither a call for 'market triumphalism' or 'market fundamentalism'. (For a collection of essays on market anarchism, see Chartier and Johnson 2011.)

(5) *I comprehend the metaphor of market of ideas as an opportunity for historians of science to criticize scientific misconduct in the established terms of political economy.* It is likely that the hostility against the metaphor of a market of ideas, especially among traditional left-wing academics, is partly rooted in the lack of economic literacy in science studies. The hostility prevents researchers in science studies from reconciling the critical market analyses of Karl Marx, K. William Kapp, Thorstein Veblen, Karl Polanyi and Nicholas Georgescu-Roegen. Such critics provide deep and broad analyses of the harmful causes in and effects of the market system.

When one sees academic scholarship as a market of ideas (or, better, as a bunch of markets of ideas), principal questions that come to mind are most likely the following: are the features of the market of commodities the same, in principle, as the features of the market of ideas in general? Are ideas and commodities really counterparts? Is, say, government intervention in the market of ideas as desirable as it is sometimes in the market of commodities?

Ronald Coase, writing on the conception of the market of ideas for the first time in the history of economics (Coase 1974), argues that, in both cases, similar considerations can be taken into account. There are such historical occasions in the market of commodities that no first-best solutions come about. Under conditions of *non*-first-best-solutions – for instance, a condition under which scholars pursue fame and fortune (Levy 1988) and no scholar aims to seek for 'the truth' – all that matters for the actors in the market is to find a way to decide on the solution with a lower cost. That is to say: (1) keep over-exploiting old

Explaining epistemic hystereses 73

methodologies and techniques insofar as they keep producing satisfying results and (2) abandon methodologies and techniques, old and new, when they do not produce satisfying results. In the market of commodities, government intervention could provide help (although limited) for the fair allocation of economic resources, but, Coase claims, a similar centralized public policy (as a remedy to market failure) would not always have the same pleasing effect in each and every case. In other words, the government might be 'inefficient' if it attempts to intervene in the market of commodities. This applies to the market of ideas as well. According to Coase, the answer to the question of (government) intervention in intellectual markets should be, 'it all depends'. There is no final answer that would fulfil all the needs and problems of scholars. What matters is a close examination of epistemic costs in the market of ideas. For instance, the metaphor of the market of ideas is not equal to saying that governments should take part in the processes of scientific research although, one can argue, certain codes of behaviour should be implemented in the processes of producing and distributing knowledge. (On the codes of academic behaviour and prefessional ethics in economics, see DeMartino 2011a, 2011b; DeMartino and McCloskey 2015). Or, take the issue of replication failure. If the epistemic cost of the replication of findings in previously published articles is too high for potential researchers, an editorial policy requiring authors to make programs and data available to the public at the stage of initial submission might be a cost-effective solution. As many of the case studies above suggest, markets of ideas do not always price the value of academic research that replicates original articles. An editorial intervention would put pressure on authors to use better software and more complete and correct data sets because journals would then give the powerful message to their readers that all research published in the journal might be monitored by potential replicators in the future. Providing the

Table 2.1 Costs in the economy and scholarly life

	World without transaction/ epistemic costs	*World with transaction/epistemic costs*
An economist interprets	Markets of goods clear 'inefficiencies'. No market failure takes place. Economic path dependence does not occur.	Markets of goods and services do not clear at all times. Non-zero transaction costs cause failure in the market of goods and services. Cumulative consequences of individual behaviour in the economy, relying on older preference sets, lead to economic path dependence.
An intellectual historian interprets	Markets of ideas correct errors. No market failure takes place. Intellectual path dependence does not occur.	Markets of ideas do not clear at all times. Non-zero epistemic costs cause replication failure in the market of ideas. Cumulative consequences of individual research in scholarly life, relying on previous results, lead to intellectual path dependence.

74 *The economic construction of sciences*

programs and data to potential researchers seeking to replicate original findings would also help reduce the barriers to entry in the process of replication. As Dewald *et al.* (1986, 590) remark, 'the editorial policy is a form of professional collective action which solves the public goods problem by combining the values of the good to individual readers'.

A world without transaction and epistemic costs is an imaginary world that exists on the blackboard only. According to Coase (2005), the view of positive (transaction/epistemic) costs states that there is a cost to every transaction in nature, including economic and scholarly lives. Intellectual history features such a property that the cost of intellectual endeavour is not at all times ignorable. Epistemic costs in intellectual transactions prevent abstract solutions from becoming real because over-exploitation, misreadings and errors in interpretation often come about, and their consequences do not easily disappear. A system, because of over-investments, locks itself into situations that can end in stasis. A system that does not adapt in the face of changing environmental conditions can result in system vulnerability. As a consequence, blackboard theorems, such as Hegel's dialectics and Popper's critical rationalism, do not hold at all times because their epistemologies do not provide us with the underlying principles as to how the institutions of academic scholarship work and set the standards for scientific knowledge. Confusion and contradictions are not always negated and falsehood does not turn into truth in time and on occasion.

When misinterpretations are not displaced by accurate interpretations and errors are not corrected, consequences of particular events are not averaged away (that is, self-corrected) and certain intellectual paths occur as a result. To assume a scholarly world without the costs of undertaking the duty of reconsidering the main findings of past research (including the errors involved in the methodologies of earlier studies) would not be 'realistic'. There *are* epistemic costs in the global market of ideas. Such costs are often high and have significant consequences in the way researchers pursue science. Were there no epistemic costs, there would be no intellectual basis for the existence of universities anywhere on the globe because the market of ideas would do the job that is done by universities today. Or, were there no transaction costs in the job market, there would be no need for contracts with and among professors because markets and individuals would construct contractual agreements in the absence of asymmetric information and this would be organized internally (Williamson 1985, 87). Also, plagiarism would not be a problem then because, no matter what the property rights say, scholars could negotiate without any cost so as to:

> acquire, subdivide, and combine rights whenever this would increase the value of [scholarly] production. In such a world, the institutions which make up the [intellectual] system have neither substance nor purpose ... Another consequence of the assumption of zero transaction costs, not usually noticed, is that, when there are no costs of making transactions, it costs nothing to speed them up, so that eternity can be experienced in a split second.
>
> (Coase 2005, 208)

Explaining epistemic hystereses 75

An absence of epistemic costs in academic scholarship is not the actual case. A PEC worldview suggests that the principle factor that makes academic scholarship look like what it is is non-zero epistemic costs in scholarly processes. In a PEC world, it is not unlikely that perfect results do not come out no matter how hard intellectuals try to obtain them. In such a world, the labour theory of value does not always tell us successfully which theory is the most valuable in the market. Nor is it possible to show at what time a theory would outperform others. Luck and other chance events play significant roles in this. Defects are abundant in the models and other explanatory patterns that intellectuals build. Disappointments in the behaviour of intellectual actors – such as unethical behaviours – are not improbable.

Then, just as markets of goods and services fail, so do markets of ideas. Failure in the market of ideas is one of the reasons for the destabilization of the growth process of knowledge. Human ideas do not always spread in ways such that better theories outperform others given sufficient time for intellectuals to complete the processes of 'shooting for the truth'. Scholars compete to win scientific authority that would allow them to speak about and act on scientific matters legitimately in authorized and authoritative ways. Legitimacy in academic scholarship can be gained only when epistemic capital accumulates (that is, producers, due to the value of their products, become respected scholars). The amount of social capital possessed by competitors in the market determines the strategies of investment and disinvestment in the research market. Research conducted by the winners of the Swedish Bank Prize and scholars at powerful institutions with which the winners of the Swedish Bank Prize are affiliated, such as the RAND Corporation, Cowles Commission and the Mont Pélerin Society (Mirowski 2002, 153–231; Horn 2009; Plehwe 2009) are highly credited and further research is often directed by the outcomes of such authors' work. This gives rise to a struggle among competitors for reputation, prestige, authority and competence.

New ideas do not always spread at fast speeds. Some are forgotten in time. Sometimes, the market of ideas turns into a giant industry featuring monopolistic properties. Jesús Zamora Bonilla (2012, 845) argues, 'epistemic competition naturally leads to monopolies because ... it is assumed that scientific problems have only one "right" answer, or, at least, that the more correct answers "displace" the worse ones'.

Pierre Bourdieu (1999, 34) explains monopolization in academic scholarship in terms of *social capital*. Social capital 'can be accumulated, transmitted, and even reconverted into other kinds of capital under certain conditions'. Markets of ideas operate, according to Bourdieu, in such a way that scholars compete to win scientific authority that would allow them to speak and act about scientific matters legitimately – that is, in authorized and authoritative ways. Legitimacy in academic scholarship can be gained only when social capital accumulates (i.e. producers, due to the value of their products, become respected scholars). The amount of social capital possessed by competitors in the market determines the strategies of investment and disinvestment in the research market.

76 *The economic construction of sciences*

The scientific field is always the locus of a more or less unequal struggle between agents unequally endowed with the specific capital, hence unequally equipped to appropriate the product of scientific labour accumulated by previous generations, and the specific profits (and also, in some cases, the external profits such as economic or strictly political benefits) which the aggregate of the competitors produce through their objective collaboration by putting to use the aggregate of the available means of scientific production.

(Ibid., 29)

According to Bourdieu, unequal endowment of social capital diminishes opportunities of gaining access to scientific problems and tools. The market becomes more restricted (i.e. costs of entry increase) to competitors who are able to produce criticism and discredit established beliefs in the market.

[N]ewcomers who refuse the beaten tracks cannot 'beat the dominant at their own game' unless they make additional, strictly scientific investments from which they cannot expect high profits, at least in the short run, since the whole logic of the system is against them.

(Ibid., 30)

In all that, the monopolization of financial resources is not a direct matter of debate: social capital may or may not be transmitted into high salaries in the jobs market and high profits in the commodities market, both of which owe much of their progress and extent to the progress and extent of the market of ideas. Monopolization in the market of ideas is an epistemic problem with economic features (i.e. command and control by a small group of scholars over the use of epistemic sources) whereas monopolization in other markets is economical in which epistemic virtues may or may not turn into (additional) pecuniary gains. For instance, Paula Stephan argues that '[p]roductivity in science is highly skewed: approximately 6 percent of scientists and engineers write 50 percent of all published articles' (Stephan 2012, 13).

The academic community is not powerful enough to fight against shifting epistemic costs onto the shoulders of intellectually weaker individuals and communities. Political commitments, sociological backgrounds, personal and group interests, as well as rent seeking and concerns about reputation and power, are all constituents of producing 'real intellectual income' in the processes of academic scholarship. When unequal endowment of social capital diminishes opportunities for gaining access to scientific problems and tools (Bourdieu 1999), academic scholarship becomes more restricted (that is, the costs of entry increase) to competitors who are able to produce criticism and discredit established beliefs in the market. Lack of pluralism dominates academic scholarship in such a way that there is only one game left in town for scholars to play.

What do scholars do?

Waking up one morning with a bright solution to the problem of trade-off between inflation and unemployment, both in the short and long runs, does not

Explaining epistemic hystereses 77

really (or, at least, always) account for the 'growth' of economic ideas. Scholarship is a collective activity. In addition to certain dynamics (mental, psychological etc.) which enable individuals to develop new ideas when they are together, scholars operate within institutions in which new individual behaviours of scholars at 'micro' levels (i.e. stories of creativity and genius) transform into 'macro' patterns (mainly 'conversations', Klamer 2007). The survival of ideas, to some degree, is dependent on the veracity of the formulation of ideas. However, if scholarly elegance is not accompanied by the 'mythic expectations of listeners', ideas stay isolated and do not always add up to the accumulated body of knowledge (March 2007).

Theories are not only selected or rejected by ways of abstract reasoning, sophisticated argumentation and additional evidence; processes of production, distribution and use of academic knowledge are so complex that intellectual history should be accounted for on institutional grounds too. The economic character of questions in epistemology, which are traditionally considered to be philosophical in nature, underscores the questions of persistence and change of institutional structure in economics.

Can failure in the market of ideas also mean that the operations of scholarly institutions are not satisfactory in correcting replication failure, fraud or plagiarism? It seems to me that institutions in the market of ideas play a double role here. The primary function of universities is to run together with, if not replace, institutionalized processes in which ideas and theories are debated and exchanged among scholars, but universities are also part of scholarly mechanisms, producing further costs to which academic scholarship can find a solution only by way of designing further institutions. Cumulative consequences of institutional design generate an entropy effect in the academic environment. Such consequences are irreversible: processes in academic scholarship are not always able to follow the same courses phase by phase in reverse order (Georgescu-Roegen 1971, 196). Plagiarized texts, fraudulent research and non-replicable data and findings are of no use for further research but rather are a product of the scholarly mechanisms that threaten the epistemic stability and sustainability. Remedies are not impossible. And yet there is no guarantee that the costs of epistemic resources forgone, used in the processes of institutional design, would not exceed the benefits of the operation of new institutions in the long run. Had there been an 'economic barometer' or 'economic clock' available to intellectual historians, such as the one in which Nicholas Georgescu-Roegen was interested in the 1930s, measuring how much harm scholars inflict upon others, this device would have given us scores, increasing in size, of the epistemic costs produced as a result of implementing (newer and better) institutional solutions to the problems of academic scholarship.

The academic environment is not *gratis* because neither scholars nor scholarly institutions are isolated. Universities, departments, academic journals and research programmes, including PhD programmes, are 'islands of conscious power' (Coase 1937), coordinating scholarly activities in which scholars collaborate and negotiate ideas within and with the help of scientific institutions.

78   The economic construction of sciences

However, such collaborations and negotiations can (and do) cause further epistemic costs in terms of, for instance, organizational problems within and among academic teams, learning how to communicate with each other, and not being individually credited for contribution to a collaborated project. Further, there is the dominance of high-ranking postgraduate programmes and orthodox curricula, such as the Chicago PhD programme and Chicago School of Economics curricula (Horn 2009, Horn and Mirowski 2009), over several other postgraduate programmes elsewhere in the USA and Europe in the post-war period. Institutionalization and standardization of education techniques (such as requirements of mathematical and statistical courses before admission to PhD programmes in economics), homogeneity of dissertation topics (such as the exclusion of Post-Keynesian, Institutionalist and Marxian issues) and ideologization in the policies of hiring new PhDs and promoting senior members of the academy – all of which have in fact happened or taken place, especially in the USA, since the 1980s (Lee 2009, 66–77) – make it less and less likely for a pluralism of methods, interests and intellectual and ideological concerns to disseminate among academic economists. All of this suggests, at least to the extent that epistemic costs are concerned, that economic aspects of academic scholarship are embedded within the institutions of academic scholarship such that academic scholarship is constructed, operated and limited by factors other than philosophical and intellectual factors. A substantial question, which might help the 'black box' of (orthodox) economic science to open up, is as follows: how do such institutions operate in a PEC world of academic economics? Or, turning back to the original question, why do economists hesitate to change their minds when they have to face challenges towards their belief systems and ideologies? Is it just 'natural' that economists are inclined to defend their 'intellectual' position or is there an internal logic, a hidden set of rules, or a social ontology, operating in more sophisticated (evolutionary) manners than naive dialectics, verificationism, or critical rationalism?

Universities are intellectual coalitions. Intellectual coalitions are one of the most important factors determining the outcome in academic scholarship. Social networks among intellectual elites, collaboration among research institutes, funding opportunities, the role of the government and different streams of thought cause variations in communication patterns among scientists. Randall Collins argues in his *The Sociology of Philosophies: A Global Theory of Intellectual Change* (1998) that intellectual causation explains how solidarity groups survive the challenges of academic scholarship. He shows that interaction among intellectuals is dense, intensifying even more when participants of a scholarly community feel that they are part of a particular community. In scholarly communities, intellectuals use specific bodily motions. They perform within certain speech acts. They also use particular metaphors to communicate (Lanteri and Yalcintas 2006). Such symbols make borders among different communities more visible, determining who is in and who is out of the scholarly conversation.

Survival of a community depends on the (re-)assembling of the participants on a regular basis in terms of time and occasion. Symbols (i.e. bodily motions, speech acts and metaphors) constitute the genes of a scholarly community. Genes

Explaining epistemic hystereses 79

act as the 'moral force' of a scholarly conversation and determine the scope of the conversation: '[charging] up individuals like an electric battery, giving them a corresponding degree of enthusiasm toward ritually created symbolic goals [even] when they are out of the presence of the group' (Collins 1998, 23). Scholars' attachment to the symbols sets the standards for the validity of ideas within the community. The social activities of a community (such as lectures and formal debates) turn individual scholars using such symbols into members of the community. Truisms arise out of the 'interaction rituals' of intellectuals.

Scholarly communities operate in repetitive patterns, reinforcing the ties between the scholars. Messages conveyed among community members in social activities are discussed, repeated and augmented every time individuals take part in a debate. Interaction rituals generate intellectual commitments among members and these commitments constitute and strengthen the social density of the 'repertoire of symbols' that determine the depth and scope of the content of a conversation. Symbols have a life. As symbols are circulated more and the sophistication in their meaning increases, there is a higher chance that they become 'parents' to a greater number of 'offspring' symbols. Symbols reproduce across generations of conversations in which creative members of the community produce large amounts of work. Large amounts of work do not always add up to more creative ideas, but they mean a better chance of survival for the symbols to which creative members are attached. The survival of a symbol depends on the degree of agreement on ideas which are crystallized in a symbol. That is to say, symbols get established when ideas that are expressed in these symbols are circulated among the community widely. As ideas make their way through different intellectual networks, there is a better chance for a symbol to become an instrument in the creativity of the scholars. Symbols spread far and wide by way of circulating ideas that are socialized among the whole intellectual community.

Intellectual paths do not necessarily amount to a hindrance or negative cumulative effect on the accumulated body of knowledge. New ideas often come about only when intellectuals invest time in examining the facts of the world until they generate intellectual paths in which they establish the borders of their science and the standards of doing it. New pathways are often created intentionally by way of entrepreneurs taking initiatives on the course of events. Such initiatives cause deviations from the possible set of actions that an individual is expected to take in reaction to certain conditions. Entrepreneurs, by so doing, win the ability to explore new pathways, thus alternatives, of motivation for proceeding further. New pathways mobilize new sequences of events in the future so that entrepreneurs escape possible long-time lock-ins. Under such circumstances, historical small events turn into starting points of creativity which involve:

the disembedding of an individual from localized structures of relevance and provinces of meaning, overcoming the inertia and momentum that he encountered, mobilizing others to work on an idea that transformed over time, all the while being flexibly resolute with a vision of what might be possible.

(Garud and Karnøe 2001, 20)

80   *The economic construction of sciences*

'Entrepreneurship', Garud and Karnøe argue (ibid., 9), 'involves an ability to exercise judgment and choice about time, relevance structures and objects within which entrepreneurs are embedded and from which they must deviate mindfully to create new paths.'

Entrepreneurial initiatives are crucial to unburden the constraints that are set in motion as a consequence of past actions. When lock-ins operate as hindrances for further progress, which is not a rule but is occasionally the case, entrepreneurships affect the fate of the course of events and change tipping points into starting points of creativity. An example of this is the development of Post-it® Notes. Many accounts of its development say it was the result of an 'accident' by Spencer Silver, one of the 3M scientists working on the original formula of Post-it® glue, to discover the 'glue that did not glue' (ibid., 17). Silver took the initiative and his experiment paid off for him with a revolutionary finding that de-framed the evolutionary pathway of the industry all at once.

When new paths are created or generated, the triggering event is not necessarily a small event. Mechanisms giving rise to path dependence may yield a recombination of further consequences. Also, other mechanisms (e.g. international dynamics or local cycles in certain regions) function in such ways that old paths are broken over time and new ones are created with enduring effects. Samina Karim and Will Mitchell (2000) argue that firms using acquisitions to achieve long-term reconfiguration generate new pathways of organization and production when they use acquisitions in the form of 'resource extension'. According to Karim and Mitchell, 'path-breaking change may occur in cases where expansion incentives and competitive pressures out-weigh path dependence. Path-breaking change occurs when acquirers retain targets' resources that are distinct from their own' (ibid., 1068). In a similar fashion, Marie-Laure Djelic and Sigrid Quack (2007) point out different mechanisms that open the way to 'processes of path transformation'. The authors argue that 'path transformation often stems from a gradual succession and combination of incremental steps and junctures' when we study more closely the national and trans-national systems (161). In the cases that they thoroughly analyze, competition regimes in Germany and the USA after 1945, they show that 'some reinforcing mechanisms generated momentum towards a new path or towards a path deviation in one case, and secured the reproduction and entrenchment of existing path dependencies in the other' (ibid., 168). According to Djelic and Quack, in the strongest versions of path dependence, path transformation is assumed to be unlikely. Only in rare cases of external shocks, systems lock out from dependencies. They claim that new paths often occur when established institutional paths confront and collide with other institutional paths – new or transitional.

Insofar as borders and standards lead to innovations in the market, intellectual paths are desirable and even necessary. As a matter of fact, standardization in high-tech industries – such as the telecommunication and computing standard of Transmission Control Protocol/Internet Protocol (TCP/IP) and secure e-commerce standard of Secure Sockets Layer (SSL) which made the World Wide Web possible – are necessary and advantageous for both producers and consumers in the market because innovation continues at a reasonable pace when it operates as an incentive to further progress. As Brian Arthur claims,

> these temporary monopolies are a prize for innovation. They're the incentive for innovation. If you took that incentive away – requiring, say, that for every lock-in you have in high tech, somebody else has to be cut in on the deal for 50 percent or there have to be at least three players – then you will see less innovation.
>
> (Arthur 1998, 24)

Economists worry about standardization and monopolization particularly when an economic actor, say, a firm, achieves a monopolistic power that lasts for a long time and uses it unfairly in the market. Under such conditions, positive feedback is a factor of risk in the market because consequences of particular events are not necessarily for the best or superior in the long run when they reinforce the monopolistic power of an economic actor. For instance, 'cultural standardization' (Pagano 2007) can seriously limit the diversity of solutions and approaches found and developed by scientists to deal with the intellectual problems of scholarly life. Cultural standardization, while making it possible for intellectual actors to interact and exchange ideas on a global scale, 'induces a global dilution of the standards of social protection' (ibid., 649). Different distributions of intellectual assets among academic circles and even nations affect the pathways of scholarly advance, in which the overall outcome of interaction and exchange of ideas can end up with inequalities among intellectual actors. Initial endowments of property rights, as a result of self-reinforcing mechanisms, such as positive feedback, transform into a dominant system of rights; the ownership of intellectual assets does not go to those who make use of them in the most efficient ways. Second 'best' solutions – that is, unequal distribution of property rights, resulting from the tendency of standardization and monopolization in 'intellectual capitalism' (Slaughter and Leslie 1997), are always likely. When this happens,

> only the agents who own the intellectual assets have sufficient safeguards to develop the ability to improve them. Only the individuals or the firms who already own the preceding version of a certain piece of software (that is, the most important input for producing the next version) will have adequate incentives and safeguards to produce improvements of the software. Thus, countries, owning a high initial stock of property rights, are likely to develop more intellectual abilities and to acquire even more intellectual property in a self-reinforcing virtuous circle.
>
> (Pagano 2007, 661)

Therefore, intellectual path dependence has both negative and positive connotations depending on the occasion in which historical small events operate. When intellectual path creation is at stake, dependence of the followers upon the innovative idea that was initially introduced by an entrepreneur should be considered as a positive occasion. In this case, path dependence leads to a short-cut that moves the evolutionary system to higher levels of sophistication. If path

82 *The economic construction of sciences*

dependence gives rise to a hindrance, there is reason for intellectual historians to consider this transition as a breakdown of the system that disallows intellectuals and entrepreneurs to achieve advancement. In each case, the tipping point is realized after a small event.

In order for us to talk about path dependence in the life history of societies, we need to observe certain characteristics regarding the initial conditions of a system. A path-dependent system is one in which the outcome of a sequence of events is not determined by initial conditions. Instead, a path-dependent system exhibits the property that outcomes are *stochastically* generated by initial conditions (Goldstone 1998). In other words, in path-dependent processes, outcomes of a sequence of events are indeterminate. They depend on the intermediary mechanisms between initial conditions and the outcome. When we 'run' a system, we have no idea (1) as to which initial conditions would give rise to path-dependent outcomes and (2) as to whether same path-dependent outcomes would come about had there been another occasion in which we could repeat the 'game'.

References

Agrawal, Ajay, and Avi Goldfarb. 2008. 'Restructuring Research: Communication Costs and the Democratization of University Innovation'. *American Economic Review* 98 (4): 1578–90.

Al-Marzouki, Sanaa, Ian Roberts, Tom Marshall and Stephen Evans. 2005. 'The Effect of Scientific Misconduct on the Results of Clinical Trials: A Delphi Survey'. *Contemporary Clinical Trials* 26 (3): 331–7.

Alchian, Armen Albert, and Harold Demsetz. 1972. 'Production, Information Costs and Economic Organisation'. *American Economic Review* 62 (5): 777–95.

American Economic Review. 1992. 'A Plea for a Pluralistic and Rigorous Economics'. 82 (2): xxv.

Anderson, Melissa S., Louis Karen Seashore and Earle Jason. 1994. 'Disciplinary and Departmental Effects on Observations of Faculty and Graduate Student Misconduct'. *Journal of Higher Education* 65 (3): 331–50.

Anderson, Richard G., William H. Greene, B. D. McCullough and H. D. Vinod. 2005. 'The Role of Data and Program Code Archives in the Future of Economic Research'. *The Federal Reserve Bank of St Louis Working Paper Series* 2005-014C.

Arrow, Kenneth J. 1962. 'Economic Welfare and the Allocation of Resources for Invention'. In *The Rate and Direction of Inventive Activity: Economic and Social Factors*, edited by Harold M. Groves, 609–26. Princeton, NJ: Princeton University Press.

Arthur, W. Brian. 1998. 'Self-reinforcing Mechanisms in Economics'. In *The Economy as an Evolving Complex System: The Proceedings of the Evolutionary Paths of the Global Economy Workshop*, edited by Philip W. Anderson, Kenneth J. Arrow and David Pines, 9–31. Redwood City, CA: Addison-Wesley.

Becker, Gary, and Kevin M. Murphy. 1992. 'The Division of Labor, Coordination Costs, and Knowledge'. *Quarterly Journal of Economics* 107 (4): 1137–60.

Bell, J. F. 1960. 'Adam Smith, the Clubman'. *Scottish Journal of Political Economy* 7 (1): 108–16.

Bernal, John Desmond. 1939. *The Social Function of Science*. London: George Routledge & Sons.

Bhattacharjee, Yudhijit. 2008. 'The Cost of a Genuine Collaboration'. *Science* 320 (5878): 859.

Bohannon, John. 2014. 'Replication Effort Provokes Praise – and "Bullying" Charges'. *Science* 344 (6186): 788–9.

Bonilla, Jesús P. Zamora. 2012. 'The Economics of Scientific Knowledge'. In *Handbook of the Philosophy of Science. Philosophy of Economics*, edited by Uskali Maki. New York: Elsevier.

Bonilla, Jesús P. Zamora. 2014. 'The Nature of Co-authorship: A Note on Recognition Sharing and Scientific Argumentation'. *Synthese* 191 (1): 97–108.

Boulding, Kenneth E. 1966. 'The Economics of Knowledge and the Knowledge of Economics'. *American Economic Review* 56 (2): 1–13.

Bourdieu, Piere. 1999. 'The Specificity of the Scientific Field and the Social Conditions of the Progression of Reason'. In *The Science Studies Reader*, edited by Mario Biagioli, 19–47. New York: Routledge.

Burman, Leonard E., W. Robert Reed and James Alm. 2010. 'A Call for Replication Studies'. *Public Finance Review* 38 (5): 647–53.

Chartier, Gary, and Charles W. Johnson (eds). 2011. *Markets Not Capitalism: Individualist Anarchism Against Bosses, Inequality, Corporate Power, and Structural Poverty.* London: Minor Compositions.

Clemens, Michael A. 2015. 'The Meaning of Failed Replications: A Review and Proposal'. *Forschunginstitut zur Zukunft der Arbeit, Discussion Paper Series No. 9000* April.

Coase, Ronald H. 1937. 'The Nature of the Firm'. *Economica* 4 (16): 386–405.

Coase, Ronald H. 1974. 'The Market for Goods and the Market for Ideas'. *American Economic Review* 64 (2): 384–91.

Coase, Ronald H. 2005. 'The Relevance of Transaction Costs in the Economic Analysis of Law'. In *The Origins of Law and Economics: Essays by the Founding Fathers*, edited by Francesco Parisi and Charles K. Rowley, 199–221. Cheltenham: Edward Elgar.

Collins, Randall. 1998. *The Sociology of Philosophies: A Global Theory of Intellectual Change*. Cambridge, MA: Harvard University Press.

David, Paul A. 2000. 'A Tragedy of the Public Knowledge "Commons"? Global Science, Intellectual Property and The Digital Technology Boomerang'. *Stanford Institute for Economic Policy Research (SIEPR) Discussion Paper 00-002.*

David, Paul A. 2001. 'The Political Economy of Public Science'. In *The Regulation of Science and Technology*, edited by Helen Lawton Smith, 33–57. London: Macmillan.

Dawkins, Richard. 1976 [2006]. *The Selfish Gene*. Oxford: Oxford University Press.

De Vries, Raymond, Melissa S. Anderson and Brian C. Martinson. 2006. 'Normal Misbehavior: Scientists Talk About the Ethics of Research'. *Journal of Empirical Research on Human Research Ethics: An International Journal* 1 (1): 43–50.

DeMartino, George F. 2011a. *The Economist's Oath: On the Need for and Content of Professional Economics Ethics*. Oxford: Oxford University Press.

DeMartino, George F. 2011b. 'On the Need for Professional Economic Ethics'. *The Economist* 6 January.

DeMartino, George F., and Deirdre McCloskey (eds). 2015. *The Oxford Handbook of Professional Economic Ethics*. Oxford: Oxford University Press.

Dewald, William G., and Richard G. Anderson. 2014. 'Replication and Reflection: A Decade at the Journal of Money, Credit, and Banking'. In *Secrets of Economics Editors*, edited by Michael Szenberg and Lall Ramrattan, 199–212. Cambridge, MA: MIT Press.

84   The economic construction of sciences

Dewald, William G., Jerry G. Thursby and Richard G. Anderson. 1986. 'Replication in Empirical Economics: The Journal of Money, Credit and Banking Project'. *American Economic Review* 76 (4): 587–603.

Djelic, Marie-Laure, and Sigrid Quack. 2007. 'Overcoming Path Dependency: Path Generation in Open Systems'. *Theory and Society* 36 (2): 161–86.

Duvendack, Maren, Richard W. Palmer-Jones and W. Robert Reed. 2015. 'Replications in Economics: A Progress Report'. *Econ Journal Watch* 12 (2): 164–91.

Dyer, Alan W. 1986. 'Veblen on Scientific Creativity: The Influence of Charles S. Pierce'. *Journal of Economic Issues* 20 (1): 21–41.

Ehrenberg, Ronald G., Michael J. Rizzo and George H. Jakubson. 2007. 'Who Bears the Growing Cost of Science at Universities?'. In *Science and the University*, edited by Paula E. Stephan and Ronald G. Ehrenberg, 19–33. Madison: University of Wisconsin Press.

Enders, Walter, and Gary A. Hoover. 2004. 'Whose Line is it? Plagiarism in Economics'. *Journal of Economic Literature* 42 (2): 487–93.

Fanelli, Daniele. 2009. 'How Many Scientists Fabricate and Falsify Research? A Systematic Review and Meta-Analysis of Survey Data'. *PLoS ONE* 4 (5): 1–11.

Feigenbaum, Susan, and David M. Levy. 1993. 'The Market for (Ir)reproducible Econometrics'. *Social Epistemology* 7 (3): 215–32.

Feigenbaum, Susan, and David M. Levy. 1996. 'The Technological Obsolescence of Scientific Fraud'. *Rationality and Society* 8 (3): 261–76.

Fine, Ben. 2013. 'Economics: Unfit for Purpose'. *Review of Social Economy* 71 (3): 373–89.

Flood, Alison 2012. 'Scientists Sign Petition to Boycott Academic Publisher Elsevier'. *Guardian*, 2 February.

Frey, Bruno S. 2003. 'Publishing as Prostitution? – Choosing Between One's Own Ideas and Academic Success'. *Public Choice* 116 (1–2): 205–23.

Gans, Joshua S., and George B. Shepherd. 1994. 'How are the Mighty Fallen: Rejected Classic Articles by Leading Economists'. *Journal of Economic Perspectives* 8 (1): 165–79.

Garud, Raghu, and Peter Karnøe. 2001. *Path Dependence and Creation*. Mahwah, NJ: Lawrence Erlbaum Associates.

Geggie, D. 2001. 'A Survey of Newly Appointed Consultants' Attitudes towards Research Fraud'. *Journal of Medical Ethics* 27 (5): 344–6.

Gentzkow, Matthew, and Emir Kamenica. 2014. 'Costly Persuasion'. *American Economic Review* 104 (5): 457–62.

Georgescu-Roegen, Nicholas. 1971. *The Entropy Law and Economic Process*. Cambridge, MA: Harvard University Press.

Glandon, Philip. 2010. Report on the American Economics Review Data Availability Compliance Project. Available at: https://www.aeaweb.org/aer/2011_Data_Compliance_Report.pdf. Accessed February 2015.

Goldstone, Jack A. 1998. 'Initial Conditions, General Laws, Path Dependence, and Explanation in Historical Sociology'. *American Journal of Sociology* 104 (3): 829–45.

Gould, Stephen Jay. 1989. *Wonderful Life: The Burgess Shale and The Nature of History*. New York: W. W. Norton Co.

Hamermesh, Daniel S., George E. Johnson and Burton A. Weisbrod. 1982. 'Scholarship, Citations and Salaries: Economic Rewards in Economics'. *Southern Economic Journal* 49 (2): 472–81.

Explaining epistemic hystereses 85

Harvey, Campbell R. 2014. 'Reflections on Editing the Journal of Finance, 2006 to 2012'. In *Secrets of Economics Editors*, edited by Michael Szenberg and Lall Ramrattan, 67–81. Cambridge, MA: MIT Press.

Herndon, Thomas, Michael Ash and Robert Pollin. 2013a. 'Does High Public Debt Consistently Stifle Economic Growth? A Critique of Reinhart and Rogoff'. *Cambridge Journal of Economics*. doi: 10.1093/cje/bet075.

Herndon, Thomas, Michael Ash and Robert Pollin. 2013b. 'Does High Public Debt Consistently Stifle Economic Growth? A Critique of Reinhart and Rogoff'. *PERI Working Paper Series 322*.

Hodgson, Geoffrey M. 1998. 'Socialism against Markets? A Critique of Two Recent Proposals'. *Economy and Society* 27 (4): 407–33.

Horn, Rob van. 2009. 'Reinventing Monopoly and the Role of Corporations: The Roots of Chicago Law and Economics'. In *The Road from Mont Pélerin: The Making of the Neoliberal Thought Collective*, edited by Philip Mirowski and Dieter Plehwe, 204–37. Cambridge, MA: Harvard University Press.

Horn, van Rob, and Philip Mirowski. 2009. 'The Rise of the Chicago School of Economics and the Birth of Neoliberalism'. In *The Road from Mont Pélerin: The Making of the Neoliberal Thought Collective*, edited by Philip Mirowski and Dieter Plehwe, 139–78. Cambridge, MA: Harvard University Press.

Hume, David. 1748 [1999]. *An Enquiry Concerning Human Understanding*. Oxford: Oxford University Press.

Ingber, Stanley. 1984. 'The Marketplace of Ideas: A Legitimizing Myth'. *Duke Law Journal* February (1): 1–91.

Ioannidis, John P. 2005. 'Why Most Published Research Findings are False'. *PLoS Med* 2 (8): e124.

Ioannidis, John P. 2008. 'Why Most Discovered True Associations are Inflated'. *Epidemiology* 19 (5): 640–8.

Johnson, Harry G. 1972. 'Some Economic Aspects of Science'. *Minerva* 10 (1): 10–18.

Kahneman, Daniel, Jack L. Knetsch and Richard H. Thaler. 1990. 'Experimental Tests of the Endowment Effect and the Coase Theorem'. *Journal of Political Economy* 98 (6): 1325–48.

Kane, Edward J. 1994. 'Why Journal Editors Should Encourage the Replication of Applied Econometric Research'. *Quarterly Journal of Business and Economics* 23 (1): 3–8.

Kapp, K. William. 1950. *The Social Costs of Private Enterprise*. Cambridge, MA: Harvard University Press.

Kapp, K. William. 1976. 'The Nature and Significance of Institutional Economics'. *Kyklos* 29 (2): 209–32.

Kapp, K. William. 1977. 'Environment and Technology: New Frontiers for the Social and Natural Sciences'. *Journal of Economic Issues* 11 (3): 527–40.

Kapp, K. William. 2011. *The Foundations of Institutional Economics*. Edited by Sebastian Berger and Rolf Steppacher. London and New York: Routledge.

Karim, Samina, and Will Mitchell. 2000. 'Path-dependent and Path-breaking Change: Reconfiguring Business Resources Following Acquisitions in the US Medical Sector, 1978–1995'. *Strategic Management Journal* 21 (10–11): 1061–81.

Kaufmann, Walter. 1968 [1974]. *Nietzsche: Philosopher, Psychologist, Antichrist*. 4th edn. Princeton, NJ: Princeton University Press.

Kaul, Inge, and Ronald U. Mendoza. 2003. 'Advancing the Concept of Public Goods'. In *Providing Global Public Goods: Managing Globalization*, edited by Inge Kaul,

86   *The economic construction of sciences*

Pedro Conceiçao, Katell Le Goulven and Ronald U. Mendoza, 78–111. Oxford: Oxford University Press.

Kean, Sam. 2006. 'Scientists Spend Nearly Half Their Time on Administrative Tasks, Survey Finds'. *The Chronicle of Higher Education*, 14 July.

Khalil, Elias. 2000. 'Survival of the Most Foolish of Fools: The Limits of Evolutionary Selection Theory'. *Journal of Bioeconomics* 2 (3): 203–20.

Klamer, Arjo. 2007. *Speaking of Economics: How to Get in the Conversation*. New York: Routledge.

Lacetera, Nicola, and Lorenzo Zirulia. 2011. 'The Economics of Scientific Misconduct'. *Journal of Law, Economics, and Organization* 27 (3): 568–603.

Lanteri, Alessandro, and Altug Yalcintas. 2006. 'The Economics of Rhetoric: On Metaphors as Institutions'. *Ankara University Faculty of Political Sciences GETA Discussion Paper Series, No: 94.*

Lee, Frederic. 2009. *A History of Heterodox Economics: Challenging the Mainstream in the Twentieth Century*. New York: Routledge.

Levy, David. M. 1988. 'The Market for Fame and Fortune'. *History of Political Economy* 20 (4): 615–25.

Locke, John. 1836 [1869]. *An Essay Concerning Human Understanding*. London: T. Tegg and Son.

Mäki, Uskali. 1989. 'On the Problem of Realism in Economics'. *Richerche Economiche* 43: 176–98.

Mäki, Uskali. 1994. 'Realisticness'. In *The Handbook of Economic Methodology*, edited by B. John Davis, D. Wade Hands and Uskali Mäki, 409–13. Cheltenham: Edward Elgar.

Mandeville, Bernard. 1714 [1962]. *The Fable of the Bees, or Private Vices, Public Benefits*. Edited by Irwin Primer. New York: Capricorn Books.

Maniadis, Zacharias, Fabio Tufano and John A. List. 2013. 'One Swallow Doesn't Make a Summer: New Evidence on Anchoring Effects'. *CeDEx Discussion Paper Series No. 2013-07.*

March, James G. 2007. 'Scholarship, Scholarly Institutions, and Scholarly Communities'. *Organization Science* 18 (3): 537–42.

Martinson, Brian C., Melissa S. Anderson and Raymond de Vries. 2005. 'Scientists Behaving Badly'. *Nature* 435 (7043): 737–8.

Martinson, Brian C., Melissa S. Anderson, A. Lauren Crain and Raymond de Vries. 2006. 'Scientists' Perceptions of Organizational Justice and Self-Reported Misbehaviors'. *Journal of Empirical Research on Human Research Ethics: An International Journal* 1 (1): 51–66.

McCabe, Donald L., Kenneth D. Butterfield and Linda Klebe Treviño. 2006. 'Academic Dishonesty in Graduate Business Programs: Prevalence, Causes, and Proposed Action'. *Academy of Management Learning and Education* 5 (3): 294–305.

McCabe, Donald L., Linda Klebe Treviño and Kenneth D. Butterfield. 2001. 'Cheating in Academic Institutions: A Decade of Research'. *Ethics and Behavior* 11 (3): 219–32.

McCullough, B. D., and H. D. Vinod. 2003. 'Verifying the Solution from a Nonlinear Solver: A Case Study'. *American Economic Review* 93 (3): 873–92.

Meyers, Morton A. 2012. *Prize Fight: The Race and the Rivalry to be the First in Science*. New York: Palgrave Macmillan.

Mirowski, Philip. 1987. 'The Philosophical Bases of Institutionalist Economics'. *Journal of Economic Issues* 21 (3): 1001–38.

Mirowski, Philip. 2002. *Machine Dreams: Economics Becomes a Cyborg Science*. Cambridge: Cambridge University Press.

Mirowski, Philip. 2009. 'Postface: Defining Neoliberalism'. In *The Road from Mont Pèlerin: The Making of the Neoliberal Thought Collective*, edited by Dieter Plehve and Philip Mirowski, 417–54. Cambridge, MA: Harvard University Press.

Mirowski, Philip, and Esther-Mirjam Sent. 2002. *Science Bought and Sold: Essays in the Economics of Science*. Chicago: University of Chicago Press.

Mirowski, Philip, and Steven Sklivas. 1991. 'Why Econometricians Don't Replicate (Although They Do Reproduce)'. *Review of Political Economy* 3 (2): 146–63.

Mirowski, Philip, and Koye Somefun. 1998. 'Markets as Evolving Computational Entities'. *Journal of Evolutionary Economics* 8 (4): 329–56.

Mokyr, Joel. 2002. *The Gifts of Athena: Historical Origins of the Knowledge Economy*. Princeton, NJ: Princeton University Press.

Pagano, Ugo. 2007. 'Cultural Globalisation, Institutional Diversity, and the Unequal Accumulation of Intellectual Capital'. *Cambridge Journal of Economics* 31 (5): 649–67.

Plehwe, Dieter. 2009. 'Introduction'. In *The Road from Mont Pèlerin: The Making of the Neoliberal Thought Collective*, edited by Philip Mirowski and Dieter Plehwe, 1–39. Cambridge, MA: Harvard University Press.

Popper, Karl R. 1963. *Conjectures and Refutations: The Growth of Scientific Knowledge*. New York: Harper and Row.

Popper, Karl R. 1972 [1979]. *Objective Knowledge: An Evolutionary Approach*. Oxford: Clarendon Press.

Rawls, John. 2011. *Political Liberalism: Expanded Edition*. New York: Columbia University Press.

Reinhart, Carmen M., and Kenneth Rogoff. 2010a. 'Growth in a Time of Debt'. *NBER Discussion Paper No. 15639*.

Reinhart, Carmen M., and Kenneth Rogoff. 2010b. 'Growth in a Time of Debt'. *American Economic Review: Papers and Proceedings* 100 (May): 573–8.

Reinhart, Carmen M., and Kenneth Rogoff. 2013. 'Debt, Growth, and Austerity Debate'. *New York Times*, 25 April.

Rockwell, Sera. 2009. 'The FDP Faculty Burden Survey'. *Research Management Review* 61 (Spring): 29–44.

Rorty, Richard. 1979. *Philosophy and the Mirror of Nature*. Princeton, NJ: Princeton University Press.

Rothbard, Murray N. 1995 [2006]. *Economic Thought Before Adam Smith: An Austrian Perspective on the History of Economic Thought, Vol I*. Auburn, AL: Ludwig von Mises Institute.

Rubin, Paul H. 2014. 'Emporiophobia (Fear of Markets): Cooperation or Competition?'. *Southern Economic Journal* 80 (4): 875–89.

Schumpeter, Elizabeth Boody. 1952 [1954]. 'Editor's Introduction'. In *History of Economic Analysis*, v–xiii. Oxford: Oxford University Press.

Shepherd, George B. (ed.). 1995. *Rejected: Leading Economists Ponder the Publication Process*. Sun Lakes, AZ: Thomas Horton and Daughters.

Siler, Kyle, Kirby Lee and Lisa Bero. 2014. 'Measuring the Effectiveness of Scientific Gatekeeping'. *Proceedings of the National Academy of Sciences* 112: 360–5.

Slaughter, Sheila, and Larry L. Leslie. 1997. *Academic Capitalism: Politics, Policies, and the Entrepreneurial University*. Baltimore: Johns Hopkins University Press.

88 *The economic construction of sciences*

Smith, Adam. 1776 [1966]. *An Inquiry into the Nature and Causes of the Wealth of Nations*. London and New York: W. Strahan and T. Cadell A. M. Kelley.

Stahl, Silke Regine 2000. 'Persistence and Change of Economic Institutions: A Social Cognitive Approach'. In *Technology and Knowledge: From the Firm to Innovation Systems*, edited by P. P. Saviotti and Bart Nooteboom, 263–84. Cheltenham: Edward Elgar.

Stephan, Paula E. 1996. 'The Economics of Science'. *Journal of Economic Literature* 34 (3): 1199–235.

Stephan, Paula E. 2012. *How Economics Shapes Science*. Cambridge, MA: Harvard University Press.

Stigler, George Joseph. 1988. *Memoirs of an Unregulated Economist*. Chicago: University of Chicago Press.

Stiglitz, Joseph E. 1986 [2000]. *Economics of the Public Sector*. 3rd edn. New York: W. W. Norton.

Stroebe, Wolfgang, Tom Postmes and Russell Spears. 2012. 'Scientific Misconduct and the Myth of Self-Correction in Science'. *Perspectives on Psychological Science* 7 (6): 670–88.

Swazey, Judith, Melissa Anderson and Karen Louis. 1993. 'Ethical Problems in Academic Research'. *American Scientist* 81 (6): 542–53.

Szenberg, Michael, and Lall Ramrattan. 2014. *Secrets of Economics Editors*. Cambridge, MA: MIT Press.

Veblen, Thorstein. 1919. *The Place of Science in Modern Civilisation and Other Essays*. New York: B. W. Huebsch.

Wadman, Meredith. 2005. 'One in Three Scientists Confesses to Having Sinned'. *Nature* 435 (7043): 718–19.

Wible, James R. 1998. *The Economics of Science: Methodology and Epistemology as if Economics Really Mattered*. New York: Routledge.

Williamson, Oliver E. 1985. *The Economic Institutions of Capitalism: Firms, Markets, Relational Contracting*. New York: Free Press.

Yalcintas, Altug. 2012. 'Yayıncılık Endüstrisinde Yapay Seçilim: Marx ve Engels'in Politik İktisat Metinleri Üzerine Bibliyografik Bir İnceleme [Artificial Selection in Publication Industry: A Bibliographical Essay on the Political Economy Manuscripts of Marx and Engels]'. In *İktisatta Bir Hayalet: Karl Marx [A Spectre in Economics: Karl Marx]*, edited by Sevinç Orhan, Serhat Koloğlugil and Altug Yalcintas, 141–80. Istanbul: İletişim.

Yalcintas, Altug. 2015. 'Intellectual Disobedience in Turkey'. In *Creativity and Humour in Occupy Movements: Intellectual Disobedience in Turkey and Beyond*, edited by Altug Yalcintas, 6–29. London and New York: Palgrave.

3 Sciences between Scylla and Charybdis

The theory of intellectual path dependence: a short review and a new introduction

The only dilemma that economists face while they are doing research is not choosing between alternative theories that yield epistemic utility. As the idiom appearing in the title suggests, economists sometimes have to choose between two options, both of which come at a cost. Economists now and again have to choose between rejecting a theory and not rejecting a theory when they are confronted with refuting evidence and falsifying data about the theory with which they are working. Rejecting a theory might amount to 'paying' the epistemic cost of time invested in the construction and application of the theory. Not rejecting a theory might amount to sticking to an erroneous theory knowingly and intentionally. Neither option would be perfect because an economist rejecting a theory would lose an epistemic tool the opportunity cost of which is months or years of understanding and explaining the facts of the world; an economist not rejecting an erroneous theory would have to work with an epistemic tool producing unreliable results. And this would inflict harm upon others in the community of scholars. Besides, the consequences of rejecting or not rejecting a theory when epistemic costs are high are often irrevocable. When economists are caught between Scylla and Charybdis, epistemic costs of doing the right thing are high. Then, it makes little sense to look for progress which is discreet rather than continuous.

In this chapter, I review the evolution of the literature on the theory of path dependence in order to be able to reflect on the ways in which we can use this theory to account for the absence of perfection or continuous progression in the history of (economic) ideas. Outlining the contributions that have emerged from the works of Paul David, Brian Arthur and Douglass North, I hope to provide insight on the theoretical components of the theory of intellectual path dependence which one can use to understand the set of complex reasons why 'progress in economics' is not continual, if possible.

The significance of a reconsideration of the meaning of scientific progress lies in the fact that the evolution of ideas has a propensity to increase the variety and sophistication of scientific knowledge whereas this process does not always operate in ways in which 'old' theories are falsified and replaced by 'new' theories.

90   *The economic construction of sciences*

Scientific perfection could have been achieved if there were only one pathway of evolution in which ideas are accumulated so as to form a larger stock of knowledge. However, scientific enquiry is a non-terminative process which requires curiosity over social and natural issues, not necessarily calculating the future consequences of the research. Since there are often multiple pathways, heading in different directions, motivating diverse groups of scholars in various ways over time, it is not possible to argue for a teleological end towards which scientific communities strive even when scholars, for instance, make every effort to 'reveal the truth'. The absence of an endpoint in the evolution of ideas is not an argument against the capabilities of the members of scientific communities; rather, it is that efforts of scientific communities do not simply add up. Several selection mechanisms, networks and contingencies, among many other factors, make scientific processes more complex as each and every small interaction has the potential to cause remote and multiple consequences. Intellectual path dependence claims that progress can only be achieved locally and temporarily, insofar as the evolutionary history of ideas is concerned, whereas intellectual history is richer in terms of the amount of variety and sophistication among theorems, ideas and viewpoints.

In evolutionary political economy, the conception of path dependence is preceded by a powerful conception: *cumulative causation* (Veblen 1919, 1898, Myrdal 1944, Kapp 1976). Path dependence and cumulative causation have a number of similarities, one of the most important of which is, perhaps, that both conceptions have been argued by unorthodox social scientists. Cumulative causation accounts for the processes that do not converge towards a predefined end point. Such processes operate in a non-teleological manner in which causal relationships between social and economic events are continual. Cumulative causation aims at explaining long-term social evolution where causal nexus among events is accounted for.

However, path dependence and cumulative causation refer to different circumstances, in which the evolution of social institutions follows different trajectories. First, cumulative causation claims that equilibrium is 'irrelevant' in social processes whereas path dependence accounts for the 'multiplicity of locally stable equilibria' featuring properties of sub-optimality (David 2007). Second, cumulative causation accounts for the dominance of 'ceremonial encapsulations' in capitalist societies resisting technological innovations (Hall *et al.*2011). Path dependence, however, is about the costs of switching to more 'efficient' technologies, therefore emphasizing lock-ins that come about as a consequence of 'technical interrelatedness, economies of scale, and quasi-irreversibility of investment' (David 1985). Third, path-dependent processes are outcomes of positive feedback mechanisms magnifying the significance of several historical accidents or chance events, whereas cumulative causation accounts for social processes in which social factors other than historical accidents and chance events, as well as negative feedback, are at play (Berger and Elsner 2007, Berger 2008).

The notion of path dependence in economics was originally applied to the historical evolution of typing machines. Paul David argued in his seminal article 'Clio and the Economics of QWERTY' (1985) that the keyboard layout in digital keyboards used in modern computers and other electronic devices today was, in fact, designed to reduce the speed of the typist. This 'inefficient' keyboard layout was introduced in order to generate a working solution to a practical problem of clashing and jamming of the mechanical parts of old typewriters. As the typist was slower in typing texts, the number of clashes and jams was reduced. Therefore, the typist could type more and longer. However, modern computers, laptops and other electronic devices do not have such problems. Digital keyboards, nevertheless, have used QWERTY as the standard layout. The industry was locked into an 'inferior' technology that obstructed progress in typing technologies. A solution was passed on to next generations, despite the fact that the problem did not exist any more.

The story in this article soon became a 'famous fable' in social sciences (Spulber 2003, 90–109; Liebowitz and Margolis 1990). Following David, economists such as Brian Arthur (1989, 1994), Douglass North (1990) and Paul Krugman (1991), among many others in other branches of social theory (Goldstone 1998, Mahoney 2000, Pierson 2000), have contributed to the research on path dependence. Today, many thinkers, with or without calling it path dependence, express similar concerns about the specificities of the evolution of social, economic and political institutions. The common concern of these thinkers is that no evolutionary process necessarily evolves towards a predefined end point. In order for a process to feature a property that allows a specific process to evolve towards a predefined end point, a 'legitimate trend', a term that Veblen used in his 'Why is Economics Not an Evolutionary Science?' (1898), should cause events to evolve in the prescribed way. However, there is no such final term to each and every evolution. There is no prearranged result for all that exists in nature and society. Exact references where this conception is discussed include John Dewey (1910b, 54, and 67; 1910a, 118–24), William James (1971), Larry Hickman (2004, 95) and Joseph Ratner (1999, 30–1).

Many publications discussing the significance of path dependence in management sciences (Sydow and Schreyögg 2013, Sydow *et al.* 2005, 2009, Driel and Dolfsma 1988), organizational action, gender studies (Sandhu 2013) and economic geography (Foss 1997, March 1996, Duhs 1998, Martin 1999) also use the notion of path dependence. Organization theorists, doing research on the problems of knowledge in firms and organizations (such as Nooteboom 1997, Sydow and Schreyögg 2010, Garud and Karnøe 2001), provide valuable insight into the processes of knowledge creation (or 'path creation'). And yet most (if not all) of these publications lack a pleasing conclusion about the lessons to be drawn from the general evolution of intellectual institutions such as universities, sciences and the scholarly methodologies and vocabularies that scientists have long used in order to communicate with each other. Conceptual and methodological works on path dependence (Cowan and Gunby 1996, Balmann *et al.* 1996, Dutt 1997, Rizzello 1997, Arrow 2000, Puffert 2003, Gartland 2005, Heikkila 2011, Vergne and Durand 2010) overlook the issue as well.

Although it is not easy to synthesize all contributions to offer a coherent definition of path dependence, many of the works in management and organization

92   *The economic construction of sciences*

studies comprehend the notion of path dependence as if firms, industries and nations could improve their capabilities if they followed certain paths of evolution. Paths in social and economic history, according to most of these authors, are, in fact, opportunities for firms, industries and nations to achieve economic growth and development. I doubt that the metaphor of path dependence indicates (or should indicate) growth and development at all. To my understanding, stasis or inertia is the primary aspect of path-dependent phenomena. Stasis occurs when there is no or little change – for instance, in routines according to which firms behave and are organized. Stasis prevents economies, industries within economies and firms within industries from improving their capacities. Now, if the theory of path dependence was to account for growth, progress and improvement of capacities of firms in several industries of the economy, what would the real contribution of the theory be other than the simple claim that 'history matters', a claim that many economic and social scholars, including the Historical School and Marxists, have made for decades? Theories explaining why progress would eventually prevail abound. In my view, using the theory of path dependence as an explanation of the ways in which we can move always forward is misleading for several reasons. As I argue in more depth below, the theory of path dependence is a theory accounting for the reasons why growth, progress and improvement are *not* continuous; it is an explanation of how several paths coexist and why better alternatives are selected out. The theory of path dependence is not just another tool showing that markets indeed work and that we are living in the best of all possible worlds. Looking for conceptions of growth, progress and improvement in the theory of path dependence is like looking for a Pollyanna in the novels of Franz Kafka. Even if one can find one, it would be against the use value of the entire theory.

My aim here is, of course, not to reach simplistic conclusions on the research conducted in fields other than the history of (economic) ideas, although path dependence research is now so broad that it involves insight into several areas of the social where institutions matter. In the history of (economic) ideas, there is an important literature focusing attention on the significance of intellectual institutions from an evolutionary viewpoint. For instance, path dependence research includes works about the 'tangled pathways of history' (Collins *et al.* 1999), the institutional history of thinking systems (Graff 1987) and 'evolution of vocabularies' that have been locked in to specific paths (Ocasio and Joseph 2005). John D. Sterman and Jason Wittenberg (1999, 322), departing from Kuhn's argument (Kuhn 2000, 104), claim that 'small changes … can have large-scale effects' and state that 'self-reinforcing processes amplify intrinsically unobservable micro-level perturbations in the environment – the local conditions of science, society and self faced by the creators of a new theory – until they reach macroscopic significance'. In a similar fashion, Albert Jolink and Jack Vromen (2001) argue that scientific knowledge and procedures are vulnerable to lock-in effects and multiple self-reinforcing mechanisms. Members of the scientific community use each others' results, build upon each others' work and seek out recognition and prestige among their peers. In fact, Christian Knudsen (1993), using the

Sciences between Scylla and Charybdis 93

conceptions of self-reinforcing mechanisms and sunk costs in existing and emerging research programmes, claims that every generation of theoretical alternatives in economics should avoid 'unification' and 'fragmentation' in order to sustain intellectual growth over long periods of time.

Intellectual path dependencies transform the (apparently) simplistic idea of the growth of scientific knowledge into a complex conception of intellectual evolution of sciences and humanities. Intellectual path dependence suggests that some of the problems in epistemology may have economic aspects alongside philosophical ones, if and when problems of theory selection, paradigm shifts and correction of errors are also economic in deeper layers of their nature. One of the distinguishing features of an evolutionary history of economic ideas is that there are path-dependent circumstances in the intellectual history of economics. Intellectual path dependence, from an economic point of view, claims that paths and dependencies come about as a result of high opportunity costs of applying or using alternative methods. Academic scholarship is not only socially constructed; it is economically constituted as well.

Intellectual path dependence comes about in various forms and fashions. For instance, intellectual path dependence is a significant problem when intellectual hegemony of a specific culture, such as the US neoliberal culture or the European imperial culture, colonizes authenticities of 'other' cultures in such a way that it becomes impossible, or culturally and epistemologically costly, to undo the consequences of intellectual dependence they have been subject to. In this book, I focus my attention on intellectual path dependence emerging when commitments and preferences of scholars in the past have degenerating effects on the present and future states of scholarship. I conjecture that new ideas do not often replace old ones. This phenomenon has much to do with the institutional conditions in which ideas emerge, struggle for survival and spread. Epistemology, as a consequence, often turns away from answering old questions and occupies itself with its own arena of dispute. Philosophy re-digs its foundations and does not always 'move forward'. In other words, ideas do not evolve by way of displacing other ideas. Instead, new ideas co-evolve with old ideas.

Criticism of the theory of path dependence

Before passing on the analysis of intellectual path dependence leading to the conclusion that evolution of ideas does not always cause the continual progress of ideas but rather that diversification among theories is the main theme of intellectual history, it is worthwhile studying the critics of the theory of path dependence.

Deirdre McCloskey, among the critics of the 'fable' of QWERTY keyboards, has raised an important issue about the notion of path dependence. During an e-seminar that took place in 1999 at the email list of Eh.net, owned and operated by the Economic History Association, many eminent economists expressed their thoughts about the notion of path dependence online. The conversation started with the summary of the path dependence literature by Stephen Liebowitz and

94 *The economic construction of sciences*

Stephen Margolis, in which they mentioned the roots of the notion in other sciences as well as their well-known critique that was published in the *Journal of Law, Economics, and Organization* (Liebowitz and Margolis 1995a). Among the participants in the conversation were Douglas Puffert, Jack Goldstone, Richard Rosenbloom and Michael Perelman.

McCloskey's claim is as follows: path dependence is certainly important for social sciences, but the example of QWERTY is not. No typing-intensive industry, since computers were introduced, has ever adopted an alternative keyboard system to QWERTY. David's theory is basically an 'urban myth' because changing keyboards has never been impossible for typists. Typists change keyboards when they use Danish, Russian, or Turkish keyboards. That we did not switch to another typing machine does not mean that QWERTY was inferior to, say, Dvorak. It rather means, simply, that no industry has found it profitable.

David's point about typing machines, McCloskey argues, is principally blackboard economics. Claiming only that 'capitalism is not perfect' – an argument McCloskey thinks David has always had in mind – is not plausible for sciences. For McCloskey, the relevant question should rather be 'How imperfect?' Capitalism is not perfect, McCloskey, too, writes in her *The Bourgeois Virtues: Ethics for an Age of Commerce* (2006). But it does sometimes work, too. The problem is to show how imperfect it is; this is where the focus should be. 'The blackboard is of limited help in this', she argues, 'not useless, but almost so, since it is obvious at the outset that any "result" whatever is possible if one is ingenious enough with the assumptions. We need measurements, simulations – not more theorems, yes?' (ibid., 1–53). Sometimes the scale is too small to matter, McCloskey thinks. One has to show quantitatively in order to know whether the second 'best' is really important.

McCloskey claims that the scientific question is one of 'oomph'. In other words, 'How important was, say, craft dignity to the old working class (thus E. P. Thompson)?' Or 'How much did the railway economy contribute to the American economic growth in the nineteenth century (thus R. Fogel 1964)?' Likewise, McCloskey renders, David must show how much a printing house with 300 typists would have gained if the company switched to a 'better' keyboard system than QWERTY. That is, how much oomph?

The question, then, is empirical. The advocates of QWERTY, according to McCloskey, should show why no typing intensive business firm has since adopted a different keyboard than QWERTY. They have to show how high the training costs of employees are, how expensive it is for a factory producing QWERTY keyboards to produce, say, Dvoraks and so forth. McCloskey argues that 'the success or failure of QWERTY as an empirical notion would not settle one way or the other whether such problems are important in the economy'. Her concern is rather to advance beyond blackboard speculations. Path dependence, of course, exists, but the question is: 'How much does it rule?' The way to show if path dependence rules significantly is to answer the quantitative question: 'Does path dependence have oomph?' She thinks the advantage of Dvoraks would not be anything like 10 per cent.

Sciences between Scylla and Charybdis   95

David responded to McCloskey in a paper he presented at the European Summer School in Industrial Dynamics in 1999. David, in his response, argued that what in fact mattered was not the magnitude of oomph: 'although,' David wrote, 'clearly the concept refers to some cardinal magnitude – since it is something that we don't seem to have "enough" of – even the appropriate unit of measurement remains unspecified' (David 1999). And he concluded:

> This suggests that the one thing that makes it worth having an *ideé fixe* – such as the belief that path dependence cannot be important in economics – is the security of knowing that there is no fact or theorem that would ever be big enough (measured in oomphs or oompha's) to dent or dislodge it from your mind. I suppose that is the comfort of religious and other dogmas. (David 1999)

I think this not quite what McCloskey meant in her criticism. In an interview (Yalcintas 2006, 195), I asked McCloskey about her views on David's response. She said:

> Paul says that I am asserting that path dependence cannot be important to economics. I am not asserting that. I have a much more modest idea: show me, quantitatively, in terms of how much. I am asserting that his particular example about QWERTY is probably empirically mistaken because, to my knowledge, and according to his, as he hasn't offered any evidence to the contrary, no typing-intensive company, of which there are large numbers in the world, has ever adapted the Dvorak keyboard. You go into insurance companies, you look around, and it's QWERTY keyboards. That suggests very strongly to me that the magnitude of gain of moving from QWERTY to Dvorak must be very, very small because it is so easy in the modern world of computers to shift from Dvorak to QWERTY. You can arrange the keyboard in the way you want. You can make an ABCDEF keyboard if you want. I can do that with my own computer. (I don't know how but it's possible.) So there's got to be something wrong with this example. I do not take the view that it's impossible for path dependence to be important in the economy. It might be. And indeed, as your argument in your [thesis] in a way shows (Yalcintas 2009), path dependence is another way of saying we're in a world of second best. And with Ronald Coase and James Buchanan and lots of other people, I think we are. Or, to put it still another way, institutions matter. And I agree with that. I think institutions do matter. I think the virtues matter. I think that family life matters. I think that lot of things change – or one can say, constrain – optimality. But that doesn't mean that you should abandon family, virtues, or religion or anything else. It just means that we are not in the world in which these institutions do not exist.

Tony Lawson, another critic of the notion of path dependence, thinks contrary to McCloskey. He argues that the story of QWERTY is valid, although some systems in economies, Lawson thinks, do not fit to this pattern, at least at the

96   *The economic construction of sciences*

moment. He argues that 'if the letter arrangement had been ABCDEFGHIJ then many of us wouldn't not regard the phenomenon as one that is at all surprising and in particular need of being explained' (Lawson 1997, 249). Lawson thinks that the case of QWERTY captures some aspects of social development, but the implications of the case cannot be generalized without more evidence and argument. In fact, 'the general emphasis which the path dependence literature places on the persistence of specific structures and technologies', Lawson writes, 'serves as a valuable corrective to certain dominant features of the contemporary mainstream' (ibid,, 251). '[Path dependence]', he also thinks, 'does seem to be against the functionalist aspect of much mainstream reasoning, along with a conception of social structure and technology as plastic' (ibid., 252).

Lawson criticizes the approach of path dependence for 'the risk of reproducing the erroneous determinism of mainstream economics ... albeit in a displaced form, turning now on evolutionism and rigidity' (ibid.). I am sympathetic with Lawson's observation that the approach of path dependence is 'being cautiously embraced by various mainstream economists' (ibid.) – and especially by those who think of the economic and social world in terms of unique equilibrium without giving up fictitious equations. I, however, think his concern in general is too farfetched for a number of reasons. Most of all, Lawson does not seem to make a philosophical claim to be generalized for the entire literature. His reading of path dependence only consists of David, and there is no mention of others at all, such as Arthur and North, whom Lawson would have most likely labelled as 'mainstream' economists. The theory of path dependence – and the entire philosophical background – is, however, not a product of David alone. It is instead a story of a number of social critics in various disciplines, who, in Santa Fe Institute, Stanford, Oxford, Washington and other places, have risen up against the mainstream view of science and philosophy.

Lawson also thinks that the attention of economists to history cannot be 'sidelined to the setting of initial conditions' (ibid., 254). History is rather an intrinsic property of economics. That is to say, the reason why economics should involve historical research cannot simply be because initial conditions yield undesirable consequences in the future. Instead, the emphasis of path dependence literature:

> must be qualified by a recognition that every social phenomenon is a production of some sort, and to some degree at least could always have been otherwise ... Even if decentralised decision-making leads to a system moving in one direction rather than another, there are likely to be intrinsic forces or tendencies which work, or could have worked, against this.
>
> (Ibid., 253)

In his critical realist critique he neglects one issue. Simply put, there are such cases in which we cannot detect 'forces' and 'tendencies' unless they are not interfered with for some reason. For instance, that the UN did not intervene in the massacre in Rwanda in 1994 does not mean that the UN had the 'force' to intervene. Likewise, that an economy does not reach equilibrium does not mean that there are 'forces' and 'tendencies' that would have carried the economy to a

Pareto-optimum state if there had been no intervention. There is often no evidence, nor any reason or cause in the form of 'forces' and 'tendencies', for an economy to reach general equilibrium. The assumption that there are such 'forces' and 'tendencies' thus sometimes becomes merely hypothetical. Besides, there are numerous cases, such as 'Polya-urn process', where we cannot talk about any 'force' and 'tendency'. Those cases are rather transparent. No reality is hidden behind the appearance. Such cases are dominated by the consequences of historical small events. In this case, realist metaphors cease to make any sense because of their emphasis that there is always something behind the scenes.

Stephen J. Liebowitz and Stephen E. Margolis, well-known critics in the literature of path dependence, provide a detailed account of the 'fable of the keys' in a number of articles (Liebowitz and Margolis 1999, 1995a, 1990, 2013, 1995b, 1998). They speak of several reasons such as 'weak' and 'strong' forms of path dependence, and argue that David's rejection of Dvorak does not report the true story about typewriters. Their basic argument is that Dvorak is not superior to QWERTY principally because there were flaws in the experiments to determine the speed of Dvorak and QWERTY. Gaps in the evidence for Dvorak and ergonomics literature have produced no support for the advantage of Dvorak. They also argue, among other things, that the theory of path dependence does not necessarily prove 'market failure with respect to the choice of a standard'. They oppose the idea that if path dependence rules, cost–benefit analysis of the individual may not offer assurance of 'optimal' or 'efficient' solutions. 'The trap constituted by an obsolete standard may be quite fragile', they write. 'Because real-world situations present opportunities for agents to profit from changing to a superior standard, we cannot simply rely on an abstract model to conclude that an inferior standard has persisted. Such a claim demands empirical examination' (Liebowitz and Margolis 1990, 21).

Liebowitz and Margolis argue that there are three different forms of path dependence. The 'first degree of path dependence' means that whatever we do in our lives has an element of 'persistence' or 'durability'. For instance, we may have saved money for 15 years; we therefore can now afford the college fees of our kids. Or, for another instance, the railway economy in the nineteenth century owed a lot to the technological advancement during the Industrial Revolution. 'Path dependence here', write Liebowitz and Margolis, 'does no harm, it is simply the fact of durability' (Liebowitz and Margolis 1998, 18).

The 'second degree of path dependence', according to Liebowitz and Margolis, has to do with information problems in the market. 'When individuals fail to predict the future perfectly', they argue,

> it is likely that *ex ante* efficient decisions may not turn out to be efficient in retrospect … In such a situation … there is a dependence on past conditions that leads to outcomes that are regrettable and costly to change.
>
> (Ibid.)

Liebowitz and Margolis are correct in pointing out that there are different forms of path dependence in the literature. In fact, this is somewhat inevitable because

98   *The economic construction of sciences*

one may not easily construct a stable definition of a metaphor such as path dependence. Liebowitz and Margolis, however, confuse the complicated notion of path dependence with another conception in the evolution of human institutions – and that is, *past dependence*. As Liebowitz and Margolis have shown, it is certainly true that the consequences of our decisions in the past determine or influence what we do today. For instance, the Dutch advanced sophisticated techniques of water management, argues Simon Schama in his *The Embarrassment of Riches: An Interpretation of Dutch Culture in the Golden Age* (1987 [1997], 24–37), and they were thus able to build a ruling Republic in the seventeenth century. The Middle Ages gave high status to adventure, Rosenberg and Birdzell argue in their *How the West Grew Rich* (1986, 67), promoting the travels of Marco Polo and the pilgrimage or Crusade to the Holy Land. The development of 'feudalism' was possible in France in the Middle Ages, argues Lynn White in his *Medieval Technology and Social Change* (1962), because stirrups improved the effectiveness of the cavalry. Such arguments, however, are too naive to make in the context of lock-ins, sunk costs, network effects and so forth because they all miss what path dependence maintains in regard to the malfunctioning of human institutions through time. That history matters is an argument as old as ancient Greek times. This argument is intuitional, too, because humans, institutions and societies have a past, determining today's conditions. What the assertion 'history matters' means when path dependence rules, however, is that history, as Liebowitz and Margolis also acknowledge elsewhere (Liebowitz and Margolis 1995a), is a tool to understand what viewpoints of rationality and efficiency do not explain. History matters when path dependence happens to be important because some historical small events cause big consequences for the future and such consequences are not explained with the tools of established views of 'rationalism'.

The argument of Liebowitz and Margolis even suggests the opposite of what Arthur, David and North meant earlier because 'first degree of path dependence', in my view, is not new to many philosophers and economists. For instance, information problems in markets – that is, the 'second degree of path dependence' – has long been known to economists. The reason why path dependence has attracted the attention of economists and other scientists is not that there is imperfect information in the market – leading to individuals make adverse selections which lead to inefficient outcomes in the future; path dependence has to do with disappointments and underachievements that economists are not able to explain with the traditional tools of 'rationality', 'equilibrium' and so forth. Path dependence is an important notion in social and natural sciences for the non-trivial reason that perfection is not always achievable. Path dependence suggests that we may have to contend with undesirable outcomes even if we had no problem of information in the past. It is a useful tool to explain why many institutions malfunction as time goes by.

As for the 'third degree of path dependence': Liebowitz and Margolis argue that:

> the main focus and novelty of the current economic literature of path dependence is on the third-degree form, and prominent examples in the literature

feature specific claims of inefficiency ... Our reading of the evidence[, however,] is that there are as yet no proven examples of third degree of path dependence in markets ... It is the third-degree path dependence claim that constitutes a new challenge to invisible-hand theorems that private optimization leads individuals to wealth maximizing allocations.

(Liebowitz and Margolis 1998, 18)

According to Liebowitz and Margolis, neither the oft-cited case of videotaping formats nor David's story of QWERTY is a demonstration of 'third degree of path dependence' because they are not examples of 'remediable efficiency' or 'inherited inefficiencies ... [that] purportedly are, or were, remediable' (ibid.).

Illustrations of path dependence in the economic literature are not flawless. For instance, the empirical evidence does not confirm the significance of path dependence in the case of QWERTY (Kay 2013). The stories of VHS/Beta videotaping systems are also incorrectly presented. As Liebowitz and Margolis write, 'the logic underlying path dependence is seductive but incomplete' (Liebowitz and Margolis 1998, 18). Nevertheless, none of these criticisms should lead us to throw away the baby with the bathwater. Many numeric and algebraic examples, such as the Polya-urn process, seem uncontroversial. The theory of path dependence is still the most powerful explanation of institutional inertia where increasing returns of scale lock the system into sub-optimal outcomes. As Jean-Philippe Vergne (2013, 1191) remarks, 'QWERTY is dead; long live path dependence'.

Increasing returns to scientific scale

Intellectual path dependence is the application of the theory of path dependence to the evolutionary history of ideas. The theory of path dependence refers to dynamic processes in the evolution of social institutions, generating consequences often irreversible and sensitive to initial conditions of the process. Under conditions of path dependence, several self-reinforcing mechanisms, such as network effects or increasing returns to scientific scale, lock in the evolutionary pathway of a system to a number of possible sub-optimal states where (negative) 'externalities' prevent systems from moving towards more efficient states.

Intellectual path dependence comes about as intellectual institutions impose costs on individuals, which individuals should seriously consider with regard to alternative providers to these institutions. Actors then, basically, have two options: they will either be content with the consequences of their actions that have evolved out of ideological judgements, or will exchange the risk that the current uncertainty creates with the risk that exploring a new path of evolution could lead to. What actors only possess in exploring a new path is their faith in getting free of the path that has been doomed to yield nothing more than it yielded in the past. Exploiting the same path of evolution, actors would rid themselves of the risk of a worse consequence of their action but would be left without the pay-offs from exploring alternatives. Switching among different paths is worth considering because pay-offs from the curiosity of exploring a new path could

100　*The economic construction of sciences*

significantly outweigh the cost that such an exploration would create. Disregarding new paths will only lead to 'widening the candidate's field of ignorance while it intensifies his effectiveness within his specialty' (Veblen 1918, 286).

Economists usually feel offended when critics ask them to elaborate on their subject matter within historical narrative (for instance, see Blaug 2001). In many econometric models, relations among economic parameters are often mathematically constructed in a timeless, ahistorical universe (Hodgson 2001, 3–21). However, the 'quest for historical economics', the central lesson to be drawn out of the literature on path dependence, does not have much to do with the anti-historical bias among neoclassical economists (David 2001). The critical debate is rather that the proportion of path-dependent processes in general is on the rise and special attention should be attached to them by way of using original analytical tools that are different from those of orthodox economics.

In path dependence research, particular attention is paid to feedback mechanisms, namely increasing returns to scale, which cause little changes to have big effects by way of turning the selection of small events in a typical process of path formation into tipping points. In economic systems, increasing returns is the principle feedback mechanism in markets magnifying the significance of the consequences of unexpected and accidental occurrences. Under conditions of increasing returns, consequences of small events give rise to aggregate outcomes. 'The earlier the events that precipitate a shift in the system occur in a series of events the more important they may be' (Walby 2007, 464). This may seem 'counter-intuitive', Malcolm Gladwell (2000) argues, because we are intellectually born into a conception of approximation among causes and consequences. Changes in social life, we presuppose, take place steadily and slowly. 'We are trained to think that what goes into any transaction or relationship or system must be directly related, in intensity and dimension, to what comes out' (Gladwell 2000, 11). However, this is not necessarily the case in the world in which we live. Consequences are often far out of proportion to initial causes when evolution takes the form of 'geometrical progression'. Under such conditions, what matter are little things, like small events.

In economics, there are various types of increasing returns to scale. The main source of increasing returns is the positive reaction of the system to any perturbation from within the system. Here, 'positive' does not necessarily mean desirable or pleasing in the popular sense of the term. Positive reaction rather refers to the amplification of individual (often small) events that have causal significance. Arthur, principally interested in detecting increasing returns in market economies in such path-dependent circumstances as Beta-VHS video systems, Silicon Valley and the Microsoft Trial (Arthur 1989, 1985, 1994, 1988, 1996, 2000; Arthur *et al.* 1987), describes path dependence, in the simplest way, as a consequence of increasing returns operating in the market. Arthur argues that we are living in a dual world of business operating according to two different principles. We, on the one hand, have such industries as construction and 'bulk production' of manufacturing automobiles and refrigerators, operating according to the principle of decreasing returns. And alongside those industries, there are

Sciences between Scylla and Charybdis   101

knowledge-based industries, such as informatics and computer industries which operate under increasing returns. They are intertwined and do not exclude each other in the operational level. What works in one industry, however, is not appropriate for the others: the two industries differ in behaviour, style and culture. They call for opposite features of management strategies of investment.

Under decreasing returns, if an economic agent increases the amount of hamburgers she eats, she would run into less satisfaction with every extra unit. Likewise, if a company, operating under the law of decreasing returns, is to keep expanding the business of growing potatoes, it would come across increasing costs of production with every extra unit. Marginal physical product of an input tends to decrease, *ceteris paribus*, as the amount of the input increases. Under decreasing returns, the more you eat or produce the less you get in return.

The economy, especially since the Industrial Revolution, has mainly been an economy of decreasing returns and of producing commodities and services in massive amounts by virtue of rigid technologies such as assembly lines. Technologies were engineered to reduce costs as production kept increasing. In industrial economics, a well-defined solution followed, generally speaking, because problems were frequently expressed in terms of decreasing returns. Problems of choice between consumption of apples and oranges and production of war tanks and refrigerators were easily solved by virtue of optimization techniques. But Arthur asked: 'Can the assumption that individuals find optimal solutions to economic problems be justified so that we can avoid studying the details of decision process? In simple cases the answer is yes. In most cases, however, it is no' (Arthur 2000, 159).

Emergence of industries based on increasing returns, such as software industries, causes numerous alterations in economic theory. The milieu of knowledge-based industries favours the flattening of hierarchies between bosses and workers, Arthur reports. 'Re-everything' changes companies, reinvents goals and ways of doing things and forces a never-stopping adaptation. People in such industries are not merely employers. They are treated as equals in the business of the company's success.

Although traditional industries of 'bulk production' still require people to carry out production and people to plan and control it, the style of competition in the world of increasing returns is more like 'casino gambling' (Arthur 1996), where the game is to choose which game to play. The principle of increasing returns maintains that optimization in the world of casino gambling – that is, the world of knowledge-based industries – is not always possible. Such industries have never been like the industries of bulk production. Actors as gamblers in the market only watched for the next wave, Arthur says, and repositioned themselves to take advantage of the new. They have been in a new world of mission orientation, Arthur claims, not a world of five-year plans (Arthur 1996).

The reasoning of actors like 'casino gamblers' largely depends on past experiences, especially when the problems that individuals face lie outside the borders of what individuals have been used to. Individuals, under such circumstances, look for ways to frame the situation. They try to make associations to simplify

102 *The economic construction of sciences*

and single out the sophistication that faces them. When past experiences are the first option for the one who seeks guidance for action, alternatives to behavioural patterns that have so far been formed by history are usually ignored. Staying away from alternatives would cause an impact of over-utilizing – 'over-exploiting', in Arthur's terms – aged methodologies and techniques. This may generate several paths of evolution with undesirable outcomes. Arthur reports that this sort of finding, where there are thresholds beyond which better alternatives become difficult to discriminate, is not familiar in economics. Borders among theories are often clear-cut, not allowing any communication with others.

Insofar as habits are the primary codes of behaviour among scholars and the entire function of scholarly activity is to produce more habits of conduct, academic scholarship is under the risk of ideologization – that is, getting locked into a set of ideological judgements about scientific method. The more intellectuals consult ideologies for more answers, the more it becomes epistemologically costly to change viewpoints, methods and paradigms. Although 'new' does not necessarily mean 'better', lock-ins amount to irreversibility which may easily turn out to be undesirable, especially in the long run. As Stephan (2012, 66) argues, '[v]intage matters in science, but the latest knowledge is not always the "best" knowledge'. This is one of the sources of intellectual path dependence in which scientific markets operate in the absence of an invisible hand that could have prevented errors from happening or corrected them in the long run. Seeds of intellectual lock-in are stored in markets of ideas due to the epistemic costs organically attached to pursuing scientific research.

Scholars, just like businessmen and politicians, do have beliefs in the absence of evidence. The social world in which we all live is not only a world of evidence and facts, but also of social networks in which we trust, respect and have responsibility for others (Boettke and O'Donnell 2015). A factual world without such social institutions would cease to exist. As John Hardwig argues, 'one can have good reasons for believing a proposition if one has good reasons to believe that *others* have good reasons to believe it' (Hardwig 1985, 336, italics in original). In other words, we are epistemologically dependent on others' beliefs and on the evidence only available to others. Some evidence may be only available to experts or to a minority of non-experts, in that one may never have the opportunity to possess facts to perform an experiment or conduct an enquiry. Then, the only opportunity, if at all, is to replicate the results of experts based on the reports prepared – that is, assess the findings in the light of new and further data in order to be sure whether one is informed or misinformed by a particular judgement. However, if this epistemic individualism were accessible for us at all times, why would we need scholarly communities at all? In practice, what we often do is check whether these experts find those experts reliable. We trust the chain of authority within a scholastic circle which disallows us to establish epistemic autonomy. Such processes are blind: 'a layperson (or scientists in a different field) cannot be rationally justified in trusting an expert' (Goldman 2001, 86).

In the world of increasing returns to scientific scale, the higher the pay-offs the higher the funds raised by government and other research institutes to finance a research project. The reason for this is that science has long ceased to operate like a local, small-scale *atelier*: it has become expensive to pursue scientific research in universities and research institutes since new technologies, such as computers, required more capital-intensive investment. This is valuable insight for, and one of the most crucial contributions of the economics of increasing returns to, science and technology policy studies in the last few decades. Publications in this field suggest that peculiarity of scientific development in the last century has been that the more industrial science has become, the more the conditions of *increasing returns to scientific scale* have prevailed in academic scholarship: 'the bigger a theoretical construct gets, the higher the pay-offs of additional contributions' (De Langhe and Greiff 2008, 4). To put it differently, academic scholarship is a game of 'winner takes all'. A small advantage that an idea possesses easily and rapidly gives rise to a big success story. This is most visible in the economics of superstars: 'small differences in talent become magnified in larger earnings differences, with greater magnification of the earnings–talent gradient increases sharply near the top of the scale' (Rosen 1981, 846).

Science does not always yield best results when scientists work on their own and on their behalf only. Science is, rather, a collaborative field of intellectual specialization; new findings require an audience to judge and replicate the novel implications and results. Granted that scholarly institutions' respect and trust, as well as 'principles of testimony' are well established and operating (Hardwig 1985, 1991), there is not much reason for the condition of decreasing returns to exist. Under such conditions, marginal returns to every scholarly contribution often rise with every novelty added to the scholarly network. Scholars are standing on the shoulders of giants, in other words, '[a]s such, the addition of one scientist to a scientific community doesn't decrease the other scientists' prospects of success ... but increase the prospect of success for the community exponentially' (De Langhe and Greiff 2008, 4).

Uncertainty, belief systems and ideologization

Path dependence of institutions is, in the first place, about complexity of popular action in which individuals make decisions and affect others in their preferences in a reciprocal fashion. An individual or a small group of individuals starting to use a different 'standard' may not bother the industry as a whole in the short run in the slightest because the low frequency of the new method would not affect large-scale practice for others. However, popularity of a certain standard may well increase as a consequence of a little trigger ('tip') and actors in the market may respond to this in a positive way because markets, under conditions of increasing returns, feed back upon new preferences in a reinforcing fashion. Individuals do not act like robots, of course. Particularly in academic scholarship, individuals act mostly in an independent manner. But they are influenced by others, as well as their past preferences. Rising of paradigms (i.e. standards prevailing) and falling of paradigms (i.e. locking out, shaking free from the influence of past events) are processes in which different factors (especially the ones

104   *The economic construction of sciences*

related to the past) affect each other in complex ways. A key issue here is that old paradigms do not fall easily, although change is not impossible. What matters is how individual preferences spread among the community – in other words, how a new method wins popularity.

Douglass North is one of the writers among the theorists of path dependence in economics whose research programme is so broad as to embrace a large variety of topics in a diverse field of social research. The notion of path dependence plays a key role in his writings and in many places he applies the notion in decision theory in economics, as well as economic history, development studies, political science and political history. He is well aware that the scope of the notion is not limited to economic science only. Path dependence is an appropriate notion applicable to other fields of knowledge, too.

One of the elements which one successively finds in the writings of North, in association with his view of path dependence, is the element of uncertainty in human decision. Individuals making up their minds in diverse and unique situations usually face difficulties that damage the desirability of the consequences of their reasoning. The difficulty is principally that individuals in economic and social life do not always have a clear and precise idea about the changing character of diverse circumstances within which they have to make decisions. They usually suppose that what they did in similar situations in the past will cause similar consequences for the present. After all, they think, alike causes generate alike consequences.

However, this principle does not hold in practice at all times. Individuals, despite the limits to their knowledge, have to keep making choices and constructing theories under conditions of uncertainty. Under such circumstances, *belief systems* serve as a basis for their decision-making. Although consequences are not always what individuals predict, North argues, the direction of the evolution of the economy, politics and intellectual life is shaped by the decisions made in light of such beliefs (North 1996).

For North, belief systems are highly influential in the way theoretical models are formed and on the way old models are abandoned and new ones are created. Acting in accordance with an established belief system is convenient – or less costly, economically speaking – especially when 'one cannot ascertain the probability of an event and therefore cannot arrive at a way of insuring against such an occurrence' (North 1990, 126). This does not mean to say that individuals acting according to their beliefs can never predict the consequences of their actions. It is rather to say that consequences that are not anticipated by the actors in advance might sometimes dominate the situation in such a way that actors facing increasing complexity of the situation may prefer to stick to the same set of beliefs instead of measuring their performance and adopting new tools if necessary. Individual actions, North argues, can thus have such consequences that choices made can create and perpetuate unproductive economic and political markets (North 1992).

In economic and social life, we have 'ignorance, incomplete information, and the resulting prevalence of ideological stereotypes as the underpinnings of the subjective models [which] individuals develop to explain their environment and

Sciences between Scylla and Charybdis 105

make choices [leading] to political markets that can and do perpetuate unproductive institutions and consequent organizations' (North 1992, 15). In other words, we reduce uncertainty by structuring human interaction. However, institutions we create need not necessarily perform as effectively under diverse circumstances.

One can think of two separate possibilities here. In the first situation, individuals have access to full information. There is no uncertainty, and neither is there risk as a consequence, because decisions are made by the actors who are conscious of the consequences of their actions. Economic models are mostly built in the assumption that actors have access to full information during market transactions. For instance, there is no ambiguity about the quality of the products that are bought and sold. Individuals know the consequences of consuming A good instead of B good or working for X company instead of Y company etc. As a result, resources are allocated in the most efficient ways; defaults in financial contracts are eliminated.

In the second, the situation is completely different. Actors now do not have access to full information. They make decisions in the face of uncertainty and therefore take the risk that consequences of their action can be other than those that they had anticipated before they took the action. In such a case, in contrast to full information – that is, no uncertainty situation – actors try to reduce the cost of the risk that can diminish the cash-value of the consequences of their decision. To do so, they build key ideas upon their perception of their environment. Those *mental models* (that is, belief systems such as myths, dogmas and taboos in 'primitive' societies and religions and ideologies in 'civilized' societies) enable actors to work out the uncertainty that they have to face. In such situations, they rely also on their habits, which they form on the basis of the past experiences where a set of tools proved to be successful. It is believed (and hoped) that the same set of tools, although the situation might have changed dramatically, would perform best as compared to the alternatives.

What all this shows is that we are involved in such circumstances that the consequences of our actions may not be the best ones at all times. Uncertainty that individuals face, and their inability to access to full information, cause such unpredictable conditions that individuals might be content with the unintended consequences of their action that reduce the pay-offs of their decision. Even if an 'efficient' outcome occurs, this would not be systematic. Repetition of the same decision might not give a way to the best outcome at every turn.

The situation can get even tougher. Uncertainty can become stronger, as (Denzau and North 1994) report, especially when:

> one is not even certain whether a particular choice will improve one's circumstances or not. The choice may be made infrequently, sometimes only once in a lifetime. Without direct experience, information about potential outcomes may not be known or easily acquired.
>
> (Ibid., 8)

The so-called *tabula rasa* situation at birth is counted as one of the instances for such a state.

106   *The economic construction of sciences*

As I claimed in the preceding chapter, epistemic costs come about as a consequence of ideological risks that are placed on the shoulders of those who pursue research. In fact, ideologies help people understand and explain the events taking place around them insofar as ideologies provide the epistemological tools of understanding to analyze the world. In some sense, ideologies are inevitable. In fact, most epistemological tools are formed via the past experiences of individuals, which proved to be useful in certain circumstances in earlier periods. However, ideologies may have further consequences for the advance of human understanding: ideologies may also set borders and rules that regulate the pathways of scientific progress. When ideologies operate so as to set borders and rules, they regulate scientific advancement towards an abstract systematic. That is to say, ideologies can organize scholarly activity in order to achieve specific goals or manners in which individuals or groups view the facts of the world. Instead of providing advantages against uncertainty, in particular, ideologies impose habits and exist by virtue of aged (epistemological) institutions.

Impossibility of continual intellectual progression

John Dewey once wrote that '"Truths" in philosophy are in fact only systematized mistakes and prejudices of our ancestors. Many of them originated in accident; many in class interest and bias, perpetuated by authority for this very reason' (Dewey 1950, 50). Kenneth Galbraith claimed something similar: 'The shortcomings of economics are not original error but uncorrected obsolescence. The obsolescence has occurred because what is convenient has become sacrosanct' (Galbraith 1958, 4). The notion of intellectual path dependence supports, at least partially, the point that Dewey and Galbraith made more than 50 years ago. Indeed, many philosophical problems are products of the unconscious adoption of assumptions built into the vocabulary in which the problems in the present were stated. We inherit philosophical problems. We reproduce erroneous thoughts without questioning the assumptions that caused the problems. According to Richard Rorty, these assumptions are mainly due to the unfortunate mistakes and confusions that are jammed into us after the writings of Descartes, Locke and Kant (Rorty 1979, 357). An important issue here is that, although such errors abound in intellectual history, there are a great many important achievements from the past. For instance, it is not wise today to look to Adam Smith for the best theory of the division of labour. Sophisticated versions of the theories of the eighteenth and nineteenth centuries are printed in many economics textbooks. The idea of government today is much more sophisticated than it was when Plato first wrote about it. In other words, there has been considerable progress in the sciences, philosophy and the arts. Boulding's question, in this sense, is very intriguing: after Paul Samuelson who needs Adam Smith? (Boulding 1971).

It is a critical error, however, to ignore the historical past of economic science as if there were a single path of institutional evolution headed towards perfection (of theorems). Economists have incorrectly assumed that whatever knowledge economics departments produce will immediately add positively to the body of economic science. Good ideas are sometimes initially completely ignored. Some texts, which were not considered important at the time they were first published, come to the forefront of economic theory years after their publication. And, sometimes, an error remains uncorrected for a long time. This shows us at least one thing: progress of scientific knowledge does not at all times follow a single path headed towards a predefined end point. An evolutionary history of ideas can, then, provide us with better explanations as to how ideas survive.

Frequency of path-dependent occasions in intellectual history is high and second 'best' outcomes do repeatedly come about. Thus, idealities of perfection or continual progression turn into mere utopias with no pragmatic content. Does the problem refer also to a philosophical condition? Why is continual progression in academic scholarship not attainable at all times?

Morris Ginsberg, founding chairman of the British Sociological Association (BSA), argues that evil has its own 'solidarity'. What he means by this is that, although misunderstandings in intellectual history often fade away as the results of new research keep providing novel findings, social and intellectual development in history may not be progressing. The flow of events has perhaps never involved the 'spirit of betterment'. In other words, we may have never been able to develop conclusive answers to the fundamental questions of intellectual history, such as those regarding the 'truth', because many small events have disturbed the so-called spirit. Ginsberg claims:

> Error and vice are in their own way cumulative and tend to produce further error and vice in individuals as well as in nations. There is no assurance that the forces making for disruption or deterioration must cancel each other out and thus bring about their own defeat.
>
> (Ginsberg 1953, 5)

Despite the importance of the matter, many historical narratives have stood fixed on the idea of continual progression without paying sufficient attention to the cumulative character of human error that has kept causing adverse consequences for the future. Few thinkers have been willing to get to the heart of this social phenomenon of scholars' capability of error. Errors are so crucial that they sometimes preclude sterilized blackboard principles from working. Scholars' underlying belief about the evolution of societies has been that of Condorcet:

> [N]ature has assigned no limit to the perfecting of the human faculties, that the perfectibility of man is truly indefinite; that the progress of this perfectibility, henceforth independent of any power that might wish to arrest it, has no other limit than the duration of the globe on which nature has placed us. Doubtless this progress can be more or less rapid; but never will be retrograde, so long, at least, as the earth occupies the same place in the system of the universe, and the general laws of that system do not effect on this globe either a general destruction or changes which would no longer permit human

108 *The economic construction of sciences*

kind to preserve or to exercise thereon the same faculties, and to avail themselves of the same resources.

(Condorcet 1795 [1949], quoted by Teggart 1949, 323, italics added)

There is, of course, not so much wrong with having ideals or different kinds of motivation for striving for what we may consider the perfect being, the best society, or the most efficient technology. The intellectual pathology here is, perhaps, the unquestioned prestige of what is 'inhuman' in various accounts of human history (see Nietzsche 1878 [1986], Mirowski 2002, 437–52.) Obviously, most people have ideals in life. They feel morally better when they preserve in their mind the idea of a perfect being or desire for a just society. Most people believe in God, pray for their beloved and think it is important to be virtuous citizens. There is no doubt that what we can achieve in our scholarly world has much to do with what we can imagine.

The images scholars have created are mostly products of fairy tales, religious theory, folklore and so forth. That they refer to a world beyond facts and experience is refreshing and progressive. Scholars' faith in different conceptions of continual progression, however, is bound up with the responsibility of their actions about images which are outside of their beliefs. In other words, the idea of continual progression is fruitful in academic scholarship insofar as there is enough space for others to think and live by alternate metaphors within various paradigms. Knowers, doers and makers of this world are responsible for their actions, no matter what sort of belief precedes or causes them – religious or secular. Beliefs are not there only for the behaviour's sake (James 2000, 198–219). Whenever we are to change public life by virtue of our passions – for example, hope, love and faith – 'the principal concern must be the extent to which the actions of religious believers frustrate the needs of other human beings, rather than the extent to which religion gets something right', argues Richard Rorty (1997, 84–5):

> although your emotions are your own business, your beliefs are everybody's business. There is no way in which the religious person can claim a right to believe as part of an overall right to privacy. For believing is inherently a public project: all we language users are in it together. We all have a responsibility to each other not to believe anything which cannot be justified to the rest of us. To be rational is to submit one's beliefs – all one's beliefs – to the judgment of one's peers.
>
> (Ibid., 88)

The ideas of continual progress (or perfection) have long dominated the academic scholarship in the USA and Europe. Continual progress means that human civilizations, slowly and gradually, advances from a state of uncertainty, ignorance and cultural deprivation towards higher levels of prosperity and wisdom (Nisbet 1994, 10). Human civilizations only move one way, thus each generation while standing 'on the shoulders of giants' progresses the civilization a step further (Pollard 1971, 20). Every generation, according to the idea of continual progress, is superior to its predecessor. Human ideas expand towards new horizons.

Sciences between Scylla and Charybdis 109

Step by step, the human mind frees itself of obstacles. The flow of events relies upon the spirit of betterment. The evolution of human institutions moves towards perfection. Perfection is a unique point; it is the final destination, predetermined. The course of progression is only to terminate where there is nothing better beyond. Betterment upon that point is not possible.

Perfection in philosophy has various meanings. It signifies a phase where no undesirable outcome is possible. It is a phase upon which evolution converges through time by means of incremental improvements. Upon such a path, there is no room for regression or depreciation. According to perfectionists,

> philosophical theories [converge] a series of discoveries about the nature of such things as truth and personhood, which get closer and closer to the way they really are, and carry the culture as a whole closer to an accurate representation of reality.
>
> (Rorty 1989, 77)

This is the view that intellectual history has long been locked into, perhaps since Plato.

Karl Popper (1962 [1971], 158–67) criticizes perfectionism in philosophy, especially inherent in Plato's philosophy, as he 'believes [it] is the most dangerous', and compares it with his alternative, piecemeal engineering, which he 'considers as the only rational strategy' in national and international politics. Perfectionism, according to Popper, requires that policy-makers have a complete blueprint of the final society before any actions are taken. Such a blueprint would identify the best ways and means to achieve maximum happiness on earth. Popper does not claim that perfectionism is unattainable. He argues that many things that were once declared unrealizable have since been realized. Institutions have been established to help secure civil peace preventing international crime and armed aggression. What he criticizes under the name of utopianism is:

> the reconstruction of society as a whole, i.e. very sweeping changes whose practical consequences are hard to calculate, owing to our limited experiences. It claims to plan rationally for the whole of society, although we do not possess anything like the factual knowledge which would be necessary to make good such an ambitious claim. We cannot possess such knowledge since we have insufficient practical experience in this kind of planning, and knowledge of facts must be based upon experience. At present, the sociological knowledge necessary for large-scale engineering is simply non-existent.
>
> (Ibid., 165)

Perfection in politics, Popper claims, can easily turn into violence in place of reason. Because of a lack of experience and the cumulative consequences of policy mistakes, unexpected results on a large scale are very likely to materialize. 'It is not reasonable', Popper argues, 'to assume that a complete reconstruction of our social world would lead at once to a workable system' (ibid., 171). Perfectionism in politics would necessarily lead to a strong centralized rule of a

110   The economic construction of sciences

select few. Such authoritarianism would discourage criticism and violent measures would be taken against those who advocate compromise and improvement via democratic methods.

Popper's political programme in *Open Society and Its Enemies* is Darwinian, in the sense that he points out the lack of necessity and even the dangers of a perfectionist view in politics. Popper argues that perfectionism in politics would only lead to further disaster, not happiness. The international political situation is not perfect and cannot be considered to have a tendency to perfection. It is instead a complex, flawed and evolving system. Just as there is no evidence for the whole of species in nature to evolve towards perfect individuals, so there is not any logic in expecting a perfect political system that would bring absolute contentment to the world's people.

The idea of continual progression and perfectionism fascinated many thinkers, especially in the Victorian period, including, of course, Darwin himself (Wright 2005, 1–28). Darwin saw the large in the small but he did not argue, as Stephan J. Gould claims, that the large would emerge out of the small by basically adding time into the process. Natural patterns are not always the outcome of uninterrupted proliferation and betterment. Darwin was puzzled by the following idea: why would there be so many diverse creatures in similar climates and geographies? Darwin (1859 [1952], 60) writes:

> but it may be objected that if all organic beings thus tend to rise in the scale, how is it that throughout the world a multitude of the lowest forms still exist; and how is it that in each great class some forms are far more highly developed than others? Why have not the more highly developed forms everywhere supplanted and exterminated the lower?

The answer would be either that there were two creators at work at the same time or that species evolved separately, tracking down different pathways at different times. It seemed certain to him that, in either case, there was no inherent direction of internal perfecting among species. 'Natural selection', Darwin claimed (ibid., 98), 'will not necessarily lead to absolute perfection; nor, as far as we can judge by our limited faculties, can absolute perfection be everywhere predicated.'

The existence of imperfections and oddities among species, according to many natural scientists, proved to Darwin that there were pathways in nature in which we could trace the particular causes that led life's history to follow this or that route (Gould 1982, 28). One could not reconcile evolution with perfection, Gould claims, because perfection does not require a history. If perfection existed, any organism in nature would have been created for the purpose to which it pertained perfectly. To put it differently, there was proof of evolution because the root of an organism did not always coincide with the 'modern form' of the organism. If these two were equal, then there was no indication of evolutionary history.

Natural selection is a mechanism that causes 'better adapted' species to win. A species' better adaptation, however, does not necessarily mean that the species are in any anatomical sense superior creatures. Natural selection involves mechanisms of positive feedbacks in which consequences of historical contingencies are sometimes reinforced in such a way that certain creatures survive, such as birds with an aerodynamic feather design or insects by way of mimicry that enable them to look like a leaf or a stick. Optimal adaptation does not always occur in life's history. 'Darwin recognized', Gould claims, 'that perfection cannot provide evidence for evolution ... that the primary evidence for evolution must be sought in quirks, oddities and imperfections that lay bare the pathways of history' (Gould 1989, 300–1).

However, as Nicholas Georgescu-Roegen argued (1971, 196), 'if science were to discard a proposition that follows logically from its theoretical foundation, merely because its factual realization has never been observed, most of modern technology would not exist. Impossibility, rightly, is not the password in science.' Indeed, from a theoretical point of view, perfectionism does not go hand in hand with evolutionism but perfect solutions have often come about in natural and social history. The difficulty here has to do with 'repeated perfection'. In the evolutionary history of a number of species oddities never occur. Some kind of an 'ordering force' interlocks evolution in certain directions. This is not a contradiction, Gould argues, because the Darwinian notion that evolution is unplanned and undirected does not cancel out the fact that 'natural selection builds good design by rejecting most variants while accepting and accumulating the few that improve adaptation to local environments' (Gould 1982, 40). Optimal solutions are prevalent in natural history. In disparate groups, abstract forms of ideal worlds exist. Final adaptation is both complex and peculiar so that in some cases physical forces may override natural selection in such a way that species obtain an optimal form by virtue of physical forces acting upon them. Complex forms are shaped by simpler mechanisms in a variety of unexpected ways. A number of natural states, Gould claims, such as hexagonal creatures or spiral leaves, are created as a consequence of only a small perturbation and modification in the form of the species. Numerous social insects, identically, relied on the division of labour and harmonious collaboration among individuals in their colonies in order to survive (Mayr 1976, 31). Nevertheless, examples of the most incredible and miraculous adaptations in nature do not serve as 'proof of intrinsic tendency toward perfection' (Mayr 1976, 46). The efficiency of an organism's instinctive reactions is not sufficient for evolutionists to conclude that nature is designed so as to perfectly serve some specific purpose. Evolutionists claim that perfect solutions arise despite arbitrariness, planlessness and accidents.

The eclipse of (intellectual) *Utopia*

The conception of perfectibility has a longstanding history. The idea of perfection has existed since the ancient Greeks, especially in the writings of Plato. It has been influential in Europe primarily since the Renaissance. It became famous, although in a very specific form, by Thomas More's *Utopia*. In his *Utopia*, More gave an account of a community in whose citizens enjoyed the perfectibility of human institutions and morality. Nature assigned no limit to the inhabitants of

112   *The economic construction of sciences*

Utopia. The ideal social order on the island was perfectly maintained. More, a 'man for all seasons', has had many admirers, from the Catholic Church, which canonized him as a saint in 1935, to the Politburo of the USSR, where a sculpture of him was erected at Lenin's behest after the revolution of 1917. His *Utopia* has influenced almost every text written on such social and philosophical issues of justice, poverty, social order and so on. The book inspired the projects of changing (and even revolutionizing) the world with a faith in perfection.

Scott Gordon (1991) argues that many writers have read *Utopia* from the view of religious freedom and secularization in political and intellectual life. In fact, *Utopia* has been influential on such diverse issues as secularization, communism and liberalism. The book has been extremely important in the process of reforming church–state relations – it was perhaps the first attempt to articulate a comprehensive religious freedom. 'Despite More's religious feelings', says Gordon,

> his *Utopia* is not notably a portrait of a perfect social order built upon religious foundations or governed necessarily by priests. In fact it was the forerunner of the form of social perfectionist writing that rose to dominance in the eighteenth century: the vision of a secular utopia ... [S]ocial science and social philosophy underwent a profound transformation from a religious to a secular orientation during the seventeenth and eighteenth centuries. This was also true of that branch of social thought most intimately connected with religion, the concept of a social order: paradise, in effect, was brought down to earth.
>
> (Gordon 1991, 160)

The conception in *Utopia* is challenging. For *Utopia* is a special utopia in which there is one unalterable world and no alternatives at all. It is a world of perfection – a world in which everything that can be thought (or imagined) can also be attained and realized. It was one of the utopias that demonstrated a world by which many thinkers such as Léon Walras and Karl Marx were inspired. It was the world in which the citizens of the Soviet Republic hoped to reside. It was not a factual demonstration, though – it was a story about a country that had never existed, for 'utopia' meant 'the place that did not exist' (Kumar 1991, 1). I have the opinion that we might have started the 'adventure of enlightenment' erroneously and we should consider the initial assumptions and preconditions once again, which means concerning ourselves with errors in intellectual history – errors that resulted in path-dependent circumstances in the history of human ideas.

Many age-old metaphors of Western thought, which were to be used to build such perfect structures, were basically symbolic figures. By virtue of such figures, according to Dewey (1950, 132):

> some have sought the good in self-realization, some in holiness, some in happiness, some in the greatest possible aggregate of pleasures. And yet these schools have agreed on the assumption that there is a single, fixed and final good. They have been able to dispute with one another only because of their common premise.

Sciences between Scylla and Charybdis 113

While Heraclites thought it was fire that was intrinsically stable and certain, Plato thought it was the rational spirit. St Augustine thought it was love of God that was fixed and final in nature and Spinoza thought it was emotion and affection. Marx thought it was class struggle that determined the course of social and economic history. Certainly, accusing intellectuals for using and over-using the same metaphors may seem pointless because this resembles accusing societies for having social values and blaming governments for having armies. Using metaphors and other place-holders turns out to be a problem, however, as Rorty once said, when the 'happenstance of our cultural development [is] that we got stuck so long with place-holders' (Rorty 1979, 83).

The problem with the majority of those figures of speech is that we have used these symbolic figures literally. In fact, such figures of speech were chosen arbitrarily, mostly with references to religious and transcendental doctrines. Utopias generate a similar effect. Utopias are, in a sense, free exercises about free worlds where constraints are loose and sometimes non-existent. They are, after all, constructed worlds – the worlds that thinkers make for themselves. Such metaphors aim to form an imaginary, balanced construction of human ideas. 'Beneath the surface of economic theorizing', Robert Nelson writes (2001, xx), 'economists are engaged in an act of delivering religious messages. Correctly understood, these messages are seen to be promises of the true path to a salvation in this world – to a heaven on earth'.

Utopia, as a metaphor, implied that it was possible to build perfect structures in the human world. It was possible, for instance, to create or discover a 'perfect language' – that is, a world of one language. Perfect language means that we name objects in such a way that we unambiguously communicate their inherent properties when we talk about them. It implies there should be one name for a tree and the name should represent the 'essentials' of the object. Names in languages would then have definite meanings. 'The dream of a perfect language', as Umberto Eco once said,

> did not only obsess European culture. The story of the confusion of tongues, and of the attempt to redeem [European culture's] loss through the rediscovery or invention of a language common to all humanity, can be found in every culture.
> (Eco 1995, 1)

One can read *Utopia* in countless ways, underscore a variety of its aspects and criticize or praise its conclusions and implications. In fact, the ideas presented in *Utopia* have long been challenged by a number of critics. Isaiah Berlin, for instance, reports that the originality of Machiavelli was his disbelief in an ideal state of affairs. 'Machiavelli ... undermines one major assumption of Western thought,' Berlin argues,

> namely that somewhere in the past or the future, in this world or the next ... there is to be found the final solution to the question of how men should live ... [But] the very search for it becomes not merely Utopian in practice but conceptually incoherent.
> (Berlin 1972, 72–6, quoted by McCloskey 2006, 247)

114   *The economic construction of sciences*

Path dependence research provides another critique of *Utopia*, conclusions of which are similar to those of Berlin.

Utopia is not always possible to attain in the evolutionary history of academic scholarship because remote consequences of small events cannot be predicted at all times. Small events shift the evolution of ideas and can cause (extra-) positive or (extra-) negative consequences to move the system away from its systematic course. As a consequence, pathways of evolution are not always non-linear. That is to say, evolution is not headed at a predefined perfect stage but rather bifurcates after several tipping points that historical small events cause without any time-regularity or periodicity. In fact, imperfections that come about as a consequence of tipping points are the central characteristic of natural selection and evolution. Richard Dawkins (1986, 91) remarks that 'evolution can be more strongly supported by evidence of telling imperfections than by evidence of perfection'.

Punctuated equilibrium in the history of ideas

The works of Dawkins (1986, 1976 [2006], 1995) are inspiring for evolutionary epistemologists explaining altruism, cooperation, complexity, replication and cumulative selection in nature and society. His works are also helpful in explaining imperfections in nature, as the preceding quote suggests, although Dawkins is not as enthusiastic as his critics Stephan J. Gould and Niles Eldredge, who introduced the theory of punctuated equilibrium in order to account for the 'conservative aspects of the history of life' (Sterelny 2007, 12). One of the conservative aspects of life, on which I focus my attention in this section, is that gene selection and mutation are not the only themes of evolution in nature. Often, species remain morphologically stable. The theory of punctuated equilibrium explains, among other things, that significant number of species have not emerged by gradual transformation but by rare and rapid shifts followed by long periods of stasis. The logic behind the theory of punctuated equilibrium is that while large populations in nature change slowly and maintain relative stability of variety among themselves, tiny populations, separated from bigger populations moving to other areas of residence, develop more rapidly and produce daughter species through speciation. Speciation is the main mechanism that leads to the evolution of new species. It takes place within a 'geographical millisecond' – that is, a thousand or tens of thousands of years – and fails to change thereafter (Eldredge and Gould 1972).

Punctuated equilibrium is a theory of differential rates of evolution among diverging pathways. It explains how a large population can come out of a small population. The total number of species increases; however, no species transforms into another. The new population need not be bigger than their parent species. It is the proliferation of stasis that generates branches that lead in different directions from their ancestors. The small sub-population after speciation gets bigger and bigger, and new pathways occur. The pathway from small to large involves short-cut generating mechanisms. There is no single pattern that determines who gets through and who does not. In other words, evolution is not directed to a single superior, perfect creature, but maybe two or even more species with 'less perfect' features. Evolutionary pathways are rather a combination of a number of evolutionary lineages. By way of several mechanisms in nature, such as speciation, diversity among species tends to increase, resulting in the coexistence of a few diverse species at the same time, which may have long been isolated from their parent species and may feature no anatomical advantages over one another.

After an increase in diversity, evolution hits such pathways where 'life settles down to generating endless variants upon a few surviving models' (Gould 1991, 47). The system locks itself into specific evolutionary lineages in which an overwhelming majority of species are destroyed and only a few survive. Species that survive may not have prevailed for a normal survival advantage. 'Perhaps, the actual reasons for survival do not support conventional ideas of cause as complexity, improvement, or anything moving at all humanward' (ibid., 48). Perhaps an earthquake hits the region, or an unpredictable environmental catastrophe provokes mass extinction. Evolution may take place dependent upon improbable courses of events, which are sensible in retrospect yet unpredictable before their occurrence. This does not mean that evolution after a chance or contingent event is senseless. It only means that the strict determinism of perfectionism may not apply. Due to some specific cause, each stage gives way to the next one, but no final term can be specified *ex ante*, even with full knowledge of the initial step of a process. Moreover, no event would occur again if we ran the system for a second time. No matter how small in size an event may be, replace it with another that seems improbable or without apparent importance and evolution would lead to a completely different pathway (Gould 1991).

So what is the significance of the theory of punctuated equilibrium with regard to the evolution of (economic) ideas? Gould and Eldredge (1977, Eldredge and Gould 1972, Gould 2002, especially Chapter 9) argue that life's history in evolutionary biology and palaeontology is often incorrectly demonstrated. They claim that conventional iconography represents natural evolution as if species in nature grow upward. This representation implies a ranking among ancestors and cousins, as 'upward' species are assumed to gain the advantages of complexity, which results from the success of species at previous stages of evolution. The problem with such iconographies is that they conceive of evolution as if there was a single pathway in life's history, directed to a perfect ideal that will inevitably result in the future. However, there is almost always more than one surviving pathway.

Figure 3.1 demonstrates the course of intellectual history as if it is headed towards a point of perfect knowledge. The production function of knowledge in Figure 3.1, represented by the curved line, is an increasing function: pieces and bits of knowledge, as time goes by, accumulate in a systematic way. However, the process of knowledge production never reaches the point of perfection, represented by the horizontal dotted line, since new findings become more difficult to acquire over time as the marginal benefits of new knowledge is smaller than the marginal benefits of previous knowledge. Therefore, Figure 3.1 does not represent the process of knowledge production by a straight line but instead as a curve

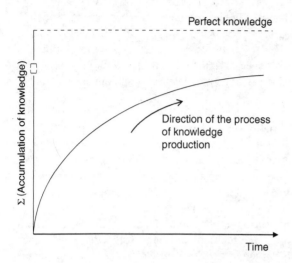

Figure 3.1 Evolution of ideas when knowledge continuously progresses

asymptotic to the maximum. This state of perfect knowledge is hypothetical in the sense that its existence is not proven and not provable by any conceivable evidence. Human knowledge is always imperfect. Figure 3.1 also represents a ladder-like pattern of evolution in which increments in the stock of knowledge are accumulated as if every small increment is perfectly fitted to what we already know in a smooth and continuous manner. Normally, a ladder-like pattern of evolution would require steps (or permanent branches) elevating the course of history to higher stages gradually and steadily. Here, steps are simplified into a flat lineage where 'unfit' additions are smoothly removed out of the process of theoretical adaptation. Finally, Figure 3.1 demonstrates a unidirectional pathway of evolution. Since there is only one pathway of evolution, converging to a perfect state of affairs, intellectual evolution features inevitability and directionality. This demonstration therefore represents a Whiggish view of history, where there is only one process, one methodology and one unidirectional pathway to the perfection of knowledge. Figure 3.1 is a result of 'uniformitarian and continuationist beliefs' (Gould 2002, 61).

Figure 3.2 represents a multi-directional course of intellectual history where intellectual evolution features rapid shifts leading to the emergence of two or more divergent pathways. After these rapid episodes in which variation arises, explanations compete with alternative explanations, and are challenged critically on their merits. Explanations survive this process by becoming a part of the numerous scholarly apparatus that helps the explanation become isolated from its parent explanation. By receiving citations from a specific network of scholars and the analysis of supportive data, explanations gain credibility and so their findings and methodologies diffuse to various fields of research. As Eldredge argues,

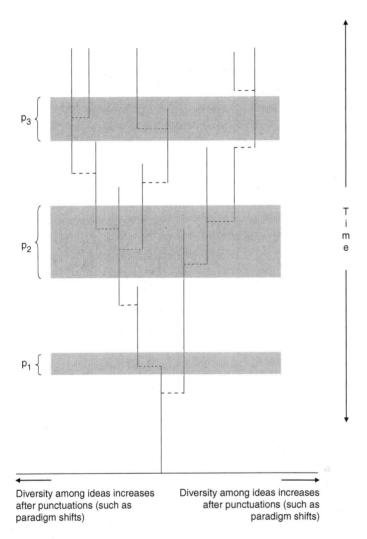

Figure 3.2 A tree of intellectual life

diffusion of knowledge is 'a matter of differential economic success biasing reproductive success' (Eldredge 1992, 113). Indeed, explanations that are able to survive are often the explanations that are able reproduce in the works of a specific network of scholars. Figure 3.2 shows that after punctuations (represented by the dotted horizontal lines), stasis (represented by the longer vertical lines) prevails within the explanation. Therefore, intellectual evolution is the sum of the processes in which (1) the variety of explanations tends to increase following rapid shifts in the perception of an explanation and (2) explanations survive the critical challenges and alternative explanations in a state of stasis (or inertia).

118   *The economic construction of sciences*

(Variety is depicted here along the horizontal axis.) Explanations do not always replace other explanations; instead, explanations co-evolve, and diversity and discontinuity of explanations is prevalent. However, as Figure 3.2 demonstrates, explanations also go extinct when emergent explanations cease to attract the attention of scholars after periods of time. Explanations are not able to reproduce themselves forever. In other words, explanations are 'spatiotemporally bounded, i.e. [explanations are] localized in time and space, with a beginning, a history, and (eventually) an end' (Eldredge 1986, 353, italics are omitted). For instance, in period p_1 three different explanations, represented by three vertical lines, are available to scholars whereas in period p_2 the number of available explanations increases to six, in period p_3 it decreases to five. After period p_3, the number of diverse explanations might increase or decrease again. Larger periods of times do not necessarily mean larger number of explanations. Subsequent periods neither lead to the 'growth' nor 'improvement' of explanations. The theory of punctuated equilibrium with regard to intellectual evolution suggests that there is no inevitability in the process of variation since contingencies leading to rapid shifts in perception might give rise to either the extinction of old explanations or the creation of new ones. This process has no definitive termination because acts of creativity cause further discontinuities in the course of history.

Both Figure 3.1 and Figure 3.2 illustrate intellectual evolution where explanations struggle for survival in academic scholarship. Intellectual evolution may not perfectly feature the specificities that are common in natural and social evolution. Additionally, the processes of knowledge production are often processes of increasing returns to scholarly scale. However, Figure 3.2 describes the process of knowledge production as if the process is one of decreasing returns. This representation is not realistic because knowledge is not a commodity with declining marginal utility. In fact, the world in which we live is a world of increasing returns and, in this world, multi-directionalities are likely. However, Figure 3.2 is not sufficiently realistic either, at least, on the grounds that it leaves one question without an answer: does continual progress require perfection? This is an open question and the answer is less than obvious. My view is that it is difficult to show whether there is progress, continual or discrete, in the absence of some kind of a measure of proximity to perfection. I think that, in most cases, continual progress requires a conception of perfection even when contingencies cause disruptions. Pathways of discrete evolution, which Figure 3.2 represents, cannot continually progress. In fact, this is the core of the theory of punctuated equilibrium, according to which discrete shifts give rise to the emergence of new pathways in which individual explanations achieve differential reproduction success rates. Reconciliation of different pathways is not always possible due to different rates of adaptation. However, different explanations often give rise to further pathways through 'new' explanations.

The theory of punctuated equilibrium has implications not only for the specific issues debated in natural and social sciences, but also for the general set of issues related to the evolutionary history of economics. The significance of the theory of punctuated equilibrium with regard to intellectual history is that it is not always possible to reconcile diverse intellectual pathways that have had unique histories. Explanations in economics do not always become more sophisticated as time goes by; they do not necessarily evolve in the direction of better knowledge. Instead, several multi-directional pathways in intellectual history cause diversity among explanations. Diversity sometimes takes place at the expense of 'intellectual improvement' because 'less fit' explanations are not always eliminated and substituted by 'fitter' explanations.

Is there progress in economics? There certainly is. Economists strive for replacing 'less fit' explanations with 'fitter' explanations in the profession. However, progression is often interrupted because such processes are often epistemologically costly and economists are hesitant in adopting new explanations to which they are not accustomed. Therefore, progress in economics is discontinuous. Is there perfection in economics? There certainly is not. In order for economics to achieve perfection, errors should have been continuously replaced when they are detected. And this does not take place. Perhaps, we need to achieve sustainability in the growth of economic knowledge if we want to get out of the spontaneous disorder in economic sciences. Indeed, sustainable growth of knowledge would be one of the ways to preserve the intellectual ecology of economic research from the harmful consequences of QRPs.

References

Arrow, Kenneth J. 2000. 'Increasing Returns: Historiographic Issues and Path Dependence'. *European Journal of the History of Economic Thought* 7 (2): 171–80.

Arthur, W. Brian. 1985. 'Strong Laws for a Class of Path Dependent Urn Processes'. *Proceedings of the Conference on Stochastic Optimization*: 287–300.

Arthur, W. Brian. 1988. 'Self-reinforcing Mechanisms in Economics'. In *The Economy as an Evolving Complex System*, edited by Philip W. Anderson, Kenneth J. Arrow and David Pines, 111–32. Massachusetts: Addison Wesley.

Arthur, W. Brian. 1989. 'Competing Technologies, Increasing Returns and Lock-in by Historical Events'. *The Economic Journal* 99 (394): 116–31.

Arthur, W. Brian. 1994. *Increasing Returns and Path Dependence in the Economy*. Ann Arbor: University of Michigan Press.

Arthur, W. Brian. 1996. 'Increasing Returns and the New World of Business'. *Harvard Business Review* 74 (4): 100–9.

Arthur, W. Brian. 2000. 'The Complexity Vision and the Teaching of Economics'. In *The Complexity Vision and the Teaching of Economics*, edited by David Colander, 51–62. Cheltenham: Edward Elgar.

Arthur, W. Brian, Yu. M. Ermoliev and Yu. M. Kaniovski. 1987. 'Non-linear Urn Processes: Asymptotic Behavior and Applications'. *IIASA Working Paper No. 87-85*.

Balmann, Alfons, Martin Odening, Hans-Peter Weikard and Wilhelm Brandes. 1996. 'Path-dependence without Increasing Returns to Scale and Network Externalities'. *Journal of Economic Behavior and Organization* 29 (1): 159–72.

Berger, Sebastian. 2008. 'Circular Cumulative Causation (CCC) a la Myrdal and Kapp-Political Institutionalism for Minimizing Costs'. *Journal of Economic Issues* 42 (2): 1–9.

Berger, Sebastian, and Wolfram Elsner. 2007. 'European Contributions to Evolutionary Institutional Economics: The Cases of "Cumulative Circular Causation" (CCC) and "Open Systems Approach" (OSA). Some Methodological and Policy Implications'. *Journal of Economic Issues* 41 (2): 529–37.

120 *The economic construction of sciences*

Berlin, Isaah. 1972. 'Originality of Machiavelli [Delivered to the British Section of the Political Studies Association in 1953]'. In *Studies in Machiavelli*, edited by Myron P. Gilmore, 25–79. Florence: Biblioteca Storica Sansoni.

Blaug, Mark. 2001. 'No History of Ideas, Please, We're Economists'. *Journal of Economic Perspectives* 15 (1): 145–64.

Boettke, Peter, J. and Kyle W. O'Donnell. 2014. 'The Social Responsibility of Economists'. In *The Oxford Handbook of Professional Ethics*, edited by George DeMartino and Deirdre McCloskey. Oxford. Oxford University Press. doi: 10.1093/oxfordhb/9780199766635.013.007

Boulding, Kenneth E. 1971. 'After Samuelson, Who Needs Adam Smith?'. *History of Political Economy* 3 (2): 225–37.

Collins, Randall, Robert A. Hanneman and Gabriele Mordt. 1999. 'How Stimulating a Compact Theory Can Reproduce the Tangled Pathways of History'. In *Macrohistory: Essays in Sociology of the Long Run*, edited by Randall Collins, 239–59. Stanford, CA: Stanford University Press.

Condorcet, Nicolas de. 1795 [1949]. 'An Historical Picture of the Progress of Human Mind'. In *The Idea of Progress: A Collection of Readings*, edited by Frederic J. Teggard, 321–48. Berkley and Los Angeles: California University Press.

Cowan, Robin, and Philip Gunby. 1996. 'Sprayed to Death: Path Dependence, Lock-in and Pest Control Strategies'. *Economic Journal* 106 (436): 521–42.

Darwin, Charles. 1859 [1952]. *The Origin of Species*. Chicago: William Benton.

David, Paul A. 1985. 'Clio and the Economics of QWERTY'. *American Economic Review* 75 (2): 332–7.

David, Paul A. 1999. 'At Last, a Remedy for Chronic QWERTY-skepticism!'. European Summer School in Industrial Dynamics (ESSID), held at L'Institute d'Etudes Scientifique de Cargèse (Corse), France. 5–12 September. http://econwpa.repec.org/eps/eh/papers/0502/0502004.pdf. Accessed November 2015.

David, Paul A. 2001. 'Path Dependence, Its Critics and the Quest of "Historical Economics"'. In *Evolution and Path Dependence in Economic Ideas*, edited by Pierre Garrouste and Stavros Ioannides, 15–40. Cheltenham: Edward Elgar.

David, Paul A. 2007. 'Path Dependence: A Foundational Concept for Historical Science'. *Cliometrica* 1 (2): 91–111.

Dawkins, Richard. 1976 [2006]. *The Selfish Gene*. Oxford: Oxford University Press.

Dawkins, Richard. 1986. *The Blind Watchmaker: Why the Evidence of Evolution Reveals a World without Design*. New York: Norton.

Dawkins, Richard. 1995. *River Out of Eden: A Darwinian View of Life*. New York: Basic Books.

De Langhe, Rogier, and Matthias Greiff. 2008. 'Increasing Returns in Science: A Model of the Dynamics of Scientific Activity'. TILPS Workshop 'Formal Modeling in Social Epistemology', October, Tilburg University.

Denzau, Arthur T., and Douglass C. North. 1994. 'Shared Mental Models: Ideologies and Institutions'. *Kyklos* 47 (1): 3–31.

Dewey, John. 1910a. 'The Intellectualist Criterion for Truth'. In *The Influence of Darwin on Philosophy and Other Essays*, 112–53. New York: Henry Holt and Co.

Dewey, John. 1910b. 'Intelligence and Morals'. In *The Influence of Darwin on Philosophy and Other Essays*, 46–76. New York: Henry Holt and Co.

Dewey, John. 1950. *Reconstruction in Philosophy*. New York: New American Library.

Driel, Hugo van, and Wilfred Dolfsma. 1988. 'Path Dependence, Initial Conditions, and Routines in Organizations: The Toyota Production System Re-examined'. *Journal of Organizational Change Management* 22 (1): 49–72.

Sciences between Scylla and Charybdis 121

Duhs, Alan. 1998. 'Five Dimensions of the Interdependence of Philosophy and Economics Integrating HET and the History of Political Philosophy'. *International Journal of Social Economics* 25 (10): 1477–508.

Dutt, Amitava. 1997. 'Equilibrium, Path Dependence and Hysteresis in Post-Keynesian Models'. In *Markets, Unemployment and Economic Policy*, edited by Philip Arestis and Malcolm Sawyer, 238–53. New York: Routledge.

Eco, Umberto. 1995. *The Search for the Perfect Language*. Oxford: Blackwell.

Eldredge, Niles. 1986. 'Information, Economics, and Evolution'. *Annual Review of Ecology and Systematics* 17: 351–69.

Eldredge, Niles. 1992. 'Punctuated Equilibria, Rates of Change, and Large-Scale Entities in Evolutionary Systems'. In *The Dynamics of Evolution: The Punctuated Equilibrium Debate in the Natural and Social Sciences*, edited by Albert Somit and Steven A. Peterson, 103–20. Ithaca and London: Cornell University Press.

Eldredge, Niles, and Stephen Jay Gould. 1972. 'Punctuated Equilibria: An Alternative to Phyletic Gradualism'. In *Models in Paleobiology*, edited by T. J. M. Schopf, 82–115. San Fransico: Cooper and Co.

Fogel, Robert W. 1964. *Railroads and American Economic Growth: Essays in Econometric History*. Baltimore: Johns Hopkins Press.

Foss, J. Nicolai. 1997. 'Equilibrium vs Evolution in the Resource-Based Perspective: The Conflicting Legacies of Demsetz and Penrose'. *Danish Research Unit for Industrial Dynamics Working Paper* Number 97-10.

Galbraith, John Kenneth. 1958. *The Affluent Society*. Cambridge, MA: Riverside Press.

Gartland, Myles P. 2005. 'Interdisciplinary Views of Sub-optimal Outcomes: Path Dependence in the Social and Management Sciences'. *Journal of Socio-Economics* 34 (5): 686–702.

Garud, Raghu, and Peter Karnøe. 2001. *Path Dependence and Creation*. Mahwah, NJ: Lawrence Erlbaum Associates.

Georgescu-Roegen, Nicholas. 1971. *The Entropy Law and Economic Process*. Cambridge, MA: Harvard University Press.

Ginsberg, Morris. 1953. *The Idea of Progress: A Revaluation*. Boston: Beacon Press.

Gladwell, Malcolm. 2000. *The Tipping Point: How Little Things Can Make a Big Difference*. Boston: Little, Brown.

Goldman, Alvin I. 2001. 'Experts: Which Ones Should You Trust?'. *Philosophy and Phenomenological Research* 63 (1): 85–110.

Goldstone, Jack A. 1998. 'Initial Conditions, General Laws, Path Dependence, and Explanation in Historical Sociology'. *American Journal of Sociology* 104 (3): 829–45.

Gordon, Scott. 1991. *The History and Philosophy of Social Science*. London and New York: Routledge.

Gould, Stephen Jay. 1982. *Panda's Thumb*. New York: W. W. Norton and Co.

Gould, Stephen Jay. 1989. *Wonderful Life: The Burgess Shale and The Nature of History*. New York: W. W. Norton Co.

Gould, Stephen Jay. 1991. 'Opus 200'. *Natural History* 100 (August): 12–18.

Gould, Stephen Jay. 2002. *The Structure of Evolutionary Theory*. Cambridge, MA: Belknap Press of Harvard University Press.

Gould, Stephen Jay, and Niles Eldredge. 1977. 'Punctuated Equilibria: The Tempo and Mode of Evolution Reconsidered'. *Paleobiology* 3 (2): 115–51.

Graff, Gerald. 1987. *Professing Literature: An Institutional History*. Chicago: University of Chicago Press.

Hall, John, Iciar Dominguez Lacasa and Jutta Günther. 2011. 'Path Dependence and QWERTY's Lock-in: Toward a Veblenian Interpretation'. *Journal of Economic Issues* 45 (2): 457–64.

122   *The economic construction of sciences*

Hardwig, John. 1985. 'Epistemic Dependence'. *The Journal of Philosophy* 82 (7): 335–49.

Hardwig, John. 1991. 'The Role of Trust in Knowledge'. *The Journal of Philosophy* 88 (12): 69–702.

Heikkila, Eric J. 2011. 'An Information Perspective on Path Dependence'. *Journal of Institutional Economics* 7 (1): 23–45.

Hickman, Larry A. 2004. 'Pragmatism as Post-Postmodernism'. In *Dewey, Pragmatism, and Economic Methodology*, edited by Elias L. Khalil, 87–101. New York: Routledge.

Hodgson, Geoffrey M. 2001. *How Economics Forgot History: The Problem of Historical Specificity in Social Science*. London and New York: Routledge.

James, William. 1971. 'Habit'. In *A William James Reader*, edited by Gay Wilson Allen. Boston: Houghton Mifflin Co.

James, William. 2000. *Pragmatism and Other Writings*. London: Penguin Classics.

Jolink, Albert, and Jack J. Vromen. 2001. 'Path Dependence in Scientific Evolution'. In *Evolution and Path Dependence in Economic Ideas*, edited by Pierre Garrouste and Stavros Ioannides, 205–24. Cheltenham: Edward Elgar.

Kapp, K. William. 1976. 'The Nature and Significance of Institutional Economics'. *Kyklos* 29 (2): 209–32.

Kay, Neil M. 2013. 'Rerun the Tape of History and QWERTY Always Wins'. *Research Policy* 42: 1175–85.

Knudsen, Christian. 1993. 'The Essential Tension in the Social Sciences: Between the "Unification" and "Fragmentation" Traps'. In *The Evolution of Scientific Knowledge*, edited by Hans Siggaard Jensen, Lykke Margot Richter and Morten Thanning Vendelø, 13–36. Cheltenham: Edward Elgar.

Krugman, Paul. 1991. 'Increasing Returns and Economic Geography'. *Journal of Political Economy* 99 (3): 483–99.

Kuhn, Thomas S. 2000. *The Road Since Structure: Philosophical Essays, 1970–1993, with an Autobiographical Interview*. Chicago: University of Chicago Press.

Kumar, T. Krishna. 1991. *Utopianism*. Minnesota: University of Minnesota Press.

Lawson, Tony. 1997. *Economics and Reality*. London: Routledge.

Liebowitz, Stan J., and Stephen E. Margolis. 1990. 'The Fable of the Keys'. *Journal of Law and Economics* 33 (1): 1–25.

Liebowitz, Stan J., and Stephen E. Margolis. 1995a. 'Path Dependence, Lock-in and History'. *Journal of Law, Economics and Organization* 11 (1): 205–26.

Liebowitz, Stan J., and Stephen E. Margolis. 1995b. 'Policy and Path Dependence: From QWERTY to Windows 95'. *Regulation* 18 (3): 33–41.

Liebowitz, Stan J., and Stephen E. Margolis. 1998. 'Path Dependence'. In *Palgrave Dictionary of Economics and Law*, edited by P. Newman, 17–22. London: Palgrave.

Liebowitz, Stan J., and Stephen E. Margolis. 1999. *Winners, Losers, and Microsoft: Competition and Antitrust in High Technology*. Oakland: Independent Institute.

Liebowitz, Stan J., and Stephen E. Margolis. 2013. 'The Troubled Path of the Lock-in Movement'. *Journal of Competition Law and Economics* 9 (1): 125–52.

Mahoney, James. 2000. 'Path Dependence in Historical Sociology'. *Theory and Society* 29 (4): 507–48.

March, James G. 1996. 'Continuity and Change in Theories of Organizational Action'. *Administrative Science Quarterly* 41 (2): 278–87.

Martin, Ron. 1999. 'Editorial: The "New Economic Geography": Challenge or Irrelevance'. *Transactions of the Institute of British Geographers* 24 (4): 387–91.

Sciences between Scylla and Charybdis   123

Mayr, Ernst. 1976. *Evolution and the Diversity of Life: Selected Essays*. London: Belknap Press of Harvard University Press.

McCloskey, Deirdre N. 2006. *The Bourgeois Virtues: Ethics for an Age of Commerce*. Chicago: University of Chicago Press.

Mirowski, Philip. 2002. *Machine Dreams: Economics Becomes a Cyborg Science*. Cambridge: Cambridge University Press.

Myrdal, Gunnar. 1944. *An American Dilemma: The Negro Problem and Modern Democracy*. New York: Harper.

Nelson, Robert. 2001. *Economics as Religion: From Samuelson to Chicago and Beyond*. Pennsylvania: Pennsylvania University Press.

Nietzsche, Frederich. 1878 [1986]. *Human, All Too Human: A Book for Free Spirits*, translated by R. J. Hollingdale. Cambridge: Cambridge University Press.

Nisbet, Robert. 1994. *History of the Idea of Progress*. New Brunswick: Transaction.

Nooteboom, Bart. 1997. 'Path Dependence of Knowledge: Implications for the Theory of the Firm'. In *Evolutionary Economics and Path Dependence*, edited by Lars Magnusson and Jan Ottosson, 57–78. Cheltenham: Edward Elgar.

North, Douglass Cecil. 1990. *Institutions, Institutional Change and Economic Performance*. Cambridge: Cambridge University Press.

North, Douglass Cecil. 1992. *Transaction Costs, Institutions, and Economic Performance, Occasional Papers/International Center for Economic Growth*. San Francisco, Calif.: ICS Press.

North, Douglass Cecil. 1996. 'Economics and Cognitive Science'. Paper provided by Economics Working Paper Archive at WUSTL in its series Economic History with number 9612002.

Ocasio, William, and John Joseph. 2005. 'Cultural Adaptation and Institutional Change: The Evolution of Vocabularies of Corporate Governance, 1972–2003'. *Poetics* 33 (3–4): 163–87.

Pierson, Paul. 2000. 'Increasing Returns, Path Dependence, and the Study of Politics'. *American Political Science Review* 94 (2): 251–67.

Pollard, Sydney. 1971. *The Idea of Progress*. Harmondsworth: Penguin.

Popper, Karl R. 1962 [1971]. *The Open Society and Its Enemies*. Princeton, NJ: Princeton University Press.

Puffert, Douglas J. 2003. 'Path Dependence'. *Eh.net Encyclopedia*. http://www.eh.net/?s=puffert. Accessed June 2014.

Ratner, Joseph. 1999. 'Introduction to John Dewey's Philosophy'. In *Useful Procedures of Inquiry*, edited by Rollo Handy and Edward Crosby Harwood. Great Barrington: Behavioral Research Council.

Rizzello, Salvatore. 1997. 'The Microfoundations of Path Dependency'. In *Evolutionary Economics and Path Dependence*, edited by Lars Magnusson and Jan Ottosson, 98–118. Cheltenham: Edward Elgar.

Rorty, Richard. 1979. *Philosophy and the Mirror of Nature*. Princeton, NJ: Princeton University Press.

Rorty, Richard. 1989. *Contingency, Irony, and Solidarity*. Cambridge: Cambridge University Press.

Rorty, Richard. 1997. 'Religious Faith, Intellectual Responsibility, and Romance'. In *The Cambridge Companion to William James*, edited by Ruth Anna Putnam, 84–102. Cambridge: Cambridge University Press.

Rosen, Sherwin. 1981. 'The Economics of Superstars'. *American Economic Review* 71 (5): 845–58.

124   *The economic construction of sciences*

Rosenberg, Nathan, and L. E. Birdzell. 1986. *How the West Grew Rich: The Economic Transformation of the Industrial World.* London: I.B.Tauris.

Sandhu, Philine Erfurt. 2013. 'Persistent Homogeneity in Top Management: Organizational Path Dependence in Leadership Selection'. PhD, Wirtschaftswissenschaften des Fachbereichs Wirtschaftswissenschaft der Freien, Free University of Berlin.

Schama, Simon. 1987 [1997]. *The Embarrassment of Riches: An Interpretation of Dutch Culture in the Golden Age.* New York: Random House.

Spulber, Daniel F. (ed.). 2003. *Famous Fables of Economics: Myths of Market Failures.* Oxford: Oxford University Press.

Stephan, Paula E. 2012. *How Economics Shapes Science.* Cambridge, MA: Harvard University Press.

Sterelny, Kim. 2007. *Dawkins vs Gould: Survival of the Fittest.* London: Icon Books.

Sterman, John D., and Jason Wittenberg. 1999. 'Path Dependence, Competition, and Succession in the Dynamics of Scientific Revolutions'. *Organization Science* 10 (3): 322–41.

Sydow, Jörg, and Georg Schreyögg (eds). 2010. *The Hidden Dynamics of Path Dependence: Institutions and Organizations.* New York: Palgrave Macmillan.

Sydow, Jörg, and Georg Schreyögg (eds). 2013. *Self-Reinforcing Processes in and among Organizations.* London and New York: Palgrave Macmillan.

Sydow, Jörg, Georg Schreyögg and Jochen Koch. 2005. 'Organizational Paths: Path Dependency and Beyond'. Conference Paper Presented at the 21st EGOS Colloqium, Berlin.

Sydow, Jörg, Georg Schreyögg and Jochen Koch. 2009. 'Organizational Path Dependence: Opening the Black Box'. *Academy of Management Review* 34 (4): 689–709.

Teggart, Frederic J. 1949. *The Idea of Progress: A Collection of Readings.* Berkeley and Los Angeles: University of California Press.

Veblen, Thorstein. 1898. 'Why is Economics Not an Evolutionary Science?'. *Quarterly Journal of Economics* 12 (4): 373–94.

Veblen, Thorstein. 1918. *The Higher Learning in America: A Memorandum on the Conduct of Universities by Businessmen.* New York: B. W. Huebsch.

Veblen, Thorstein. 1919. *The Place of Science in Modern Civilisation and Other Essays.* New York: B. W. Huebsch.

Vergne, Jean-Philippe. 2013. 'QWERTY is Dead; Long Live Path Dependence'. *Research Policy* 42: 1191–4.

Vergne, Jean-Philippe, and R. Rodolphe Durand. 2010. 'The Missing Link Between the Theory and Empirics of Path Dependence: Conceptual Clarification, Testability Issue, and Methodological Implications'. *Journal of Management Studies* 47 (4): 736–59.

Walby, Sylvia. 2007. 'Complexity Theory, Systems Theory, and Multiple Intersecting Social Inequalities'. *Philosophy of the Social Sciences* 37 (4): 449–70.

White, Lynn Townsend. 1962. *Medieval Technology and Social Change.* Oxford: Clarendon Press.

Wright, Ronald. 2005. *A Short History of Progress.* New York: Carroll and Graf.

Yalcintas, Altug. 2006. 'Otomobillerimiz var, Pizzalarımız da … Deirdre McCloskey ile bir Söyleşi [We have automobiles, and pizzas, too: An Interview with Deirdre McCloskey]'. *Mulkiye Dergisi* 30 (251): 185–97.

Yalcintas, Altug. 2009. 'Intellectual Paths and Pathologies: How Small Events in Scholarly Life Accidentally Grow Big'. PhD Thesis, Erasmus Institute for Philosophy and Economics, Erasmus University Rotterdam.

4 Error

A common tragedy in sciences

Darren Oldridge reports a remarkable trial that was held in Rothenbach in 1485 (Oldridge 2005, 1–19). The trial was about a woman who was suspected of witchcraft. The Court of Fürstenberg decided to try the woman with a method called 'trial by red iron'. The method required the person to hold a piece of hot iron and carry it for three paces. The person's hand would then be bound for three days. After three days, the wound would be inspected. If the wound was healed completely, the person would be declared innocent. But if it was still weeping and discoloured, the person would be condemned. The trial ended with an impressive result. The woman took the iron from the furnace, walked more than three paces and asked if she was required to walk further. After all that, she was acquitted and freed.

The story tells that the woman was accused of a crime (witchcraft) that would seem to be 'strange' to a reasonable (lawful) mind: she was set free on the basis of a completely arbitrary reason (i.e. passing the test of red iron). The cause of the strange event was cancelled out not as a result of some systematic cause (of history), but due to another cause that was no less absurd: that she seemed unaffected by the red iron. Oldridge writes that such trials stopped not because people started to think them illogical, but, rather, because the Church Father thought that they were against the Christian doctrine. Such instances suggest that many absurd, strange, erroneous events could have conceivably existed in history, lasted for long periods and disappeared after some time not because of some systematic tendency inherent in the course of history, but, rather, by further absurdities, strangeness and erroneousness.

Errors, and other types of irregularities alike, have always existed in intellectual history. Although no philosophical or scientific enquiry since the ancient Greeks has been separated from reflections on error, there is not much space devoted to the imperfect character of human doings (i.e. capability of error) that is repeated for so long until we eventually start to think that it has long been wrong. The issue here is not to argue or show whether or not errors played any role in the course of events in our past. Rather, it is to develop an answer as to whether they had any significance, either by way of self-reproducing or self-correcting themselves, in generating pathways in life's history. This chapter

126 *The economic construction of sciences*

examines whether errors are significant in the evolutionary course of academic scholarship and, if so, why. It is argued that scholarly errors are among the factors that generate intellectual pathways in which consequences of historical small events feed back on each other positively. Pathways maintain intellectuals' dependence on the consequences of errors which interact upon each other and prevent intellectual path dependencies from disappearing fully. As a result, ideas do not converge towards perfection. Evolutionary accounts of errors suggest that errors in the history of ideas matter, even though they are often corrected.

Types of error: a brief survey

It is possible to elaborate on the term 'error' in a number of ways. According to Aristotle, Canguilhem argues, a monster could be an error because it intervened unfavourably in the ways in which plants and animals behaved so as to achieve harmony in nature. Error could be attributed to an objective criterion, too. For a calculator, it is a substantial error to calculate nine as the square root of 64. Some errors are not harmful such as (some of) those made by children (Gigerenzer 2005). When a child who has just started to speak uses 'gived' instead of 'gave' she is usually recognized as following a normal and necessary developmental path. Such errors are 'good errors'. Sometimes, experts make good errors as well. 'After the invention of the telephone', Gerd Gigerenzer reports, 'a group of British experts concluded that this invention had no practical value, at least in their country: The telephone may be appropriate for our American cousins, but not here, because we have an adequate supply of messenger boys' (Gigerenzer, 2005, 195).

We can choose from a multitude of examples from history to illustrate this point. For instance, blackness (the so-called 'Negro Problem') or homosexuality have for a long time been (and even still are by some) regarded as (neurotic) pathologies. What must strike the enquirer here is that cultural factors influence the way biological and mental pathologies are defined. The opposite is also true: how we define pathology influences the way the culture is constructed. In other words, there is a feedback relation between the two. Under such conditions, pathologies re-express and reconstitute the values of the society in which those pathologies are defined. In the case of homosexuality, social culture's horror of homosexuality has given rise to the efforts to 'cure' the condition. All homosexuals were thought to have a common dysfunctioning. Such 'pathology' caused societies to see it as the root of a number of problems, such as cultural degeneration. And this has made the examination of the pathology a more critical issue. A number of serious measures were taken in the social and cultural sphere. This intensified society's horror of sexuality and the circular logic was thus constructed.

Another illustrative example of this phenomenon is the case of defining blackness as pathology. The result was the widespread sharing of a descriptive norm as a social norm. Benjamin Rush (1823), although a strong ally of the black-skinned population in America in the eighteenth century, claimed to have

Error: a common tragedy in sciences 127

discovered a pathology that he called 'negroism' or 'negritude', which, Lawrie Reznek reports, was a mild form of congenital leprosy whose only symptom was the darkness of the skin (Reznek 1987, 18). Rush argued that being a 'negro' or black was a hereditary pathology. Whites should not intermarry with the blacks, Rush declared, as it 'would infect posterity with the "disorder"'.

In a similar fashion, Samuel Cartwright (1851) named two diseases peculiar to black-skinned peoples – 'drapetomania' and 'rascality'. Drapetomania was a disease causing the slaves to run away. And dysaesthesia aethiopica was a disease that caused rascality, writes Cartwright,

> peculiar to negroes, affecting both mind and body in a manner as well expressed by dysaesthesia, the name I have given it, as could be by a single term. There is both mind and sensibility, but both seem to be difficult to reach by impressions from without. There is a partial insensibility of the skin, and so great a hebetude of the intellectual faculties, as to be like a person half asleep, that is with difficulty aroused and kept awake. It differs from every other species of mental disease, as it is accompanied with physical signs or lesions of the body discoverable to the medical observer, which is always present and sufficient to account for the symptoms. It is much more prevalent among free Negroes living in clusters by themselves, than among slaves on our plantations, and attacks only such slaves as live like free Negroes in regard to diet, drinks, exercise, etc.

When pathologies are at stake, cumulative causation operates in disfavour of numerous disenfranchised and minority groups. Cumulative causation, as I have already discussed in the previous chapter, referring to the works of such writers as Thorstein Veblen (1898, 1919) and Gunnar Myrdal (1944), accounts for how final effects of greater magnitude come into existence as causes of the initial efforts. In such causal mechanisms, components and variables respond to a change of any cause in the same direction with a follow-up effect upon the first components and variables. The causal system is dynamic in the sense that the system moves as a consequence of the cumulative effects of initial and consecutive pushes as well as the interaction between them. Variables are causally interconnected, leaving no place for the 'first cause'; 'everything is cause to everything else' so that the system is interlocked. Myrdal assumes interdependence between all the factors in the 'Negro Problem'.

> White prejudice and discrimination keep the Negro low in standards of living, health, education, manners and morals. This, in its turn, gives support to white prejudice. White prejudice and Negro standards thus mutually 'cause' each other. If things remain about as they are and have been, this means that the two forces happen to balance each other. Such a static 'accommodation' is, however, entirely accidental. If either of the factors changes, this will cause a change in the other factor, too, and start a process of interaction where the change in one factor will continuously be supported

128   *The economic construction of sciences*

by the reaction of the other factor. The whole system will be moving in the direction of the primary change, but much further. This is what we mean by cumulative causation.

(Myrdal 1944, 76)

Malcolm Gladwell (2000) makes a similar analogy and likens the spread of social behavioural patterns to the epidemics of contagious diseases. Ideas diffuse among different social circles, Gladwell argues, just like viruses do. Epidemics 'tip' – that is, the spread of virus reaches critical mass and its graph shoots straight upwards. This happens very rapidly because the virus carriers are (or at least can be) socialized into different groups among which there are powerful ties. In the 1990s it was thought that crack cocaine was the cause of the spread of HIV in New York because it led to risky sexual behaviour. 'It brings far more people into poor areas to buy drugs', Gladwell reports, 'which then increases the likelihood that they will take an infection home with them to their own neighbourhood. It changes the patterns of social connections between neighbourhoods' (ibid., 15). Social and intellectual path dependencies work in the same way. The emergence of fashion trends, the ebb and flow of crime rates and the phenomena of word of mouth are examples in which a social pattern crosses a threshold and its expansion takes the form of 'exponential overdrive' (ibid., 7). This may seem like a strange thought, Gladwell claims, because we are intellectually born into a conception of approximation among causes and consequences. Changes we render in social life take place steadily and slowly. 'We are trained to think that what goes into any transaction or relationship or system must be directly related, in intensity and dimension, to what comes out' (ibid., 11). This is not necessarily the case 'in the real world'. Consequences are often far out of proportion to initial causes when evolution takes the form of 'geometrical progression'. Under such conditions, what matters are little things, like small events.

Crime is always considered to be a consequence of social injustice, structural economic inequities, unemployment, racism and so forth. If policy-makers want to reduce the crime rate, they have to solve the big social problems; they have to deal with big causes. Indeed, this was what the New York Police Department and many criminologists said was done in the 1990s, when the crime rate in New York fell more than 60 per cent within a decade. Policing strategies improved noticeably, they claimed. The crack trade was stopped. Employment opportunities increased.

Such changes are certainly important in increasing the quality of life of a community – but only in the long run. As a matter of fact, New York's economy did not improve significantly between 1980 and 1990. Crack cocaine was an influential factor in the increase of crime rates, Gladwell reports, but it had already been in steady decline by the time the crime rate dipped. The reason why the crime rates declined in New York was more complicated. Big social factors could not account for why the rates did not fall so sharply in other cities that implemented the same social policies and why it took place in such a short time only in New York.

Error: a common tragedy in sciences 129

Gladwell argues that the 'broken window theory' of two criminologists, James Wilson and George Kelling, provides the best explanation. 'If a window is broken and left unrepaired', writes Gladwell,

> people walking by will conclude that no one cares and no one is in charge. Soon, more windows will be broken and the sense of anarchy will spread from the building to the street on which it faces, sending a signal that anything goes.
>
> (Ibid., 141)

This is an epidemic theory of crime, saying that crime is contagious and it can start with a broken window and spread to the whole community. Gladwell shows that the problem in New York was solved by way of changing specific and relatively small elements that served as tipping points. The authorities decided to remove all the graffiti in the subway system. This would show New Yorkers, authorities thought, that they were taking the problem seriously. The graffiti problem was considered the symbol of the collapse of the system. The authorities considered that at the heart of the problem lay the winning of the battle against graffiti on the trains. And, just as they thought, such minor changes had dramatic effects on how people behaved. Authorities fixed the broken windows, cleaned up the graffiti and removed any other signals in public places that would invite people to commit crime. The crime rate fell dramatically. After the tipping point people started to behave differently. The New York subway experiment showed, according to Gladwell, that it was 'possible to be a better person on a clean street or in a clean subway than in one littered with trash and graffiti' (ibid., 168).

Many errors in the history of human ideas are trivial or self-corrective. Such 'errors' do not always cause intellectual path dependence. Jevons, for instance, thought there was a connection between sunspots and business cycles, but it was soon corrected. 'The Earth [was] at rest', Ptolemy thought, 'it [was] in the centre of the Universe, and that fixed stars move[d] together as a sphere' (Field 1981, 349). His astronomy was wrong but it nevertheless worked well and helped navigators produce land and sea maps using measurement and observatory techniques. It was then corrected, too. Sungook Hong reports that Guglielmo Marconi's invention of the transmission of wireless signals across the Atlantic Ocean was based upon a small error. We now know that he was wrong (Hong 2005).

While some errors in history are harmless or even temporarily fruitful, others generate enduring paths of evolution. Many errors in history are either left uncorrected or their significant consequences linger on through time (although, occasionally, at decreasing scales). In such cases, we keep repeating the same errors. Uncorrected errors of the past sometimes generate disappointments about concrete situations in the future. Life then starts to get more complicated and more tragic. Kenneth Prewitt (2005) argues that there are many instances in the history of social science of 'truths' that have lasted for centuries without being touched upon. The example he gives is a 'mistake whose origin is to be found in the assumptions, preferences, and prejudices brought to the research question'

130 *The economic construction of sciences*

(ibid., 219). Samuel George Morton, a nineteenth-century anthropologist and zoologist, Prewitt reports, thought to have proved a hierarchy of races in which Caucasians were blessed with the most capacious array of skills and Negros, together with a number of aboriginal groups, with the smallest. Morton's categorization was used to formulate the 1850 census that was introduced to determine whether or not cross-race reproduction caused mentally defective offspring. Merton's 'race science' – as well as Herbert Spencer's survival-of-the-fittest argument – resulted in many unhappy stories in the USA and Europe in the twentieth and, even, twenty-first centuries. 'The social science mistake was an elementary one', writes Prewitt, '[a]s noted by Stephan Jay Gould, it was "the claim that worth can be assigned to individuals and groups by measuring intelligence as a single quantity" (Gould 1981)' (Prewitt 2005, 221).

Such examples suggest that some errors are significant but nevertheless temporary. That is, the consequences of errors sometimes fade away in time, causing less and less damage as time goes by. Some other errors, however, take more time for intellectuals to realize that they have basically been locked onto a pathway that was inaccurate. Such errors are reinforced by further errors and they linger on and on. The consequences are copied by themselves multiple times. On such occasions, errors are difficult to cope with. They generate significant intellectual *path*ologies in history.

Intellectual pathologies

'In all cases, error since the seventeenth century has been understood as a case of pathological belief, of credit extended recklessly or lazily or slavishly' (Daston 2005, 6). My question, likewise, is the following: are errors ignorable or are they among the factors that give rise to intellectual paths?

Path dependence, in general terms, is regarded as *blind* processes that do not consummate with a certain end point. In epidemiology, blindness is usually considered to be a pathological situation that causes a person to lack visual perceptions (see the WHO Fact Sheet No 282, November 2004). In fact, blind processes, from a philosophical point of view, can be considered pathological, too, in the sense that, in nature and society, they lead to path-dependent circumstances in which individuals practise their capability of error and capability to repeat it in the general course of events.

The manner in which the 'normal' and the 'pathological' are constructed in such disciplines as medicine, psychology and sociology is crucially important in uncovering the significance of historical small events and mechanisms related to the evolution (of ideas), consequences of which dominate various fields of intellectual life. Pathologies in the history of medicine and psychology often show us the central role of historical small events, usually in the form of errors and contradictions, in the making of social and economic institutions: initial conditions (errors), self-reinforcing themselves, often turn into bigger occurrences (pathologies). An error is considered to be any factor that generates formal flaws featuring hereditary interruptions and suspensions in social processes (Canguilhem 1966 [1978], 278).

Error: a common tragedy in sciences 131

Under such conditions, harm can be truly significant and radical. Errors transform into pathologies within the relation between the organism and its environment. An error is no longer defined as a simplistic phenomenon, taking place only once, with predictable results. Instead, it is considered to feature complexity in the sense that linear causal relations lead the system into non-linear states, generating substantial outcomes randomly.

The notion of pathologies, though, should not necessarily be imbued with a negative meaning or circumstance. The distinctive element in the notion of pathology is the positive feedback loops inherent in the evolutionary history of a specific epidemic. Intellectual paths in the institutional evolution of human ideas are pathologies in the sense that numerous self-reinforcing mechanisms magnify the effects of small causes in such a way that consequences of initial conditions are much greater for the intellectual community in the end. Whether the outcome is desirable or not is another issue.

The study of intellectual paths matters because these paths help us explain the mechanisms which disallow thinkers to diverge from pathologies in history. Had there been only a single path of modern civilization or intellectual advancement since thinkers started to ask questions about nature and society – that is, if the best-of-all-possible-worlds argument were true and we lived in such a world – we would have never been interested in the roles that small events have played in the course of history. There have been many. There have been numerous spatial and temporal paths in history, in which particularities and specificities played important roles in the course of events. Irregularities come about in such 'processes' in response to assorted variables in the direction indicated by the first push. Investigations into such pathologies require more effort than deriving abstract generalizations or doing 'blackboard science'.

Alchemy and fortune-telling are still alive and well in the minds of many people who read astrology magazines. We have long forgotten the business of witchcraft, but witchcraft remains (at least conceptually) in our daily lives. Charles Mackay's *Extraordinary Popular Delusions and the Madness of Crowds* (Mackay 1841 [1995]) focuses on manias, follies and delusions in human history. He covers such issues as 'The South-Sea Bubble', 'The Witch Mania' and 'The Slow Poisoners', about which he wrote in 1852:

> We find that whole communities suddenly fix their minds upon one object, and go mad in its pursuit; that millions of people become simultaneously impressed with one delusion, and run after it, till their attention is caught by some new folly more captivating than the first.
>
> (Ibid., xv)

Many are not aware of the stories of madness from the past, but we live by the consequences of idiocy, insanity and irony such as those that Mackay mentions in his book.

Matthijs van Boxsel (2004) provides numerous examples of ironies in history. He argues that stupidity is the foundation of our civilization. The best way to get rid of the terrible feeling after a stupid act, according to Boxsel, is to repeat it.

132   *The economic construction of sciences*

This turns stupidity into a joke and makes it funny. Thus, stupidity turns into a conscious act. It is institutionalized and has become a condition for intelligence.

Errors as historical small events

Historians have pointed out some events that have dramatically changed the course of happenings in exceptional ways. Such events tend to attract more attention nowadays than the 'iron laws of history' and mysterious 'forces behind the appearance regulating the economic behaviour in global markets'. Some events hardly fit the general picture drawn by historians and their consequences accumulate in a noticeably different fashion. They are *casual* events of history that have *causal* significance for today. Following the writings of Brian Arthur on complexity, increasing returns and path dependence (Arthur 1988, 1989, 1994), such events are now called 'historical small events'. According to (Arthur 1989, 118), historical small events are:

> those events or conditions that are outside the ex ante knowledge of the observer – beyond the resolving power of his 'model' or abstraction of the situation … [T]he small events … determine … the path of market shares; the process is non-ergodic or path dependent – it is determined by its small-event history.

There is a tendency in social sciences to analyze the evolution of human institutions as if the history of human civilizations were only a story of wars and social uprisings and profitability of a solution or some technique or invention in the market. According to this type of reasoning, 'big changes' come about only after 'big causes' (Landes 1994). The history of human civilizations, however, cannot be reduced solely to the consequences of such 'big events' of our past. Neither can it merely be a bunch of 'big' success stories. There are such occasions in history that a blind chance event unexpectedly gives rise to a remarkable success story or accidentally to an ultra-disappointing drama. Big consequences do not follow big causes at all times. The difference of magnitudes of significance among events often matters. Institutional path dependence principally addresses the condition in which consequences of some events should stand out as significant but their causes are still considered small. Historical small events do not necessarily provide the most accurate explanation about each and every social event, but only a retrospective understanding of smallness of some events in regard to the magnitude of their significance at the time they first appear.

There are countless occasions in history where 'big' events lead only to 'big' consequences (and 'small' only into 'small'). Under such circumstances, the difference of significance among subsequent events does not matter at all. In other words, every event is equally significant. Evolutionary analysis of path-dependent patterns, in which historical small events play significant roles, is an alternative to 'one-size-fits-all epistemology' (Tetlock and Belkin 1996, 16).

Error: a common tragedy in sciences   133

There is no uniform model or pattern of explanation that would account for how the outcomes have come into existence. Blackboard notions fail to function here.

Tangled pathways of intellectual history emerge as consequences of small, seemingly unimportant events of the past. There are scores of scholarly examples in which small events or objects are argued to have changed the course of history in dramatic ways. Lynn White argues in his *Medieval Technology and Social Change* (1962) that feudal nobles achieved their status during the Middle Ages by virtue of a small but sudden shift in the methods of warfare. Horses, although domesticated since 4000 BC, became a serious power on the battlefield only after the rider was equipped with a technological invention in the eighth century: stirrups. A stirrup was a little wooden or iron ring hung under the saddle to support the rider's foot, without which the seat of the rider on the horse was instable. Horses gifted the riders a great advantage of mobility over the footmen in the field long before the introduction of stirrups, but without stirrups the rider was limited in his methods of fighting: the spear was used with the strength of the shoulder muscles and there was always the risk of the rider finding himself on the ground after a powerful attack. After stirrups, the blow was delivered with the combination of muscles and charging horse. The mounted rider was thus much more stable and powerful.

William Rosen argues in his *Justinian's Flea: Plague, Empire, and the Birth of Europe* (2007) that in the transformation of the Mediterranean into medieval Europe and proto-nation states, a very little factor – a flea and a bacterium that it carried, *Yersina Pestis* – played the most significant role and gave rise to very big results in respect to its initial size. This bacterium brought about the plague that caused widespread death throughout Europe. Such transformations in history usually come about as a consequence of big events only, but, as Rosen shows, 'a moment in history' is sometimes sufficient to turn everything upside down at catastrophic speed.

Edward N. Lorenz, the author of *The Essence of Chaos* (1993), presented a paper at the 139th meeting of the American Association for the Advancement of Science in Washington DC in 1972 in which he showed how the 'flap of a butterfly's wings in Brazil [may] set off a tornado in Texas'. The paper was the very occasion in which the expression 'butterfly effect' appeared in the scientific literature for the first time. Butterfly effect, now a 'symbol of the small that can produce the great' (ibid., 15), highlights the fact that minuscule disturbances in weather conditions disallow us to accurately predict the occurrences in the atmosphere in distant futures.

Size matters – that is, the small is important. Although it is true, in the physical and anatomical sense, that cannon balls are bigger than stirrups, and fleas and butterflies are smaller than cows and horses, that is not the point. In fact, what matters here is not the actual size of the objects involved in the stories; rather, it is the specificity of seemingly less significant causes that gives rise to more significant consequences. What matters is the amplification process – not necessarily the objects themselves, such as stirrups or fleas or butterflies. The specificity of the occasion in which size matters is the relative relation between inputs and outputs where causes are amplified and give rise to big consequences.

134　*The economic construction of sciences*

Historical small events highlight a difference of size among events in terms of their significance in a specific occasion. It is no surprise for history students to hear that the amount of production is closely related to how efficient the inputs employed by industry are. And, therefore, it would not amaze them to read that the steam engine caused a tremendous increase in industrial production. For readers to understand the history of the Industrial Revolution it is necessary to see the 'causal connections' in the course of events. It is easy to do: the steam engine increased the amount of industrial product be*cause* machine tools were able to work with metal objects of great size at high speeds, which offered technical possibilities and commercial profits that workmen could not (Hicks 1969, 145–8). But, there are some events that make a big difference in an unexpected fashion.

The results of such events can be counterintuitive. They surprise the researcher, as multiplication of the consequences of neglected events is never expected. Small events can create a similar effect to the crises that cause 'paradigm shifts' in the Kuhnian sense (Kuhn 1970). James Gleick writes,

> In science as in life, it is well known that a chain of events can have a point of crisis that could magnify small changes. But chaos meant that such points were everywhere. They were pervasive. In systems like the weather, *sensitive dependence on initial conditions* was an inescapable consequence of the way small scales intertwined with large.
>
> (Gleick 1987, 23, italics added)

Friction, for instance, is a factor the effect of which is often neglected in physics – as well as in economics, for that matter, in the form of transaction costs where transaction costs are seen as market friction or 'frictional costs' (Jacobides and Winter 2003). But friction is something that depends on speed – and vice versa – and with friction and speed things can get complicated. Neglecting one small factor – that is, friction – an equation or a system can generate unforeseen or unexpected consequences. This can be why an economy does not reach an equilibrium. This can also be why we do not reach general equilibrium in the economy, and why the 'truth' cannot be established in philosophy.

We can compare the accumulation of the consequences of some small events to the way the probability of drawing the same-coloured balls in the so-called Polya-urn processes increases (Arthur 1985, Arthur *et al.* 1987). The process runs as follows: suppose there are initially equal numbers of red and black balls in an urn. We randomly draw a ball. Then we return the ball to the urn, with another ball of the same colour. That is, if the ball that we draw is red we return the red ball with another red one. If there were initially one red and one black ball in the urn, there would now be three balls in the urn – two reds and one black. We draw another ball. We repeat the game. The consequence of the process is that, as we make further draws, the probability of drawing the same-coloured ball increases. The process, in other words, is reinforced by the small event of drawing a red ball from the urn.

A possible objection for the role of small events in the evolution of social institutions is that they are not easily detectable. No event, after all, is small or

Error: a common tragedy in sciences 135

big. 'Small event', however, is only a name – just like path dependence is. And the adjective 'small' might metaphorically refer to many things in diverse contexts. This makes it difficult for us to produce a standard definition of the term – just as for path dependence. 'Small events', in the broadest sense, are the events, as demonstrated above, that are usually neglected, sometimes overlooked and erroneous or contingent. They, in most cases, are the causes of path dependence in the evolution of human institutions. They occasionally bewilder the researcher – and they do it in such a way that consequences are, in general, ironic and underachieving.

Behind the classification of events according to their size lies the following dictum: causes and consequences are not proportional. The sum of the parts of a system is often bigger than the whole. In other words, multiplications of the causes within a system do not exactly enable us to predict the behaviour of the system at all times. The reason for this is that the output of the system is fed back into the system. Interaction among causes amplifies the impact of each cause on each other cause.

The distinguishing property of disproportionateness is that it runs against Newton's Second Law. The law, $f = ma$, states that 'an object that is subject to a force responds by accelerating at a rate *proportional* to that force' (Bak 1996, 3). That is, what comes in the equation (force) is the equivalent of what goes out of it (velocity). Inputs and outputs are thus proportional. The case of historical small events implies the opposite of the law: when path dependence occurs, causes are smaller and consequences are bigger in the sense of *the magnitude of their significance* in the course of events. In order to help us better understand the semantics of the 'small event' and 'big event' taxonomy, let us elaborate on the matter via the matrix in Table 4.1.

According to the matrix, events in the course of natural and social evolution can be classified in two ways. First, *events* are the cause or the consequence of a happening. In other words, the unit of analysis is events, not objects or things, in nature and society. We are interested in the changes in a state of affairs (Hare and Madden 1975, 15). What matters for us here is how, for instance, silicon made it possible for the computer engineers to produce micro-chips and how this gave a

Table 4.1 Events and their sizes

		Events as causes	
		small	big
Events as consequences	**small**	(1)	(2)
	big	(4) path dependence	(3)

136 *The economic construction of sciences*

way to a revolution in the global economy. We are not interested in the tiny sili-con chips only. We pay primary attention to the *stories* attached to such objects and things. A story about the silicon micro-chip might take the following form: a micro-chip is an essential component of a computer. They enable engineers to produce highly complex machines like computers. By virtue of computers, economic agents are able to move their assets with a click of a mouse among numerous world markets. This generates complex patterns of asset flows on a global scale for the analysis of which scientists again use computers, etc.

The matrix tells us, second, that each event can be classified according to its size, either as small or as big. Events – that is, both causes and consequences – are therefore subject to a sub-classification which tells us that the role of some events does not sustain their significance at a constant pace, but amplifies with every follow-up event that feeds itself back into the process. The process grows, as a result, exponentially and its more accurate examination requires discrimination of the sizes of events that have causal impacts on future occurrences.

This provides us with the following scheme:

1. The cause and consequence of a happening can both be small.
2. The cause of a happening can be big but its consequence small.
3. The cause and consequence of a happening can both be big.
4. The cause of a happening can be small but its consequence big – that is, path dependence.

For simplification, let us use the following terminology in order to remark on the combinations of events in a period of time: let 'small *events*' and 'big *events*' mean, respectively, 'small events as *causes*' and 'big events as *causes*'. Likewise, let 'small *consequences*' and 'big *consequences*' mean, respectively, 'small events as *consequences*' and 'big events as *consequences*'.

The four possibilities mentioned above are the following:

1. *Small event–small consequence scheme*: In this scheme, causes and conse-quences are not relevant or important for the issue at stake. We can ignore them completely. An example of this might be the economic historian examining the conditions that gave rise to the Industrial Revolution in the eighteenth century, and assuming that the density of seawater in the North Sea was an important factor. In fact, no one has ever opened a debate about the significance of the density of seawater in the Industrial Revolution so far. To determine whether this played a role, we should ask the question 'How much?': how much of a role did seawater density play in the Industrial Revolution? Perhaps, the difference between the densities of the seawater in the North Sea and Mediterranean affected, in some hitherto unaccounted fashion, the way engineers built cargo ships and the wood was carried from Scandinavia to Great Britain. But, in order for this to be a scientific fact, it is necessary for the scientist to show quantita-tively how big the effect was. In other words, size matters for an event to be considered a cause.

Error: a common tragedy in sciences 137

Measurement, therefore, is certainly an issue. Deirdre McCloskey has long debated the issue in a number of different contexts. 'Oomph' is a term that she coined in order to imply the question of 'How much?', which she thinks economists have ignored in their work (McCloskey 1986, 1992; Ziliak and McCloskey 2004). She argues that there are such phenomena in our economic and social lives and that they do not really matter as the magnitude (and, therefore, significance) of their consequences is not very big. Economists have long been obsessed with finding out (or just making up) qualitative correlations among data that they could find (or generate) and completely put aside the true economic question: 'How much?' Such correlations that economists prove by way of numerous econometric tools – such as significance tests – do not prove whether the tested variables are economically significant. In economic life, in other words, some small events cause small consequences only, although there is a strong correlation between them. However, 'what matters is oomph', she writes (McCloskey 2003, 195),

> oomph is what we seek. A variable has oomph when its coefficient is large, its variance high and its character exogenous. A small coefficient on an endogenous variable that does not move around can be statistically significant, but it is not worth remembering.

Significance is about measurement. And we need empirical material to judge. We need the material not because we are necessarily willing to be empiricists in the British tradition of philosophical empiricism, but, rather, because having an understanding of the issue of size in the course of events is being a 'good empiricist' in the sense Paul Feyerabend (1968) used the term. This requires quantification and comparison of the phenomenon as well as openness to diverse theories about the (very same) observation – say, *how much* did the market transaction of hiring a foreigner cost a shipping firm in the 1780s and *how much* does it cost to an IT firm today? The 'method of reasoning in science is look-see', McCloskey argues (McCloskey and Ziliak 2001, 255). To put it differently, viewing the subject from within epistemology, 'capitalism is bad' or 'markets are efficient' do not constitute scholarly statements for those who are interested in the ways in which the evidence they possess transforms into something else. And neither are such statements sufficient for many evolutionary scientists because they would like to see the course of change, not merely the end product, which enhances (or in some cases decreases) the significance of the initial conditions helping the species survive in a specific environment or causing the water molecules to start a turbulent flow. Such an outlook is about measuring the steps or stages that give rise to the transformation of magnitudes.

2. *Big event–small consequence scheme*: The importance of 'oomph' reveals itself also when a big event results in a small consequence. Again, in big event–small consequence scheme, the consequence is too small to be relevant. But the difference from the previous case is that, this time, consequences are either counterintuitive or disappointing in the sense that the significance of the consequence

138   *The economic construction of sciences*

is smaller than expected. 'The Santa Barbara earthquake caused the collapse of numberless chimneys', is an example in the scheme of big event–small consequence (Ducasse 1993, 125). Or, as the Roman poet Horace (65–8 BC) wrote in his *Ars Poetica*: '*Parturient montes, nascetur ridiculus mus* – Mountains will be in labour and the birth will be a funny little mouse' (*Brewer's Dictionary of Phrase and Fable* 1987, 760). Mighty effort is made for a small effect, in other words. Likewise, the English idiom 'to make a mountain out of a molehill' is used in order to mean unnecessary stress on a small matter (*Oxford Dictionary of Phrase and Fable* 2000, 711). Nicholas Udall paraphrased Erasmus (1548–9) in the following lines: 'The sophicists of Greece would through their copiousness make an elephant of a fly and a mountain of a molehill' (*A Concise Dictionary of Phrase and Fable* 1993, 213). Such phrases are used precisely to imply the big event–small consequence scheme in natural and social history.

The phenomena of post-millennialism and Y2K can be considered big events that many expected to produce big consequences. But they produced only small ones. Millennialism was originally an apocalyptic story of Christian traditions (Gould 1997, 6). It implies a 'blessed end of time'. The religious and political implications of millennialism are present throughout history. As we approached the year 2000, the definition of millennium transformed into a calendrical meaning. People's concern was now the number 1,000. It turned into a 'number mysticism' (Gould 1993). Traditionalists started to think that 4,000 years must have elapsed between the creation of earth and the birth of Jesus; therefore, an apocalypse would take place in year 2000.

No such apocalypse came about, however. The argument was flawed; the promises and prophecies by the forerunners of post-millennialism, such as Jonathan Edwards, did not materialize. '[T]he classic argument for linking the apocalyptic and calendrical millennium may seem awfully weak and disappointing', writes Gould (1997, 45), 'for the junction requires a symbolic interpretation that will probably strike most of us today as fatuous and far-fetched'. If Satan had been bound for 1,000 years, as described by Saint John the Divine (Book of Revelation, Chapter 20), and Christ returned and brought back to life the Christian martyrs of the last 1,000 years, it would have resulted in the biggest consequence for humans ever – that is, a 'blessed end of time'.

'Calendrics' were not alone in claiming that the year 2000 would generate big consequences. Computer and network experts, too, warned the world that, by the end of the 1990s, a software problem that they called Y2K would cause turmoil in such critical industries as overseas flights, water and electricity monitoring, global finance and so forth, which could soon turn into a critical trigger that might cause a serious crisis worldwide. The problem was that engineers equipped computers with an internal digital clock which was able to show the time in six digits only. When 31 December 1999 (31.12.1999) turned to 1 January 2000 (01.01.2000) the digital clock in the computer would switch to 01.01.00, thinking that it was readjusted to show 1 January 1900 (01.01.1900). It did not take too long for the engineers and network experts to envisage that all of the computers (especially the old ones) should be checked. Thomas Friedman claims (2006, 126–36) that Y2K was

Error: a common tragedy in sciences   139

initially a very big thread for the world economy, as well as an important opportunity – especially for Indian computer engineers because India had educated a vast amount of well-qualified engineers who were certainly able to fix the problem cheaply. Indeed, Y2K soon caused the Indian computer industry to boom.

No significant failures for the world economy occurred, however. Neither was it an opportunity for the Indian economy as a whole. The problem was overstated.

3. *Big event–big consequence scheme*: This is one of the most widely used schemes in accounting for natural and social phenomena that has long been the dominant paradigm in classical science theory. In the big event–big consequence scheme, causes and consequences are proportional. The general characteristic of this scheme is the reversibility of outcomes and determinism of connections in the course of events. Knowing the circumstances of an object or event at a certain moment, one can identify the consequences that the object or event would lead to. The system is predictable. Phenomena, in this scheme, are those that we explain in deterministic terms; there is no place for historical small events. In the course of events, effects cancel each other out and, typically, errors are corrected sooner or later. No surprises occur. In the big event–big consequences scheme, events in nature and society are accounted for as if they were components of a smoothly running clock. Results are universal. Mechanisms identified in such courses of events are generalizable to other cases without respect to the specificities peculiar to each case. We usually classify wars, social uprisings, policy reforms etc. under the big event–big consequence scheme. In economics, constant returns to scale may be considered as an example.

Such systems are also called ergodic. Ergodic systems are those that 'come near almost every possible state over time but do so in a regular manner' (Jansen 1990, 99). Ergodic systems give rise to predictable consequences when the system is not sensitive to its initial conditions. Future states of an ergodic system are the same without regard to the states in which these systems started out. In statistics, when a system is ergodic, there is zero possibility for the system to be in any other state. The only factor that is necessary for this to happen is time. When there is a sufficient amount of time, the moving system will arrive at a unique stationary state ('ensemble average') whatever the initial states were. 'Stir a large pot of treacle in a vigorous way', writes John Barrow (1991, 48),

> and it will quickly settle down to the same placid state no matter how you stirred it. Drop a rock in air from a sufficiently great height and it will hit the ground at essentially the same speed no matter how hard you threw it initially because the competing effects of gravity accelerating the stone and air resistance slowing it down always act to create a situation where they have an equal and opposite effect, and thereafter the stone feels no net force at all and falls at constant speed.

4. *Small event–big consequence scheme*: Atoms in nature and individuals in society, however, do not quite work that way most of the time. In other words, some

140 *The economic construction of sciences*

of the initial conditions will never be damped down sufficiently and the system will remain sensitive to such conditions. Complexity of the system and numerous positive feedback mechanisms magnify the consequences of initial events exponentially. Each time, amplification of causes evolves the system from a given initial state to a 'far from equilibrium' *attractor*. An attractor is a rest point to which a system eventually settles down. The world is full of unpredictable consequences stemming from relatively small causes in earlier stages. Small-scale errors and uncertainties, under certain mechanisms, such as positive feedbacks, become larger and larger. There is no short-cut to predict the evolutionary future of the system. Henri Poincaré argued in 1903,

> A very small cause which escapes our notice determines a considerable effect that we cannot fail to see, and then we say that the effect is due to chance ... It may happen that small differences in the initial conditions produce an enormous error in the latter. Prediction becomes impossible, and we have the fortuitous phenomena.
>
> (Quoted by Crutchfield *et al.* 1990, 81)

The effects of historical small events multiply in unforeseen and unexpected ways – especially when neglected or overlooked in scientific experiments. Such events are sometimes the *errors* that researchers overlook. James D. Fearon (1996, 42) argues that the model known as 'cellular automaton' helps us best in understanding the behavioural pattern in which 'a little neglect breeds mischief'. A cellular automaton is a computer simulation first developed by John van Neumann and Stanislaw Ulam in the 1940s. It mimics a certain outcome of individual behaviour in nature and society. Suppose you have a chessboard on the screen of your computer, made up of a number of cells larger than 8×8, say, 100 x 100. Every cell has either of the two colours: black or red. In every successive period, cells of the board will change colour according to a simplistic algorithm. Let the algorithm be the following: red if two neighbouring cells are red, and black otherwise. When you run the simulation, colours of cells will change following the deterministic rule that is set *ex ante*. You may know the deterministic rule but it may be impossible to generate a formula that would tell you which colour pattern the entire chessboard will have in the end. Merely knowing the initial conditions, you would not be able to project the system's behaviour. It is essentially unpredictable. The only way to find out the pattern of the system is to run it numerous times and observe the varying outcomes each time.

The simulation shows that even deterministic behaviour in nature and society may generate highly chaotic and complex aggregate patterns. There is no long-run equilibrium in such models upon which the system converges. Instead, it follows stochastic pathways. Changing the colour of only one cell and re-running the simulation, you may have an unrecognizable outcome. And once the structures are formed, they may endure for longer periods until another factor is included to disintegrate the system.

The only way to understand how such a world would most likely work is to observe the system running and develop inferences about the regularities across

Error: a common tragedy in sciences 141

changing cases. Such regularities would tell you only how the behavioural pattern is in the short intervals. What if we had started with more blacks than reds? What if the number of blacks had been larger than the reds? No matter how perfect your knowledge of the changing patterns, it is not possible to have a general law-like statement telling you the long-run behaviour of the system every time you run it. Only knowing the simple deterministic regularity would not be sufficient to draw out the consequences of a particular antecedent at all times. The larger the system the more complex it is and the more likely it is that only short-term regularities are possible to predict. Deriving the systematic regulatory rule that would have told you the long-run state of the system is less and less likely.

⋅ The large comes out of the pathway in which early (small) events interact with and feed back upon each other. However, sensitivity to initial conditions does not, at all times, lead to big consequences. Initial conditions are also in operation when causes and consequences are proportional (i.e., causes and consequences are of the same size). In other words, even in the first or third scheme, initial conditions can be in operation. Consider chess. In principle, each move by both chess players is equally significant. In other words, the significance of every move is statistically equivalent. Every time a new game starts, however, players play a different game. The outcomes are different because possibilities are immense – practically infinite. The player builds a model and ignores some variables or is not able to calculate all the possibilities. The model is not a complete one but the player can win even if her model is not perfect – it only needs to *better* than her rival's. Start a new game and a new model will be built. Strategies, as well as the winners, will change every time at a high probability.

The reason for such outcomes is that certain mechanisms – such as positive feedbacks – become randomly effective in the routine course of events. Via such mechanisms, random outcomes follow only because initial conditions are altered. This is the principal difference between linear and non-linear systems: linear systems feature negative feedbacks which regulate the system and move it to equilibrium, whereas non-linear systems feature positive feedbacks which amplify the magnitude of certain causes and push the system far from equilibrium. When there are positive feedbacks within an equation, the terms of the equation generate disproportional impacts on other terms; terms are repeatedly multiplied by themselves (Briggs and Peat 1989, 24). When a microphone is located in front of a loudspeaker, the output from the microphone is fed back into the system as the microphone picks up the signal and sends it back to the loudspeaker. The same outcome comes about when we place a camera in front of a mirror. The mirror reflects the image on the screen into the camera which reflects it through the screen back onto the mirror. This goes *ad infinitum* and the same image is reproduced and magnified during the experiment.

Niall Ferguson's analysis (1999) has shown that the World War I was not inevitable and that it could have been avoided or it could have given rise to alternative outcomes if Britain had not appealed to France and Russia on imperial and later continental issues after 1905 or if Germany had been able to strengthen its security before 1914 or if Germany had been pushed to sign a peace agreement.

142   *The economic construction of sciences*

The reason for the war was a number of factors which were causally related to all others. Ferguson claims that the Anglo-German confrontation was one of the most over-determined events in modern times, which caused transformation of a continental conflict into a war. Britain thought that if it stood aside and allowed France to be crushed by Germany, Germany would have become the supreme power on the continent and Britain isolated. Such a thought was dominant in Britain and became even more powerful with the media influence over the public. Also, theatres and cinemas, as well as journals and newspapers of the time, propagated the view that all European states had imperial plans, so Britain should take immediate action. 'The combination of censorship and the spontaneous bellicosity of many newspapers tended to discourage arguments for compromise and to encourage demands of annexation and other war aims which only a complete victory could achieve', writes Ferguson (ibid., xli).

Another perspective on the way in which positive feedback loops generate turbulence at the macro level is developed by Ilya Prigogine and Isabelle Stengers (1984). According to Prigogine and Stengers, every system involves sub-systems that work independently from a regular principle. Occasionally, such sub-systems can be affected by a number of positive feedbacks which result in the destruction of the past states of the system. Prigogine and Stengers call the phenomenon 'bifurcation'. After bifurcation takes place, it is not certain in which direction the system will move. Microscopic changes under the influence of numerous positive feedbacks revolutionize the system at the macro level. The system stabilizes itself by virtue of exchanging energy with other factors in the environment. The entropy consumes the energy of the system and minimizes the differences among the systems. The new stabilized systems are called 'dissipative structures'. Although randomness, with the help of certain positive feedback mechanisms, causes such systems, dissipative structures, once occurred, are ruled by deterministic principles. The course of events after bifurcation evolves along the lines of predictable rules; however, it is not possible to predict when the next bifurcation will occur. A puzzling issue here is whether the presence of small events precludes the role of deterministic structures in the course of events. Neither thermodynamics nor the occurrence of dissipative structures, as is illustrated by Prigogine and Stengers as well as many others, is a story of random occurrences *alone*. Random events play an important role when positive feedbacks destabilize the macro states of a system by way of causing determinate consequences at micro levels to move in the same direction as their causes. Determinist structures fail to function in the predicted way at the very moment of the bifurcation, giving rise to unaccountable changes. This causes fluctuations in the system, but it eventually results in dissipative structures whereby the occurrence of indeterminate small events is less probable and determinate relations prevail.

After every bifurcation, the world is divided into numerous 'parallel universes', so to speak. In every universe, events take place either according to deterministic laws or according to random occurrences and mechanisms. Which game is selected, we never know unless we stop thinking and take one of the paths. In other words, exact prediction of the future values of the terms of a system is

Error: a common tragedy in sciences 143

theoretically and practically impossible. Contrary to what Albert Einstein claimed in the 1920s, God plays dice.

In fact, the real question is not even whether God plays dice or not. As Ian Stewart once put it, it is *how* she plays it (Stewart 1989, 1–3). Erwin Schrödinger illustrated the case with a thought experiment in a paper published in *Die Naturwissenschaften* in 1935 [1980]. He wanted us to think of a cat imprisoned in a steel chamber along with a tube full of hydrocyanic acid and a device which was programmed to detect the existence of radioactive substances in the chamber. Radioactive substances were released when atoms decayed and this did not follow a deterministic pattern. If the device detected the decayed atoms, it would trigger a hammer which would break the tube of hydrocyanic acid and kill the cat inside the chamber. The issue here is that one could not know whether an atom had decayed prior to observation and that the probability of the cat in the chamber to be alive is just 50 per cent. Schrödinger's example demonstrates that one cannot be sure of the outcome unless the observer opens the box and observes the case. The result cannot be predicted beyond statistical measures. The experiment tells us that macroscopic states of objects, such as a cat in a chamber, cannot have unique deterministic descriptions. Every system becomes either this or that only at the very moment that one observes the system. There is no 'truth' about possible states of a system unless observation takes place. 'It is typical of these cases', wrote Schrödinger,

> that an indeterminacy originally restricted to the atomic domain becomes transformed into macroscopic indeterminacy, which can then be resolved by direct observation. That prevents us from so naively accepting as valid a 'blurred model' for representing reality. In itself it would not embody anything unclear or contradictory. There is a difference between a shaky or out-of-focus photograph and a snapshot of clouds and fog banks.
>
> (Schrödinger 1935 [1980], 124)

The lesson to be drawn from Schrödinger's thought experiment is that an outcome does not exist without measurement. It does not really make any sense (at least scientifically) to prove any theorem on the blackboard only without observing or testing it with the facts of the world. A possibility could be claimed to be 'true', such as the claim that the cat in the chamber is 50 per cent alive and 50 per cent dead. But the claim is practically insignificant. We are not always able to predict the direction that the terms of an equation or the components of a system will move in before we run the equation or put the system in motion. The relations among terms and components are not always deterministic. Several mechanisms can send events off course at any time. Thus, small perturbations may result in large occurrences. What matters is the measurement of possible states of the system. We must observe how big the effect of each term is on others.

The issue here is that we do not know *ex ante* whether and when an event becomes dependent on a feedback mechanism which amplifies the magnitude of

144   *The economic construction of sciences*

the effect of a small event. To put it differently, knowing the initial conditions of a system does not mean we can predict the result. It is probable that a random occurrence might dominate the entire course of events. This does not rule out the deterministic relations after such an event happens. Whether the system will lead to this (deterministic) or that (random) result is only a matter of probability.

We should, of course, underline the fact that consequences of blind chance events are not always amplified so as to lead up to path dependence, although they may still cause the general course of events to diverge from its systematic course. A chance event can trigger a 'domino effect', for instance, in which, all of a sudden, an unexpected cause generates a remote consequence. A remote consequence does not necessarily mean that the outcome is bigger than its cause. A domino effect is a special circumstance in which a small event does not translate into a big consequence, but rather gives rise to further small changes in a linear fashion. It produces like changes in sequence and no difference among events is present in terms of the magnitude of their significance. Under such circumstances, the direction of the change can be blind but the changes do not need to be bigger than their antecedents. Instead, they are all lined up in such a way that the process is usually out of the experimenter's control or it is simply a sudden occurrence with a definite end point.

During the Cold War, international politics was influenced by a particular view. It was thought that communism would spread around the world, with states falling like dominoes. The analogy of falling dominoes was often employed to illustrate the, perhaps paranoid, ideas of proponents of this viewpoint. Most of us are familiar with the phenomenon of dominoes, stood on the narrow end and lined up in a close proximity to each other, which will, when the first is pushed towards the next, all fall in succession. Proponents of the 'domino theory' asserted that if the USA did not prevent a country from the influence of communist ideas, the tainted country would turn communist and influence all the countries neighbouring it, which would succumb as well to communist ideologies. Capitalism would then disintegrate and disappear from that region of the world. The principle was openly proclaimed by one of the presidents of the USA, Dwight David Eisenhower, in the 1950s. It was such a powerful idea at the time that it motivated the USA to intervene politically and militarily in Vietnam in the 1970s and to support anti-communist militias in the Middle East and Afghanistan in the 1980s and 1990s (Mamdani 2002, 52–7). It turned out, however, that the doctrine was incorrect because after China was revolutionized in 1949 many countries, such as Thailand, resisted the winds of change, even without US interference. In any case, it was an influential ideology that shaped international politics during one of the most critical moments in modern history.

Another example where difference is still involved, but blind chance events happen to produce big changes without giving way to path-dependent circumstances is the 'chain reaction' in chemistry and physics. Such systems are quite common and have inspired a number of innovative ideas in the sciences, such as nuclear reactors and atomic bombs (with unhappy consequences), since the 1930s. Chain reactions cause a system to diffuse the type of change that takes place in the very beginning of the process. Subsequent changes are reactive to the preceding ones, can be self-sustaining for a period and the process usually does not die out quickly. Such systems are sometimes even ergodic (not always though) in the sense that, without regard to the initial conditions, only one specific outcome is produced in the end. The process is usually under the control of the experimenter and the outcome is, as a rule, intended.

Historical small events, by way of amplifying mechanisms such as positive feedbacks, could cause the evolution to diverge from its systematic course. The primary property of such amplification processes is that initial conditions when the course of transformation of sizes commences are blind chance events in which no causation need be involved. That is, one may never know which butter-flies will flap their wings, when and for how long. Nor can one ever predict the ways in which a plague will hit a region or an invention take place and twist the direction of the historical pathways of societies. There could, however, be a plurality of self-reinforcing counteracting mechanisms that might move the system in the opposite direction.

The path-dependent evolution of natural and social events might be a conse-quence of the irregularities caused by the increasing entropy that comes about as a result of a working system. The entropy law states that the heat produced within a system moves the system away from equilibrium. This does not mean, however, that no further entropies will ever occur in the future states of the system so as to counteract and generate a tendency that would smooth out the irregularities in the course of events. Further and bigger entropies, under such conditions, could move the system back to equilibrium and thus, diminishing the significance of chaos, could cause a perfect equilibrium. To put it differently, the vicious circles caused by positive feedback loops are broken by other vicious circles caused by other positive feedback loops. 'This sounds like an attractive scenario', writes John Barrow (1991, 49),

> [t]he main problem is that the smoothing of irregularities is [only] one of those processes that is governed by the second law of thermodynamics. Irregularity in the expansion can only be reduced if this partial reduction in disorder (or 'entropy' as it is called) is paid for by an even larger production of entropy in another form.

In other words, it is certainly not true that small events subject to positive feed-back loops will necessarily cause big consequences or path dependence. It all depends on the specificity of the evolution of events – that is, the type of ampli-fication process – in which every single event is connected to each other in the most varied ways. Conditions and particularities in the environment matter at the same time.

The only way for a small event to be big, obviously, is amplification by virtue of which the significance of events simply grows – not all types of amplification have this effect, though. What we mean by amplification is the system of accu-mulation in which contiguous events feed back upon each other so as to increase the impact of earlier causes and lead to path dependence. In order to demonstrate

146 *The economic construction of sciences*

a case in which no feedbacks take place to give rise to non-linear outcomes, think of an amplifier converting the signals that a guitar or an electronic piano produces at a certain amount of energy into identical signals with higher energy. Such devices work in a linear fashion in that no feedbacks are permitted in the task that the device accomplishes. This is an ideal situation for the device to work within. Such amplification processes are predictable.

The ideality does not hold at all times, however, and feedbacks occasionally occur unintentionally. Under such conditions, the process can go off track and end up with unpredictable results. Signals are amplified in unlikely ways. This is when path-dependent circumstances are most likely to come about.

The logic of amplification, however, does not necessarily coincide with blindness or randomness either. Speaking in general terms, blind chance events need not always play the same roles in the course of history as those of small events. Consider gambling, for instance. While throwing dice or playing poker in a casino, the outcome is, after all, a blind chance event. The distinctive property of gambling is that the probability of having a number or drawing a card on the table is always constant. In other words, it is not possible to classify the coming of a double six or an ace as small or big. All possibilities are equal, causes are essentially equivalent and they can be foreseen (although at low levels of statistical probability). In the case of small events, the significance of the consequences of some events is disproportionately bigger than the significance of their causes. It is not possible at all times to tell *ex ante* which event is smaller or bigger, before we push the play button of the universe. They are historically conditioned – that is, consequences of some events become bigger in the long run, although their significance in the short run was smaller. Their size, in other words, changes only as time goes by and we recognize path dependence only *ex post*.

The differences that positive feedbacks engender are, by and large, irreversible (that is, time-dependent). The reason why the consequences of institutional evolution are mostly called irreversible has to do with an analogy between institutional history, thermodynamics and evolutionary biology. The point here is that we cannot easily subtract the accumulated effect of a factor from its evolutionary past because, under such conditions, consequences of certain events do not add up; they multiply. In order to contrast this case with the one in which causes only add up, consider the following example. *The Economist* (9–15 June 2007) reported in a short article, entitled 'It All Adds Up', that every summer, millions of small engines mow the lawns, whack its weeds and trim its borders in the USA. Each engine produces little smoke, but using a chainsaw for two hours adds up to an amount of pollution equal to what would be produced when ten cars drive 400 km. The carbon dioxide emissions, escaping fuel vapours and leaking oil make them dirty machines for their size. Although operated only for short periods, lawn mowing contributes a lot of pollution, which the federal government now is planning to take action against.

Such problems of policy-making are simplistic in the sense that 'unnecessary contingencies' in the way the problem is stated ('it all adds up') are shaved away. Simple problems satisfy the conditions of 'Ockham's Razor' – a statement by a fourteenth-century English logician William of Ockham, who claimed that 'entities

Error: a common tragedy in sciences   147

should not be multiplied beyond necessity'. Klaus Mainzer (1996, 185) reports that 'Ockham's razor from philosophy demands that we cut away superfluous hypotheses, remain economical with the postulation of metaphysical entities, and restrict hypotheses to the minimal number that seems indispensable for empirical research'.

Problems of policy-making, as well as academic scholarship, are often complex, however. While the consequences that the adding up of causes leads to might be smoothed out if necessary precautions are taken in time, consequences that are generated by way of multiplication of a number of causes are not always eliminable. Such phenomena are irreversible. We call, for instance, a chemical reaction in chemistry and an evolutionary pathway of a species in biology irreversible when the system cannot return to its initial condition once the chemical reaction or evolution starts. A system is irreversible when it loses memory of its past conditions at the very start. Chemical systems are irreducibly irreversible because the heat that comes out as a consequence of a chemical reaction can never be recovered again in the subsequent stages. Such a 'loss' is an inevitable outcome of every chemical reaction (Prigogine and Stengers 1984, 75–7). Likewise, in evolutionary biology, Stephan Jay Gould argues, a particular historical item or organism – such as dinosaurs – cannot be recovered. 'If all information about a historical event has been lost', writes Gould,

> then it just isn't there anymore and the event cannot be reconstructed. We are not lacking a technology to see something that actually exists; rather, we have lost all information about the thing itself, and no technology can recover an item from the void.
>
> (Gould 1993, 52)

Initial conditions and numerous small events by virtue of a number of spatio-temporal mechanisms give rise to irreversible consequences; they reinforce the influence of their own causes upon future happenings. Once they happen, they never un-happen again (David 2001). Therefore, the systematics of the general course of natural and social events is threatened by historical small events at all times. But this does not guarantee that every similar coincidence will end up with path-dependent circumstances. Consequences of small events can be small as well as big. Moreover, small events are not always what one should be looking for in order to account for the occurrences in which outcomes are sufficiently big to surprise the observer because big events often generate big consequences. 'Smallness' and 'significance' are not opposite terms. 'Small' does not always mean uninteresting or weak or superficial or ignorable. 'There is very little difference between one man and another', claimed William James (1992, 648), 'but what little there is, is very important'.

References

A Concise Dictionary of Phrase and Fable. 1993. Lincolnwood, Chicago: NTC.
Arthur, W. Brian. 1985. 'Strong Laws for a Class of Path Dependent Urn Processes'. *Proceedings of the Conference on Stochastic Optimization*: 287–300.

148 *The economic construction of sciences*

Arthur, W. Brian. 1988. 'Self-reinforcing Mechanisms in Economics'. In *The Economy as an Evolving Complex System*, edited by Philip W. Anderson, Kenneth J. Arrow and David Pines, 111–32. Massachusetts: Addison Wesley.

Arthur, W. Brian. 1989. 'Competing Technologies, Increasing Returns and Lock-in by Historical Events'. *The Economic Journal* 99 (394): 116–31.

Arthur, W. Brian. 1994. *Increasing Returns and Path Dependence in the Economy*. Ann Arbor: University of Michigan Press.

Arthur, W. Brian, Yu. M. Ermoliev and Yu. M. Kaniovski. 1987. 'Non-linear Urn Processes: Asymptotic Behavior and Applications'. *IIASA Working Paper No. 87-85*.

Bak, Per. 1996. *How Nature Works: The Science of Self-Organized Criticality*. New York: Copernicus.

Barrow, John D. 1991. *Theories of Everything: The Quest for Ultimate Explanation*. Oxford: Oxford University Press.

Boxsel, Matthijs van. 2004. *Encyclopedia of Stupidity*. London: Reaktion.

Brewer's Dictionary of Phrase and Fable. 1987. London: Cassell.

Briggs, John, and F. David Peat. 1989. *Turbulent Mirror: An Illustrated Guide to Chaos Theory and the Science of Wholeness*. New York: Harper & Row.

Canguilhem, Georges. 1966 [1978]. *On the Normal and the Pathological*. Dordrecht and Boston: D. Reidel.

Cartwright, Samuel. 1851. 'Diseases and Peculiarities of the Negro Race'. *De Bow's Review, Southern and Western States* 11. Available at: http://www.pbs.org/wgbh/aia/part4/4h3106t.html. Accessed December 2015.

Crutchfield, J. P., J. D. Farmer, N. H. Packard and R. S Shaw. 1990. 'Chaos'. In *Chaos II*, edited by Hao Bai-Lin. Singapore: World Scientific.

Daston, Lorraine. 2005. 'Scientific Error and the Ethos of Belief'. *Social Research* 72 (1): 1–28.

David, Paul A. 2001. 'Path Dependence, Its Critics and the Quest of "Historical Economics"'. In *Evolution and Path Dependence in Economic Ideas*, edited by Pierre Garrouste and Stavros Ioannides, 15–40. Cheltenham: Edward Elgar.

Ducasse, Curt. 1993. 'On the Nature of Observability of the Causal Relation'. In *Causation*, edited by Ernest Sosa and Michael Tooley, 125–36. Oxford: Oxford University Press.

Fearon, James D. 1996. 'Causes and Counterfactuals in Social Science: Exploring an Analogy between Cellular Automata and Historical Process'. In *Counterfactual Thought Experiments in World Politics: Logical, Methodological, and Psychological Perspectives*, edited by Philip E. Tetlock and Aaron Belkin, 39–68. Princeton, NJ: Princeton University Press.

Ferguson, Niall. 1999. *The Pity of War: Explaining World War I*. New York: Basic Books.

Feyerabend, Paul. 1968. 'How to Be a Good Empiricist: A Plea for Tolerance in Matters Epistemological'. In *The Philosophy of Science*, edited by P. H. Nidditch, 12–39. Oxford: Oxford University Press.

Field, J. V. 1981. 'Ptolemaic Astronomy'. In *Dictionary of the History of Science* edited by W. F. Bynum, E. J. Browne and Roy Porter. Princeton, NJ: Princeton University Press.

Friedman, Thomas. 2006. *The World is Flat*. New York: Farrar, Strauss and Giroux.

Gigerenzer, Gerd. 2005. 'I Think, Therefore I Err'. *Social Research* 72 (1): 1–24.

Gladwell, Malcolm. 2000. *The Tipping Point: How Little Things Can Make a Big Difference*. Boston: Little, Brown.

Gleick, James. 1987. *Chaos: Making a New Science*. New York: Viking.

Error: a common tragedy in sciences 149

Gould, Stephen Jay. 1981. *The Mismeasure of Man*. New York: W. W. Norton Co.

Gould, Stephen Jay. 1993. 'Dinomania'. *New York Review of Books* 40 (14): 51–6.

Gould, Stephen Jay. 1997. *Questioning the Millennium*. New York: Harmony.

Hare, Peter H., and Edward H. Madden. 1975. *Causing, Perceiving, and Believing: An Examination of the Philosophy of C. J. Ducasse*. Dordrecht and Boston: D. Reidel.

Hicks, John. 1969. *A Theory of Economic History*. Oxford: Clarendon Press.

Hong, Sungook. 2005. 'Marconi's Error: The First Transatlantic Wireless Telegraphy in 1901'. *Social Research* 72 (1): 1–18.

Jacobides, Michael G., and Sidney G. Winter. 2003. 'Capabilities, Transaction Costs and Evolution: Understanding the Institutional Structure of Production'. *Working Paper of the Reginald H. Jones Center WP 2003–04*. The Wharton School, University of Pennsylvania.

James, William. 1992. *Writings 1878–1899*. Cambridge, MA: Harvard University Press.

Jansen, R. 1990. 'Classical Chaos'. In *Chaos II*, edited by Hao Bai-Lin. Singapore: World Scientific.

Kuhn, Thomas S. 1970. *The Structure of Scientific Revolutions*. Chicago: University of Chicago Press.

Landes, David S. 1994. 'What Room for Accident in History?: Explaining Big Changes by Small Events'. *The Economic History Review* 47 (4): 637–56.

Lorenz, Edward N. 1993. *The Essence of Chaos*. Seattle: University of Washington Press.

Mackay, Charles. 1841 [1995]. *Popular Delusions and the Madness of Crowds*. London: Three Rivers Press.

Mainzer, Klaus. 1996. *Thinking in Complexity: The Complex Dynamics of Matter, Mind, and Mankind*. Berlin and New York: Springer.

Mamdani, Mahmood. 2002. 'Good Muslim, Bad Muslim: A Political Perspective on Culture and Terrorism'. In *Critical Views of September 11: Analyses from Around the World*, edited by Eric Hershberg and Kevin W. Moore, 44–60. New York: New Publisher.

McCloskey, Deirdre N. 1986. 'Why Economic Historians Should Stop Relying on Statistical Tests of Significance and Lead Economists and Historians into the Promised Land'. *Newsletter of the Cliometrics Society* 2 (2): 5–8.

McCloskey, Deirdre N. 1992. 'Other Things Equal: The Bankruptcy of Statistical Significance'. *Eastern Economic Journal* 18 (3): 359–61.

McCloskey, Deirdre N. 2003. *How to Be Human – Though an Economist*. Ann Arbor: University of Michigan Press.

McCloskey, Deirdre N., and Stephen Thomas Ziliak. 2001. *Measurement and Meaning in Economics: The Essential Deirdre McCloskey*. Cheltenham: Edward Elgar.

Myrdal, Gunnar. 1944. *An American Dilemma: The Negro Problem and Modern Democracy*. New York: Harper.

Oldridge, Darren. 2005. *Strange Histories: The Trial of the Pig, the Walking Dead, and Other Matters of Fact from the Medieval and Renaissance Worlds*. London and New York: Routledge.

Oxford Dictionary of Phrase and Fable. 2000. Oxford: Oxford University Press.

Prewitt, Kenneth. 2005. 'The Two Projects of the American Social Sciences'. *Social Research* 72 (1): 219–36.

Prigogine, Ilya, and Isabelle Stengers. 1984. *Order Out of Chaos: Man's New Dialogue with Nature*. 1st edn. Boulder, CO: New Science Library.

Reznek, Lawrie. 1987. *The Nature of Disease*. London and New York: Routledge & Kegan Paul.

150   *The economic construction of sciences*

Rosen, William. 2007. *Justinian's Flea: Plague, Empire, and the Birth of Europe*. New York: Viking.

Rush, Benjamin. 1823. *An Inquiry into the Effects of Ardent Spirits upon the Human Body and Mind*. Boston: James Loring.

Schrödinger, Erwin. 1935 [1980]. 'The Present Situation in Quantum Mechanics: A Translation of Schrödinger's "Cat Paradox" Paper (Translator: John D. Trimmer)'. *Proceedings of the American Philosophical Society* 124: 323–38.

Stewart, Ian. 1989. *Does God Play Dice?* New York: Basic Blackwell.

Tetlock, Philip E., and Aaron Belkin. 1996. *Counterfactual Thought Experiments in World Politics: Logical, Methodological, and Psychological Perspectives*. Princeton, NJ: Princeton University Press.

Veblen, Thorstein. 1898. 'Why Economics is not an Evolutionary Science'. *Quarterly Journal of Economics* 12 (4): 373–94.

Veblen, Thorstein. 1919. *The Place of Science in Modern Civilisation and Other Essays*. New York: B.W. Huebsch.

White, Lynn Townsend. 1962. *Medieval Technology and Social Change*. Oxford: Clarendon Press.

Ziliak, Stephen Thomas, and Deirdre N. McCloskey. 2004. 'Significance Redux'. *Journal of Socio-Economics* 33 (5): 665–75.

Part III
Concluding remarks

5 Economics as part of a system of research ethics

I agree with K. William Kapp (1949 [1963], 3) who sees 'economics as part of a system of applied ethics'. The issue here is whether self-interested scholars can increase the intellectual welfare of the scholarly community if they are utility maximizers only. Absent a system of ethics, I argue, intellectual welfare cannot be continuously increased. If concerns about the harmful consequences of erroneous theories remain external to scholarship, issues about the morality of research remain external as well. Economists, like other social and natural scientists, should take into account the negative 'externalities' of QRPs.

I also agree with Imre Lakatos (1970, 122) that 'sophisticated methodological falsificationism' gives scholars the opportunity to behave according to particular 'standards for intellectual honesty'. New research programmes lead to 'progressive problemshifts' and such 'problemshifts' require scholars to accept the theories that are proven and to reject the theories that are falsified and unfalsifiable. However, as I hope I have shown in the preceding chapters, there are such scholarly processes that errors are continuously reproduced; even 'sophisticated falsificationists' do *not* replace the theories refuted by the facts of the world. Lakatos does not clearly explain such processes, writing:

> Sophisticated methodological falsificationism offers new standards for intellectual honesty. Justificationist honesty demanded the acceptance of only what was proven and the rejection of everything unproven. Neojustificationist honesty demanded the specification of the probability of any hypothesis in the light of the available empirical evidence. The honesty of naive falsificationism demanded the testing of the falsifiable and the rejection of the unfalsifiable and the falsified. Finally, the honesty of sohisticated falsificationism demanded that one should try to look at things from different points of view, to put forward new theories which anticipate novel facts, and to reject theories which have been superseded by more powerful ones.
>
> (Ibid.)

Economics should be part of a system of ethics. Reason without an understanding of morality can lock intellectual systems into pathways where the intellectual welfare of a scholarly community cannot be increased unless the consequences of QRPs are fully corrected. In other words, reason does not always cause

154 *Concluding remarks*

knowledge and meaning to continuously accumulate. Had reason been the sole source of intellectual evolution, types of knowledge belonging to different spheres of life could have easily been united into a homogenized body of knowledge. In fact, rational construction of sciences has long been desired by philosophers – from Plato to Hegel. However, a homogenized body of knowledge has merely been a phantasm that is not attainable, an ideality that is observable in Hollywood movies only.

Indeed, popular culture has exploited this idea of rationalistic construction of sciences to the limit. How? Libraries, for instance, are often thought of as inventories where knowledge is homogeneously and rationally deposited. If an individual needs the most sophisticated explanations on a particular subject, she only needs to spend a sufficient amount of time on the internet or reading a few publications in a nearby library where books are very well catalogued. For instance, in *The Ninth Gate* (1999, Roman Polanski), Dean Corso (Johnny Depp), a book dealer searching for the 'truth' about a rare book written in the seventeenth century, visits a library in New York to learn more about the book. In the first book that Corso picks from one of the first shelves of one of the first halls in the library, he runs into a match and thinks he finds what he is looking for. In *Seven* (1995, David Fincher), Detective William Somerset (Morgan Stanley), spending a few hours in a public library in Los Angeles, discovers that the serial killer, John Doe (Kevin Spacey), whom Somerset and his partner David Mills (Brad Pitt) have been chasing, has been motivated by Dante's *The Divine Comedy*. In such movies, and numerous other works of popular art, such as *Star Wars Episode II: The Attack of the Clones* (2002) and *Ghostbusters* (1984), knowledge is stored, catalogued and presented to the general public in such a way that individuals, those interested in science, who are curious about the details of a subject, can easily gain access to the most developed version of knowledge about virtually any subject. Individuals can reach reliable conclusions about the problem at issue. Puzzles can thus be solved. Secrets are revealed. Is this really how sciences work?

In actuality, science often does not work like that. Scientific knowledge is *not* rationally constructed. Imperfections are not always cleared out. Puzzles are not fully resolved. Some errors remain uncorrected. The question, then, is how should scientists deal with the processes where such inconsistencies, anomalies and irregularities are not automatically eliminated?

Philosophers have long elaborated on irregularities caused by erroneousness in academic scholarship. According to Friedrich Hegel, the history (of philosophy) progressed from contradiction to logic through dialectics. 'Dialectical philosophy', Terry Pinkard argues (1988, 19), 'explains the possibility of apparently incompatible categorical beliefs by trying to show that the apparent incompatibility is only apparent, that the contradiction is avoided once one expands one's framework of discourse in the appropriate way'. History is self-determined to true knowledge. It runs through negativity: a proposition ('thesis') is negated (that is, passed over into its opposite) by another proposition ('anti-thesis') that is dialectically in contradiction with the former proposition and transforms into a new beginning ('synthesis') which, in turn, is the proposition of a new generation

Economics as part of a system of research ethics   155

of dialectical discourse. 'What propels the dialectic is the emergence of new contradictions in the explanation that avoided the old ones, and the dialectic continues until no more contradictions emerge' (ibid.). This general 'process of change' was the pathway from 'abstract' to 'concrete', from 'possibility' to 'actuality', from 'falsehood' to 'truth'. Upon the path, contradictions and confusions were all negated, one after another. Accidents and contingencies were not part of the big story. The 'process' featured necessity. It was completely teleological.

> The only requisite for the acquisition of the Scientific progression – and the very simple insight into this is what essentially concerns us – is the cognition of the logical proposition that the negative is equally positive, or that that which contradicts itself does not dissolve into Zero [*Null*] but essentially only into the negation of its particular content, or that such a negation is not all negation but the negation of the determinate subject-matter [*Sache*] which dissolves and is thus determinate negation, so that that from which it results is essentially contained in the result – which actually is a tautology, for otherwise it would be something immediate and not a result.
>
> (Hegel 1812 [2010], quoted by, Rosen 1982, 31)

A difficulty here is that we do not know – or, at least, we cannot show it with concrete evidence – if there is in nature such a principle, or *Geist*, that negates errors, partially or wholly, in such ways that the history (of philosophy) becomes error-free. In contrast to Hegelian dialectics, the theory of intellectual path dependence holds that we may not get rid of imperfections in the form of errors in either the short or long term. It is likely that we have to live by the consequences of past errors for long periods of time. In other words, an 'anti-thesis' may never replace a 'thesis' and an 'anti-thesis' may never lead to a 'synthesis'. Most of the 'theses' either survive the intellectual challenges, such as philosophers' efforts to negate the arguments of their opponents, or they co-evolve with their 'anti-theses', spontaneously giving rise to parallel truths. In both cases, contradictions do not go extinct. Despite philosophers' will and effort to replace refuted theorems, the history (of philosophy) is not always exempt from erroneous claims that exist even though they are invalidated by evidence and counter-argumentation. Hypothetically, 'syntheses' may even evolve into their own 'theses', although 'theses' are shown to be negated by their 'anti-theses'. However, due to the irreversibility of the consequences of some errors in intellectual history, many of which I reported in the opening part of this book, false propositions are not always replaceable with true or truer propositions. Scholars do not change their minds, even when counter-propositions are available to the members of the community of scholars. Scholars keep behaving according to negated beliefs. Such beliefs are ideologies, or *false consciousness*, a useful phrase that Friedrich Engels used – unfortunately, only once, in a private letter to Franz Mehring (Engels 1893 [2004]). As Engels also claims, scholars are almost never able to refrain from false consciousness and false consciousness is a reason why errors remain uncorrected.

156   *Concluding remarks*

Karl Popper's view on critical rationalism is also based on the understanding that errors are an essential part of scientific research. According to Popper, there is no way to avoid errors in the explanation of the unknown. But science is, nevertheless, capable of correcting them. In order for this to happen, scientific knowledge should be able to be falsified by further evidence and testing. Scientific activity is based on 'negative argument' – that is, criticism and propositions that put things right (or closer to the truth). If a proposition is not criticizable (i.e. falsifiable), it is not scientific. By way of criticism, more errors in the scientific discourse can be singled out and we can move on to new theories that feature more truth-value. What matters is the cure – not the prevention of error (Popper 1984, 9–14). According to Popper, critical rationalism is the only way for science to grow. Verification cannot be the way of attaining the 'truth' because it does not have a critical rationalist basis and it is flawed with the problem of induction: no matter how many times one observes an event, one cannot provide any proof as to whether the same happening would take place next time. By way of falsification, Popper argues – that is, choosing theories that have higher empirical content or verisimilitude – one could 'move forward' as false theories are thus eliminated from the intellectual sphere. The 'truth' is an endless enquiry, requiring a critical rationalist view on new theories. Popper (1972 [1979], 286) claims:

> [W]e, too, are not only producers but consumers of theories; and we have to consume other people's theories, and sometimes perhaps our own, if we are to go on producing.
>
> 'To consume' means here, first of all, 'to digest,' as in the case of the bees. But it means more: our consumption of theories, whether those produced by other people or by ourselves, also means criticising them, changing them, and often even demolishing them, in order to replace them by better ones.
>
> All these are operations which are necessary for the growth of our knowledge; and I again mean here, of course, knowledge in the objective sense.

Popper claims that processes of theory consumption in which we criticize theories in order to eliminate errors and replace them with better theories are continuous processes where old problems (P_1) lead to new problems (P_{1+n}). Progress or growth of knowledge is the 'distance and expectedness' between (P_1) and (P_{1+n}); this is 'a competitive struggle which eliminates those hypotheses which are unfit' (Popper 1972 [1979], 261). Criticism and elimination of unfit explanations will thus get scientific claims nearer to the 'truth'.

Despite Popper's powerful evolutionary rhetoric to solve the problem of demarcation between science and pseudo-science, I do not think that his critical rationalism resembles a Gouldian programme, as outlined in the previous part. Falsifying evidence is sometimes not enough for errors and their consequences to disappear. For instance, multiple errors may lead to a condition in which consequences of errors counteract each other and errors may cease to have further consequence (or any cause). In this case, processes of trial and error would increase the number of errors, instead of eliminating errors. But errors, when they

Economics as part of a system of research ethics 157

are over-determined, do not produce any effect; in a sense, they become invisible. As Roy Bhaskar (1975) remarks, *absences are real.* My interpretation of Bhaskar's claim is that just because an event does not take place in actuality does not mean that causes of a particular event are non-existent. On the contrary, there may be multiple causes and multiple causes may nullify each effect and neutralize the overall result; errors have ontological status although they may not be observed in actual terms – that is, errors keep having causal powers but consequences do not materialize. One may not experience multiple errors in one particular case but the total effect of singular errors may be devastating. This does not mean that errors are corrected; it only means the simplistic relationship between errors and corrections no longer exist. In such conditions, falsification is not a sufficiently complex conceptual tool to account for the significance of errors in intellectual history. In Chapter 4, entitled 'Error: a common tragedy in sciences', I reported examples suggesting that more errors cause better results than more corrections. Such accounts, which should be seen as alternatives to Hegelian negation and Popperian falsification, cannot, perhaps, explain why two errors do not make one right, but they can explain how two or more than two errors can counter-impact on each other, so that the expected consequences, which would have emerged if errors had not counter-impacted on other errors, do not materialize.

Imre Lakatos argues, too, that there is a rational basis for progression in science. Research programmes, according to Lakatos, are progressive if and when a new theorem is an attempt to discover novel facts and provide more precise predictions about novel facts. Growth of knowledge is not necessarily a matter of accepting or refuting single theorems according to a scientific criterion. In other words, the Popperian problem of demarcation – distinguishing science from pseudo-science – is not the only problem. (It is not even an important one.) What matters is an assessment of research programmes in which a scientific community operates with a number of very general hypotheses – 'hard core' – in terms of their ability to provide explanations about new facts. The key issue here is that new theorems must help develop new experimental techniques and provide insights about new facts. In a progressive research programme, theorems do not need to pass the test of falsification (or comply with any other abstract rule). Neither do theorems need to displace another theorem. The problem is to lessen the amount (or significance) of inconsistent observations that newly accepted theorems point at. In the Popperian methodology, inconsistencies would end up with the abandoning of the theorem. In the Lakatosian methodology, abandoning a research programme is not necessarily the only option for a forward-looking scientist who is confronted with theoretical challenges that come about as a result of the observance of new facts. Actually, it is a moral duty for scientists to face negative 'crucial experiments'. Solving the problems that crucial experiments give rise to, scientists are more able to achieve 'problem shifts', which eventually results in cumulative progress of knowledge. When negative experiments lead to more inconsistencies – or what Thomas Kuhn once called 'anomalies' – 'positive heuristic' helps scientists to overcome these difficulties. Positive heuristic

158   *Concluding remarks*

consists of the principles instructing scientists as to the path to follow in order to get them 'closer to the truth'. Lakatos (1970, 173) describes the requirement for 'continuous growth' in science:

> There are no such things as crucial experiments, at least not if these are meant to be experiments which can instantly overthrow a research programme. In fact, when one research programme suffers defeat and is superseded by another one, we may – with long hindsight – call an experiment crucial if it turns out to have provided a spectacular corroborating instance for the victorious programme and the failure for the defeated one ... if a scientist in the 'defeated' camp puts forward a few years later a scientific explanation of the allegedly 'crucial experiment' within (or consistent with) the allegedly defeated programme, the honorific title may be withdrawn and the crucial experiment may turn from a defeat into a new victory for the programme.

To put it simply, Hegel, Popper and Lakatos presupposed that big systematic forces of history, such as dialectics, critical rationalism and sophisticated methodological falsificationism, would eventually dominate the course of natural and social events in such a way that the consequences of historical small events, usually in the form of small errors and contradictions in analysis, giving rise to intellectual path dependence, would cancel out the effects of each other. Historical small events existed, according to Hegel, Popper and Lakatos, but their role was only temporary and such events could not have long-lasting causal influences. At best, they could be side effects which would be cancelled out one way or the other over the course of time.

In my view, one of the main reasons why intellectuals are held dependent on several evolutionary pathways is that intellectuals develop *habits of thought* according to which they think, behave and act. Think about it. Many of us like reading newspapers on Sunday mornings. We use words from a specific, limited vocabulary of pet names to address our lovers. And, historians of ideas use specific sets of metaphors to explain the evolution of the phenomenon that they are interested in. Certainly, historians' use of specific sets of metaphors is not necessarily because they do not know any others. It is rather because they are *used to* doing science with those words. A good reader of Nietzsche would immediately guess which texts might belong to him because Nietzsche chose a specific set of words to explain philosophy. It is the same in the music of the Beatles and the paintings of Johannes Vermeer. But an intellectual path *independency* worldview suggests that we are not really entitled to begin talking about intellectual and practical problems in the terms that we are accustomed to, especially when we are more knowledgeable than past generations about the shortcomings and imperfections of the constructions that we continue to make. We do not need *one* theory of economics providing us with solutions to *all* the worldly problems of human societies that have existed in history and all around the globe. There should be no presumption that corrections in the history of economics will cure all the imperfections in and of the past (thus irreversibility). In other words,

Economics as part of a system of research ethics   159

markets often fail to fully reverse the consequences of errors for a complex set of reasons. We should underline the fact that errors *and* corrections, considered together, are two of the non-eliminable constituents of the evolutionary history of scholarly institutions. The relationship between the two is complex: they interact upon each other, they co-evolve and they generate irreversible and unpredictable outcomes.

So why?

It is not only economists who are reluctant to change their minds in the face of refuting argumentation and data. I hope I have been able to show that the argument of the book holds true for other branches of social and natural sciences as well. Although it is not an easy task for me to comment on the specifics of scientific misconduct in fields other than economics, I can, perhaps, include a section in which I propose a generalized claim about one of the consequences of the existence of errors in sciences, humanities and the arts. My question in the final section of this book is the following: why are intellectuals *willingly* dependent on pathways which emerged ahead of them? To put it differently, is it only economic pressures that force scholars to lock into certain pathways of thought or is it also connected to scholars' reluctance to un-follow the footsteps of their predecessors? This query does not reduce the significance of the role of economics in the processes of scientific knowledge production. My aim is to open up further space for a specific topic for further research which I believe has been missing in discussions on evolutionary epistemology of sciences. And this research topic is *creativity*.

'What then', Etienne de la Boétie in his 1548 essay, *The Politics of Obedience: The Discourse on Voluntary Servitude* (1548 [1975], 44–5), asked,

> if in order to have liberty nothing more is needed than to long for it, *if only a simple act of the will is necessary*, is there any nation in the world that considers a single wish too high a price to pay in order to recover rights which it ought to be ready to redeem at the cost of its blood, rights such that their loss must bring all men of honour to the point of feeling life to be unendurable and death itself a deliverance? (Italics added)

The point in his question is important. In fact, the 'willers' have done their best to achieve their purpose. Intellectuals with the *will to perfection* have made every possible move in their lifetimes in order to reach the perfect state of academic scholarship. Economists have provided proofs for the existence of a general equilibrium of markets. Social engineers have designed fictive societies in which the problem of scarcity does not exist. Philosophers have hoped that the 'truth' will soon come out as human knowledge accumulates. But most of them have not succeeded – almost none. Their attempts have failed one after another.

When the objective is to change the order of things, what matters most is the act of will itself. 'From all these indignities', de la Boétie writes,

160   *Concluding remarks*

such as the very beasts of the field would not endure, you can deliver your-selves if you try, not by taking action, *but merely by willing to be free.* Resolve to serve no more, and you are at once freed. I do not ask that you place hands upon the tyrant to topple him over, but simply that you support him no longer; then you will behold him, like a great Colossus whose pedestal has been pulled away, fall of his own weight and break in pieces.

(Ibid., 47, italics added)

De la Boétie's concern is to understand how tyrants get the power, and how they maintain it. He attempts, in fact, to illustrate how 'so many men, so many villages, so many cities, so many nations, sometimes suffer under a single tyrant who has no other power than the power they give him' (ibid., 40). He concludes that all servitude is voluntary. That is, servitude is the consequence of the will of individuals imprisoning them to tyranny – the individuals who do not have the courage and interest to defeat the power that governs them and drives them to servitude.

The question is therefore the following: why have thinkers chosen voluntary servitude instead of, say, the will to independence? Why is it, in other words, that individuals wittingly accept being tyrannized? Let us ask ourselves: what is it that encourages people to be dependent on a path of evolution that produces undera-chieving consequences? Why is it that we are locked in a path that yields us undesired results? Is path dependence inevitable? Or, is it *the will of the depend-ees* that generates servitude to the tyranny of institutions in general? And, in line with de la Boétie, what is there to be done if, in order to have path independence, nothing more is needed than to long for it, *if only a simple act of the will is necessary*?

The present state of doing things – doing economics, reading art history, asking philosophical questions, almost anything, in fact – is basically determined by our commitments in the past, commitments which are not completely in accord with the requirements of the present. The way parents approach issues related to the education of their children, the way professors lecture at universities and the way graduate students read economic textbooks today are inherited from, if not deter-mined by, their history. The fact that we inherit our habits of behaviour from the past is a factor disallowing us to free ourselves from dissatisfactory outcomes in the present; it forces us to do things in the way we are accustomed to doing them. Veblen once said:

Institutions are products of the past process, are adapted to past circumstances, and are therefore never in full accord with the requirements of the present ... At the same time, men's present habits of thought tend to persist indefinitely, except as circumstances enforce a change. These institutions which have thus been handed down, these habits of thought, points of view, mental attitudes and aptitudes, or what not, are therefore themselves a conservative factor. This is the factor of social inertia, psychological inertia, conservatism.

(Veblen 1889 [1994], 133)

Economics as part of a system of research ethics 161

'Social inertia, psychological inertia[, and] conservatism' do not always help solve the difficulties in our daily lives. Sometimes change, radical or gradual, is necessary. If change does not come about when it is needed, one ought to conclude, it is *us* who do not ask for change. We sometimes just do not have the *will* to change things, although we clearly see that many things can work out for us if we work at them. Why do we not have the will to change things? Why not take another path that would make all the difference – as in Robert Frost's famous poem, 'The Road Not Taken'? Why not find a new job? Why not move to another city? Why not read a new book? (Or, why not stop reading at all?) Why not try to see things from another viewpoint? Why not change the constitutive metaphors in our fields of enquiry?

> I shall be telling this with a sigh
> Somewhere ages and ages hence:
> Two roads diverged in a wood, and I –
> I took the one less traveled by,
> And that has made all the difference. (Frost, 'The Road Not Taken,' 1920)

Below are some possible answers to these questions. One should not proceed with the idea, however, that all the writers mentioned below argue their point so perfectly as to provide an exclusive understanding for the political economy of obedience. The ideas presented below are nevertheless illuminating. Research on intellectual path dependence should increase understanding of the psychology of the 'will to bondage', although such issues call for further investigation. But one should mention them in the hope that they will shed some light on the present confusion.

One possible reason for the will to bondage is the ignorance of scholars. By ignorance, I refer to a Rawlsian *original position* where scholars embark upon new research projects. At this initial state, scholars take the *status quo* for granted. Then, they introduce themselves to the debates, the conceptions and the truisms that past scholars have reached. Scholars internalize the givens into their own research. In the sense John Rawls (1971 [1985], 136–42) uses the term, scholars are behind a veil of ignorance.

Once the veil is lifted – that is, once the scholars proceed in their research, become knowledgeable about what other scholars have claimed and establish their own truths – it is epistemologically costly to change the consequences of their original position even when they are required to do so. For instance, theories may be falsified and invalidated. Then, scholars may know what needs to be fixed to establish or increase intellectual welfare. However, since changing their initial preferences is costly, scholars are reluctant to make the subsequent moves. It is less costly for the scholars to stick to their initial preferences, believing that they best advance their intellectual interests and goals. The scholars thus remain behind the veil of ignorance. The enduring consequences of the original position cause an intellectually poor state of scholarship.

Indeed, in the case of 'Coase Theorem', as well as in many others that I mentioned throughout the book, economists have taken the initial *status quo* for

162 *Concluding remarks*

granted, not taking significant action to change the situation thereafter. Remember, Ronald Coase claims that the world in which we live is a world of positive transaction costs, a claim in complete contrast to what his so-called theorem says. Even after economists were shown that 'Coase Theorem' was not what Coase meant, they did not change their original position. Had there been no veil of ignorance – that is, had the scholars *not* been born into an intellectual network where members believed that Coase meant a world of zero transaction costs – the scholars would perhaps have not taken the given intellectual path. The consequence of the original position could be 'just', in the sense Rawls uses the term, if economists had changed their original position when refuting evidence and counter-arguments were provided. An intellectually rich state is a state where scholars abide by the fundamental scholarly convention: *reject theories when they are refuted and lock out the intellectual pathways in which certain debates, conceptions and truths are not replicated for their validity*. In the absence of this fundamental scholarly convention, it is impossible to set up and sustain a community of intellectual welfare.

Neglect is also a factor that generates intellectual path dependence. Neglect is the condition in which actors are indifferent among dissimilar outcomes which may emerge when actors do not behave in a particular way. Neglect is not a consequence of incomplete information or conceptual imprecision or indeterminacy of the conditions in which actors ought to behave. Neglect is the lack of an attitude against a condition where a great degree of compromise may be necessary for an actor to prevent a specific outcome. (Compromise can be giving up personal habits or disobedience against institutional principles and rules.) It sometimes refers to inertia in which actors resist reasons that call for change. Certainly, neglect is not always a vice and it does not at all times give rise to undesirable results within a particular context. But it may lead to conditions in which actors may fail to foresee the positive consequences of their behaviour. Neglect of the possibility of cumulative results, each of which feed back upon another, is sometimes one of the most important factors generating intellectual path dependence. In other words, when scholars neglect (or simply do not care about) the consequences of not behaving in epistemologically responsible and moral ways, it is not unlikely that intellectual pathologies create degenerating consequences over the evolution of the scholarly lives of intellectuals.

Another reason why individuals choose to be dependent is, perhaps, the 'emulation' effect of society over individuals. The originator of the term is Thorstein Veblen, who argues that the failure to consume freely and of the best quality of food, drink, narcotics and so forth becomes a 'mark of inferiority and demerit' and is discredited as 'moral deficiency' or 'elements of indecency', while some ways of life turn into norms of reputability within society. In every society, some jobs are credited as noble and others discredited as ignoble. 'Customary expenditure' provides considerable pecuniary reputability and relative economic success for the leisure class. Emulation is manifested in several ways – and the will to get the attention and admiration of other fellows is just one. Veblen writes:

Economics as part of a system of research ethics 163

In order to stand well in the eyes of the community, it is necessary to come up to a certain, somewhat indefinite, conventional standard of wealth; just as in the earlier predatory stage it is necessary for the barbarian man to come up to the tribe's standard of physical endurance, cunning, and skill at arms. A certain standard of wealth in the one case, and of prowess in the other, is a necessary condition of reputability, and anything in excess of this normal amount is meritorious.

(Veblen 1889 [1994], 21)

Does Veblen's emulation explain the dependence of intellectuals? Yes, to a certain extent, it does because scientists, philosophers and artists, too, struggle to attain status within intellectual circles. People's will to be like some others somehow grants intellectuals considerable reputability. Instead of exploring a new path of ideas that would, perhaps, yield *rhetorical satisficing*, scientists, philosophers and artists keep exploiting the same worn paths – that is, they choose to stay intellectually path dependent – which will surely yield them reputation, but 'predatory inefficiency' too. Predatory inefficiency, for Veblen, is deeply ingrained in our habits of thought.

Another evolutionary approach to the puzzle is provided by the 1978 Nobel Prize winner Herbert Simon. Simon reflects upon altruism and docility in order to advance an evolutionary understanding of the (weak and strong forms of) 'unrequited sacrifice of fitness for the benefit of other organisms' (Simon 1983, 57). He describes the 'kinship model' and 'structured deme' which, he argues, explain why and how societies reward individual behaviour that has no relation to the fitness of the individual in the short run. Such behaviour is selected for because 'the long term survival of the behaviour may be determined by the fact that it contributes to the fitness of the whole society, hence is rewarded by the society' (ibid., 64).

Simon argues:

Docility may be defined as the propensity to behave in socially approved ways and to refrain from behaving in ways that are disapproved. Docility, like any other trait, is presumably developed under the influence of the processes of natural selection. That is, the level of docility will tend to rise if docility contributes positively to individual fitness, and to decline if it damages fitness. Remember though, that docility is a propensity to behave not in specific ways but in ways defined as appropriate by the society. Hence some of the behaviours imposed on the individual by this mechanism may increase his fitness; others may decrease it.

(Ibid., 65)

Simon's approach certainly contributes to the resolution of the puzzle. He quite clearly develops a tool to understand why children enjoy a long period of dependence as well as voluntary servitude. It applies to adults as well. His point is that 'obeying behaviour', which causes the individual to sacrifice fitness in the short run, is selected by virtue of the compensation that the individual receives in the form of long-run rewards. On balance, the individual equalizes the

164 *Concluding remarks*

marginal cost of his voluntary servitude or the will to dependence in the short run to the marginal benefit of docility in the long run. Any specific form of behaviour is 'fitter', according to Simon, although social dependence causes immediate sacrifice. His approach suggests that individuals calculate the consequences of their behaviour beyond time horizons. Individuals have a capability to look ahead – in contrast to a myopic kind of rationality – that help them see the ways in which they should behave. Individuals choose voluntary servitude because they think they can easily convert short-run disadvantages into long-run advantages.

His explanation is illuminating in a number of respects. I have sympathy for his approach, especially in his statement that 'evolutionary theory is anti-utopian' (ibid., 73). I, however, do not think the consequence of his explanation for individuals is a happy one. As Keynes famously said, in the long run we will all die. This suggests that path dependence can be interpreted as a dismal metaphor. Perhaps it was Keynes, back in the 1930s, who first recognized the significance of path-dependent structures in the economy and society – or so it can be hypothesized.

Last, but not least, I will consider Friedrich Nietzsche's writing on the issue. Path dependence, as has already been emphasized, means that history matters. It is now widely accepted without question among economists, even by the critics of the theory of path dependence, that institutions matter and historical enquiry is a crucial component of social research. One might have the impression, however, that, in line with Nietzsche, there seems to be a borderline here – a borderline that demarcates two different ways of interpreting the phrase 'history matters'.

The 'degree of history', according to Nietzsche, is important for understanding individuals and cultures but 'the unhistorical and the historical are equally essential … [In] an excess of history the human being stops once again; without that cover of the unhistorical he would never have started or dared to start' (Nietzsche 1873 [2005], 8). Individuals are historically committed to past habits and patterns of behaviour, but they also have the capacity to will to overcome dependence on the past, the will to forget the burden of the past and so forth. And this quality is equally essential. The 'unhistorical' is what allowed Johannes Vermeer to paint *Girl with a Pearl Earring*. It is what allowed Joan of Arc to resist the British and win victory for her country. It is what allows the Kurds and the Palestinians to fight for freedom. True, a painter, a general and a people are dependent on the past; the past is what determines their present circumstances. They achieve success, however, only when they cure themselves of taking the past excessively seriously. It is, in other words, their own will that holds them dependent on the past. 'I believe, in fact', wrote Nietzsche, 'that we are all suffering from a consumptive historical fever and at the very least should recognize that we are afflicted with it' (ibid., 4).

In my view, the line that demarcates the styles of interpreting the phrase 'history matters' also distinguishes between two different conceptions that I find important for understanding the critical point that the approach of path dependence brings forth. The consequence of the evolution of an institution can be

Economics as part of a system of research ethics 165

two-fold. In the first case, which we can call path dependence, locking in the same old problem could yield undesirable and underachieving results, although (technological or analytic) efficiency at each and every single stage of evolution could have been actualized. The argument for path dependence, however, is not complete if we overshadow the achievements of the past. That is to say, we should not call every kind of institutional evolution path dependent. In the second case, which we can call *past* dependence, becoming dependent upon, or even locking into a particular path of evolution is of no great importance. Past dependence means 'history matters', too, but the significance of past dependence would be that arguing for the consciousness of the institutional dependence on the past – just as institutional economists have kept warning orthodox economists – would be nonsense and useless. It would be irrelevant, too, to insist on the significance of historical knowledge in understanding today's institutions. For sometimes history does not matter much.

Nietzsche argues that there are different ways of reading history. He writes, of what he calls 'antiquarian history':

> Antiquarian history knows only how to preserve life, not how to generate it. Therefore, it always undervalues what is coming into being ... antiquarian history hinders the powerful willing of new things; it cripples the active man, who always, as an active person, will and must set aside reverence to some extent. The fact that something has become old now gives birth to the demand that it must be immortal, for when a man reckons what every such ancient fact, an old custom of his fathers, a religious belief, an inherited political right, has undergone throughout its existence, what sum of reverence and admiration from individuals and generations ever since, then it seems presumptuous or even criminal to replace such an antiquity with something new and to set up in opposition to such a numerous cluster of revered and admired things the single fact of what is coming into being and what is present.
>
> (Ibid., 20)

Nietzsche, in the above quote, seems to formulate the conservative reading of history. Antiquarian history praises the traditional, the inherited and the antiquity, whereas it damns any creativity, novelty and digression from what has already been established. Antiquarian history calls for continued dependence on the past – despite the possibility of the will to independence. Nietzsche thinks, however, that it is an abuse of history. For dependence on past institutions makes sense and is useful if institutions keep producing solutions today. For instance, we are using combustion engines and are dependent on petroleum – automobiles still allow us to travel long distances. No problem. Antiques look good displayed on shelves. No problem here, either. In the past, we developed numerous techniques to solve many social and economic problems, and we are now fine with using such techniques even today. We do not find it problematic, therefore, to be dependent on the past because we think it can still be useful.

166   *Concluding remarks*

Dependence is not necessarily a bad thing. Humans and institutions, in one way or another, evolve through time in different moral geographies. It is almost inevitable that we belong to – and are thus dependent upon – a past determined by the social and cultural features of a particular geography. The problem, however, is not determined by the past. It is not dependence on the past. The problem is that we lock into one particular path of institutional evolution and lose the ability, equipment and desire to switch to another path when institutions previously constructed by a society do not meet present-day requirements.

William James writes that 'the history is to a great extent that of a certain clash of human temperaments' (James 2000, 8). I completely agree. People believe in friendship and love. People have faith in a better future, so that they struggle for it. People also have faith in perfect beings who they think can care for their loved ones and make things better for everybody, even if there is, I think, no conveniently recognized reason for it. Intellectual path dependence is not an argument against any of these. The lesson to be drawn from the metaphor and the story where the metaphor plays the key role is that we should develop new vocabularies and metaphors. We should want to be creative. We should do this not because we wish to break with the old; we should do this primarily because we *can* do it. It is pragmatically possible and definitely fruitful.

References

Bhaskar, Roy. 1975. *A Realist Theory of Science*. Leeds: Leeds Books.

De La Boétie, Etienne. 1548 [1975]. *The Politics of Obedience: The Discourse of Voluntary Servitude*, translated by Harry Kurz. Auburn, AL: Misses Institute.

Engels, Friedrich. 1893 [2004]. 'Engels to Franz Mehring'. In *Karl Marx Friedrich Engels Collected Works*, 134. London: Lawrence and Wishart.

Hegel, Georg Wilhelm Friedrich. 1812 [2010]. *The Science of Logic*. Cambridge: Cambridge University Press.

James, William. 2000. *Pragmatism and Other Writings*. London: Penguin Classics.

Kapp, K. William. 1949 [1963]. 'Economics as Part of a System of Applied Ethics'. In *History of Economic Thought: A Book of Readings*, edited by K. William Kapp, 3–4. New York: Barnes and Noble.

Lakatos, Imre. 1970. 'Falsification and the Methodology of Scientific Research Programmes'. In *Criticism and the Growth of Knowledge*, edited by Imre Lakatos and Alan Musgrave, 191–6. Cambridge: Cambridge University Press.

Nietzsche, Frederich. 1873 [2005]. *On the Use and Abuse of History*. New York: Cosimo Classics.

Pinkard, Terry. 1988. *Hegel's Dialectic: The Explanation of Possibility*. Philadelphia: Temple University Press.

Popper, Karl R. 1972 [1979]. *Objective Knowledge: An Evolutionary Approach*. Oxford: Clarendon Press.

Popper, Karl R. 1984. *Popper Selections*, edited by David Miller. Princeton, NJ: Princeton University Press.

Rawls, John. 1971 [1985]. *A Theory of Justice*. Oxford: Oxford University Press.

Economics as part of a system of research ethics   167

Rosen, Michael. 1982. *Hegel's Dialectic and Its Criticism*. Cambridge: Cambridge University Press.

Simon, Herbert A. 1983. *Reason in Human Affairs*. Stanford, CA: Stanford University Press.

Veblen, Thorstein. 1889 [1994]. *The Theory of Leisure Class*. New York: Penguin.

Index

2008 Financial Crisis, the 13, 17, 21, 65

absence 12, 51–5, 60, 62, 66–7, 74–5, 89–90, 102, 118, 157, 162
academic capitalism 72
accountability 65
accounting, intellectual 47
action; individual action 3, 21, 62, 104; collective action 21, 74
agoraphobia 72; *see also* emporiophobia
Althusser, Louis 30
Altman, Morris 19
Amarglio, Jack L. 25
American Economic Association 31, 68
American Economic Review 16, 18, 23, 31, 66, 68
Aristotle 63, 126
artificial selection *see* selection 51–4
as if 4–6, 26, 92, 106, 115, 116, 118, 132, 139
assumption ix, 5–7, 10, 13, 55, 71, 74, 94, 97, 101, 105, 106, 112, 113, 129

belief systems 55, 71, 78, 103–6
Bernal, John Desmond 14, 57
Berne Convention for the Protection of Literary and Artistic Works 56
Bhaskar, Roy 157
blackboard (economics) ix, xi, xii, 4, 7, 74, 94, 107, 131, 133, 143
Blaug, Mark 18, 23, 30
Boétie, Etienne de la 159, 160
Bonilla, Jesus Zamora 75
Boulding, Kenneth E. 59, 106
Bourdieu, Pierre 75–76
Brian, Arthur 81, 89, 91, 96, 98, 100–2, 132
broken window theory 129
business cycle 21, 129

Cambridge Journal of Economics 24, 66
Cambridge Society for Economic Pluralism 33
capitalism; capitalist 17, 71, 72, 81, 90, 94, 137, 144
causality; causation; cumulative causation; intellectual causation 4, 23, 25, 60, 61, 69, 70, 78, 90, 127, 128, 145
Chaplin, Charlie 31
Chicago Boys 17, 21
Chicago School of Economics xi, 9, 21, 78
Christian Economics 5
Coase, Ronald H. ix, xi, xii, 3–12, 54, 62, 63, 72–4, 95, 162
Coase Theorem Proper, the xi, xii
"Coase Theorem," the 8–9, 11–12, 18–26, 29, 44, 76–7, 175–6
Cobb-Douglass 21
Coleman, William 18
Collins, Randall 78
commodity 55, 56, 118
Commons, John C. xi
competition 27, 28, 33, 55, 75, 80, 101; imperfect competition xii; perfect competition 4, 8
complexity 103, 104, 144, 115, 131, 132, 140
confirmation bias 16, 20, 30
(conservative) conservatism xi, xii, 8, 28, 29, 114, 160, 161, 165
contingency 60, 61, 71, 90, 111, 118, 146, 155
continuity 18; continuous 9, 11, 14, 47, 48, 50, 59, 89, 92, 116, 119, 127, 153, 154, 156, 158
controversy 5–7, 15, 18, 32
convention xi, xii, 22, 30, 48, 72, 115, 162, 163
convergence 50, 90, 109, 126, 140

Index 169

conversation xii, xiii, 18, 25, 28, 48, 69, 77–9, 93, 94

correction 18, 28, 32, 48, 54, 93, 157–9; *see also* self-correction

cost; cost-free 49; cost-benefit analysis 46, 47, 97; epistemic cost ix–xii, 8–11, 15, 28, 29, 45–57, 68, 73–8, 89, 102, 106; frictional cost 134; opportunity cost 10, 23, 49, 89, 93; positive epistemic cost (PEC) ix, 8, 9, 11, 46, 49, 50, 57, 75, 78; private cost xii, 8, 28, 45, 46, 56; social cost ix, xi, 3–6, 8, 28, 45–47, 50; transaction cost xi, xii, 4–11, 16, 49, 73, 74, 134, 162; "unpaid cost" 48

counterfactual 60

Cowles Commission 75

Coyle, Diane 21

creativity 55, 77, 79, 80, 118, 159, 165

critical rationalism x, 14, 69, 74, 78, 156, 158

critical realism *see* realism

CrossRef 32

Darwin, Charles 110, 111

data: data sharing 64; data availability 31, 65, 67, 68, 73; fabrication of data x, 65; manufacturing of data x

David, Paul 16, 89–91, 94–9

Davis, John B. 30

Dawkins, Richard 59, 114

DeMartino, George 73

Depp, Johnny 154

Dewey, John 63, 91, 106, 112

dialectic(s) x, 14, 54, 74, 78, 154, 155, 158

divergence x, 5, 24, 26, 27, 48, 116, 131, 144, 145, 161

division of labour 26, 106, 111

docility 27, 163, 164

domestication 52, 133

Duvendack, Maren 68

Econ Journal Watch 31

Econometrica 31, 67, 68

econometrics 16, 20, 26

economic: economic criticism xiii, 22–4, 27, 28; economic philosophy (philosophy of economics) xiii, 22–4, 26; economic methodology (methodology of economics) 26; economic philosophizing 24

Economic History Association 22, 93

Economic Journal 23, 68

Economic Thought: History, Philosophy, and Methodology 24

Economics and Philosophy 23–4

economics: experimental economics 22, 64; historical economics 100; institutional economics xi, 90, 165; neoclassical economics 71, 100; orthodox economics xi, xii, 8,13, 23–8, 33, 47, 78, 100, 165; unorthodox economics 11, 24, 28

economics of scientific knowledge (economics of science) ix, 48, 56

efficiency xii, 4, 6, 11, 16, 48, 73, 81, 90, 91, 97–9, 105, 108, 111, 134, 137, 165; inefficiency 11, 73, 91, 98, 99, 163

Einstein, Albert 143

Eldredge, Niles 114–18

emergence x, 24, 60, 101, 116, 118, 128, 155

emporiophobia 72 *see also* agoraphobia

emulation 162, 163

Engels, Friedrich 52–4, 155

entropy 77, 142, 145

environment x, 25, 47–9, 52, 56, 59, 64, 74, 77, 92, 104, 105, 111, 115, 131, 137, 142, 145

epistemic hysteresis 22, 28, 34

Erasmus Journal of Philosophy and Economics 45–82

ergodic 132, 139, 145

error; error-free 48, 50, 155; coding error 17, 65; erroneous x, xi, xii, 7, 10, 13, 20–2, 28, 29, 47–9, 53, 55, 66, 69, 70, 89, 96, 106, 112, 125, 135, 153–5; generic error 56

ethics; professional ethics 33; research ethics xiii, 51, 55, 56, 67, 153

Europe 5, 24, 66, 78, 108, 111, 130, 133, European countries/economies 65, 66, 93, 95, 113

evidence x, 19, 21, 22, 28, 30, 63, 65, 69, 77, 89, 95–9, 102, 110, 111, 114, 116, 153, 155, 156, 162

evolution; evolution of ideas 12, 13, 15, 18, 28, 52, 58, 69, 78, 81, 89, 90, 91, 93, 99, 107, 110, 111, 114–19, 126, 130, 145, 159

explanation x, xii, 22, 24, 26, 27, 47, 48, 58, 59, 64, 69, 92, 99, 107, 116–19, 129, 132, 133, 154–8, 164

externality xi, 6, 45, 47; negative externality(-ies) 3, 4, 9, 45, 46, 48, 50, 51, 56, 70, 72, 99, 153; positive externality(-ies) 45, 50

extinction: extinction of theorems (explanations) 118; extinction of species 115

170   *Index*

failure *see* replication; *see* market of (economic) ideas
false consciousness 155
falsification x, 13, 52, 56, 64, 65, 69, 153, 156–8
fast thinking 30
"Federal Communications Commission, the" 3
feedback (loop) 100, 126, 143, 146; negative feedback(s) 90, 141; positive feedback(s) 9, 61, 62, 66, 81, 90, 111, 131, 140–2, 145, 146
Ferguson, Niall 141, 142
Feyerabend, Paul 24, 137
first-best xii, 72
Fish, Stanley 24
Frey, Bruno 51
friction 5, 134
Friedman, Milton 3, 29
Frost, Robert 161

Galbraith, John Kenneth 14, 106
game theory 17, 22, 59
GDP 21, 65, 66
gene 59, 78, 114; *see also* meme
Georgescu-Roegen, Nicholas 72, 77, 111
Gladwell, Malcolm 100, 128, 129
Gleick, James 134
Gould, Stephan J. 60, 110, 111, 114–16, 130, 138, 147, 156
government 3, 4, 6, 21, 22, 45, 66, 72, 73, 78, 102, 106, 113, 146

habit 102, 105, 106, 162, 164; habits of thought 28, 55, 102, 158, 160, 163
Hall, Robert E. x
Harberger, Arnold 3
harm, harmful x, xi, 3–6, 17, 28, 32, 45, 47, 50, 55, 57, 61, 63, 65, 69–72, 77, 89, 97, 119, 126, 129, 131, 153
Hegel, G. W. Friedrich x, 13, 63, 74, 154, 155, 157, 158
Herndon, Thomas 17, 65, 66
Heterodox Economics Newsletter 66
history: history of economics, history of economic thought ix, xiii, 3, 8, 12, 15, 18, 20, 22, 24, 71, 72, 93, 118; history of ideas 9, 18, 51, 90, 99, 114, 126; history matters 92, 98, 164, 165; intellectual history 9, 12, 18, 48, 51, 52, 54, 61, 70, 71, 74, 77, 90, 93, 106, 107, 109, 112, 115, 116, 118, 119, 125, 133, 155, 157
History of Political Economy 24
Höffler, Jan 68

honesty x, 153
how much? 18, 77, 94, 95, 136, 137
Hume, David 60

ideology 8, 9, 23, 28, 144; ideologization 5, 9, 50, 51, 55, 78, 102, 103
imperfection xii, 110, 111, 114, 154, 155, 158
increasing returns to scientific scale 99–103
inefficiency *see* efficiency
inertia 79, 92, 99, 117, 160, 161, 162
innovation, innovative x, 21, 27, 32, 51, 69, 80, 81, 90, 144
Institute for New Economics Thinking, the 33
integrity x, 32, 55, 56, 63, 65
intellectual: intellectual merit 63; intellectual minima 47
intention xiii, 5, 8, 23, 49, 51–3, 59, 60, 61, 69, 70, 79, 89, 146
intervention 4, 22, 52, 62, 72, 73, 97
invalid ix, x, 13, 14, 27–9, 47, 48, 60, 63, 69, 155, 161
invisible hand x, xi, 8, 14, 99, 102
irreversibility 12, 18, 32, 52, 65, 77, 90, 99, 102, 146, 147, 155, 158, 159

James, William 91, 147, 166
Jevons, Stanley 15, 129
JMCB Project, the 67
Jolink, Albert 11, 92
Journal of Economic Issues 24
Journal of Economic Literature 67
Journal of Economic Methodology 24
Journal of Institutional Economics 67
Journal of Law and Economics 3
Journal of Money, Credit, and Banking 31, 67: *see also* JMCB Project
Journal of Philosophical Economics xiii 24
Journal of Political Economy 23, 31, 67, 68

Kafka, Franz 54, 92
Kahneman, Daniel 4, 10, 29, 30, 32, 63
Kapeller, Jakob 66
Kapital, Das 53
Kapp, K. William xi, 5, 45, 47–9, 72, 153
Klamer, Arjo 10, 25, 26
Krugman, Paul 91
Kuhn, Thomas 24, 27, 92, 134, 157
Kurds, the 164
Kyklos 24

Index 171

Lakatos, Imre 24, 153, 157, 158
Lakoff, George 24
Lawson, Tony xii, 25, 26, 95, 96
legitimation 15, 27, 52, 69, 75, 91
liability 45
Liebowitz, Stephen J. 16, 93, 94, 97–9
life's history 110, 111, 115, 125
life's tape 60, 61
lock in 10, 62, 71, 79–81, 90, 92, 98, 99,
    102, 159, 166
Locke, John 60, 106
London School of Economics 9, 24
Lorenz, Edward N. 133
Lyotard, Jean-François 27

Mäki, Uskali 25
malpractice x
Mankiw, N. George 29, 30
marginal 46, 50, 101, 103, 115, 118, 164
Margolis, Stephen E. 16, 94, 97–9
market of (economic) ideas ix–xi, 7–10,
    14, 56, 65, 70–7; failure of the market of
    (economic) ideas 71
Marshall, Alfred 45
Marx – Engels Gesamtausgabe
    (MEGA) 54
Marx / Friedrich Engels Collected Works
    53, 54
Marx, Karl 30, 52, 53, 54, 72, 78, 92,
    112, 113
McCloskey, Deirdre N. 7, 16, 18, 19,
    24–7, 30, 93–5, 113, 137
McCullough, B. D. 19, 20, 57
McGee, John 3
mechanism x, 3, 8, 10, 12, 25–7, 45, 48,
    51, 59, 62, 63, 69, 70, 77, 80, 81, 82, 90,
    92, 93, 99, 100, 110, 111, 114, 115, 127,
    130, 131, 139–43, 145, 147, 163
Medema, Steven 5, 16
meme 59; *see also* gene
metaphor ix, 26, 62, 71–3, 78, 92, 97, 98,
    108, 112, 113, 135, 158, 161, 164, 166
military 17, 22
Mill, John Stuart 15
Mirowski, Philip 17, 22, 25
misinterpretation 14, 52, 70, 74
misrepresentation 4, 9, 10, 61
Mokyr, Joel 27, 46
monopoly, monopolization 33, 55, 57, 75,
    76, 81
Mont Pélerin Society 75
moral, morality x, 5, 6, 28, 30, 31, 32, 34,
    51, 55–7, 79, 108, 111, 127, 153, 157,
    162, 166

Myrdal, Gunner 127
myth 13, 77, 94, 105

natural selection *see* selection
NBER 65, 66
negation x, 3, 4, 13, 14, 155, 157
Nelson, Julie 16, 20, 25
neoliberalism xi, 9, 17, 71, 93
Nietzsche, Friedrich 54, 108, 158, 164, 165
Nobel Prize 3, 7, 55, 62, 163; Swedish
    Bank Prize 5, 30, 75
North, Douglass 89, 91, 96, 98, 104
North, Gary 5, 6

Ockham's Razor 146, 147
*Oeconomia – History / Methodology /
    Philosophy* 24
one-size-fits-all methodology 21, 132
ontology xii, xiii, 11, 26, 78
oomph 94, 95, 137
operations research 17, 22, 59
optimal xii, 29, 55, 56, 71, 90, 95, 97, 99,
    101, 111

Palestinians, the 164
paradigm xi, xiii, 9, 22, 93, 102–4, 108,
    117, 134, 139
past dependence 98, 165
patent 46, 49
pathology 108, 126, 127, 131
peer review 15, 24, 51, 56
perfect: perfection 18, 89, 90, 98, 106–19,
    126, 159; perfect competition 4, 8;
    perfect markets xii, 9, 71; *see also*
    progression
Pigou, Arthur Cecil 3, 7, 8, 45
Pinker, Steven 15
Pitt, Brad 154
plagiarism x, 16, 45, 56, 57, 65, 67, 74, 77
pluralism 14, 33, 55, 76, 78
Poincaré, Henri 140
Polanyi, Karl xi, 72
Polanyi, Michael x
Polya-Urn processes 97, 99, 134
Popper, Karl R. x, 14, 25, 68–70, 74, 109,
    110, 156–8
positivism 23, 24, 30, 68–70
postmodernism 24, 27, 30
practicing economist 23, 25, 27, 48
pragmatism 24
Prigogine, Ilya 142, 147
private ownership 6
"Problem of Social Cost, the" 9, 10, 11,
    17–25

172   *Index*

process of knowledge production 46, 47, 75, 115, 116, 118
progression 100, 106, 109, 119, 128, 155, 157; continual progression (*see also*: perfection) 11, 12, 59, 89, 107, 108, 110; discreet progression 89
public commodity (good) 55, 56, 74
public space 72
punctuated equilibrium 114–19; *see also* speciation

Quarterly Journal of Economics 23
Questionable research practices (QRPs) ix, x, xi, xiii, 8, 21, 22, 28, 31, 32, 46–8, 51, 52, 56, 57, 61, 62, 65, 119, 153; *see also* responsible research practices
QWERTY 16, 90, 91, 93–7, 99

Rad Lab 22
Rand Corporation 15, 22, 31, 75
rational (rationalism) ix, x, 14, 23, 38, 30, 48, 54, 69, 74, 78, 98, 108, 109, 113, 154, 156–8, 164; *see also* critical rationalism
Rawls, John 55, 161, 162
realism (in economics) xiii, 24–8; critical realism xiii, 96; hyper-realism 59, 60
realistic (realisticness) ix, xii, 13, 33, 48, 49, 52, 54, 60, 68, 74, 118
refereeing *see* peer review
refutation 15, 32, 57, 66, 75, 76, 163
reinforcement 9, 48, 49, 57, 58, 61, 79–81, 92, 93, 99, 103, 111, 130, 131, 134, 145, 147
Reinhart, Carmen M. 17, 65, 66
Reiss, Julian 21
replication xiii, 8, 9, 10, 11, 15, 16, 18, 31, 50, 73, 74, 77, 102, 103, 114, 162; replication failure (*see also*: reproduction) xii, 9, 10, 57–70, 73, 77
reproduction x– xii, 10, 27, 28, 47–52, 58–63, 66, 70, 79, 80, 96, 117, 118, 125, 130, 141, 153; *see also* replication
research misconduct 69
research programme x, xi, 9, 10, 14, 15, 22, 58, 63, 70, 77, 93, 104, 153, 157, 157, 158
responsible 3, 4, 26, 29, 47, 53, 102, 108, 162; responsible research practices 63; *see also* questionable research practices
retraction 16, 31, 32, 66
Review of Economic Studies 31
Review of Economics and Statistics 23
Review of Social Economy xiii, 56
Revue de philosophie économique 24

rhetoric xiii, 19, 23, 24–9, 34, 62, 69, 156, 163
Ricardo, David 15
right: property right 3, 4, 45, 55, 74, 81; copyright 28, 31, 46, 48, 49, 63; legal right 6; moral right 31, 32, 56
Rogoff, Kenneth 17, 65, 66
Rorty, Richard 24, 62, 63, 106, 108, 113
Rothbard, Murray N. 16, 57
Ruccio, David F. 25

sabotage xi
Samuelson, Paul 7, 8, 45, 106
scarce (scarcity) ix, 9, 14, 57, 58, 159
Schrödinger, Erwin 143
Schumpeter, Joseph A. 30, 54
second "best" 95
selection 15, 51, 52, 59, 90, 93, 98, 100, 114; artificial selection 51, 52, 54; natural selection 110, 111, 114, 162 *see also* domestication
self-correction 28
self-corrective (self-correction) ix–xi, 9 14, 18, 48, 61, 74, 129; *see also* correction
self-deregulation 28
self-interest 28, 71, 153
self-regulation xi, 56, 72
significance: statistical significance 16, 18, 19; intellectual significance 61, 63
Simon, Herbert 163, 164
small event xiii, 9, 12, 61, 70, 79–82, 97, 98, 100, 107, 114, 128, 130–48, 158
Smith, Adam 7, 8, 16, 30, 45, 54, 57, 106
software 17, 19, 20, 55, 56, 67, 70, 73, 81, 101, 138
Spacey, Kevin 154
speciation 114,115; *see also* punctuated equilibrium
spill-over 5, 45
Stanley, Morgan 154
stasis 74, 92, 114, 117
Staveren, Irene 25
Stengers, Isabelle 142, 147
Stephan, Paula 76, 102
Stigler, George xi, 3–11, 16, 63, 71
stochastic 82, 140
sub-optimality *see* optimality
survival x, 52, 71, 77–9, 93, 115, 118, 130, 163
Swedish Bank Prize *see* Nobel Prize
symbol xii, 10, 46, 78, 79, 112, 113, 129, 133, 138
System 1 30

Theory of Moral Sentiments, the 30
Theory of Price xi, xiv, 4, 9
think-tank x
thought collective 9, 15, 47
tipping point xii, 10, 80, 82, 100, 114, 129
Tragedy of Commons, the 28
transaction *see* cost
truism 8, 79, 161
trust 32, 57, 102, 103
truth seeking xii
truth, the 14, 25, 29, 60, 62, 72, 74, 75, 90, 106, 107, 109, 129, 134, 143, 154–6, 158–62

uncertainty 12, 55, 99, 103–6, 108
under-labour 60
unfit x, 51, 116, 156
unintended 45, 105
utility 6, 49, 50, 118, 153; epistemic utility 49, 50, 55, 89; utility function 49
Utopia 107, 109, 111–14, 164

Valdés, Juan Gabriel 17, 22
value x, 6–8, 11, 21, 32, 54, 57, 58, 73–5, 92, 105, 113, 126, 142, 156, 165; labour theory of value 75
Veblen, Thorstein B. xi, xiii, 5, 72, 90, 91, 127, 160, 162, 163
verification 27, 69, 78, 156
Vermeer, Johannes 158, 164
Vromen, Jack 92

wealth 16, 27, 30, 45, 46, 57, 99, 163
Wealth of Nations, the 16, 30, 45
Web of Science 5
welfare 8, 21, 28, 32, 46, 48, 153, 161, 162
Whiggish view of history 116
Wible, James ix, x, xiii, 14, 56
will to perfection 159
Williamson, Oliver 5
workmanship 11

Ziliak, Stephan T. xiii, 16, 18, 19, 25, 137